PENGUIN BOOKS

THE LIFE OF THE PARTY

Robert Kuttner is the economics correspondent of *The New Republic* and a columnist for *Business Week* and *The Boston Globe*. His previous books are *The Economic Illusion*, which was nominated for the National Book Critics Circle Award, and *Revolt of the Haves*.

ROBERT KUTTNER

THE LIFE OF THE PARTY

DEMOCRATIC PROSPECTS IN 1988 AND BEYOND

PENGUIN BOOKS

PENGUIN BOOKS
Published by the Penguin Group
Viking Penguin Inc., 40 West 23rd Street,
New York, New York 10010, U.S.A.
Penguin Books Ltd, 27 Wrights Lane,
London W8 5TZ, England
Penguin Books Australia Ltd, Ringwood,
Victoria, Australia
Penguin Books Canada Ltd, 2801 John Street,
Markham, Ontario, Canada L3R 1B4
Penguin Books (N.Z.) Ltd, 182–190 Wairau Road,
Auckland 10, New Zealand

Penguin Books Ltd, Registered Offices:
Harmondsworth, Middlesex, England

First published in the United States of America by
Viking Penguin Inc., 1987
Published in Penguin Books 1988

Portions of this book first appeared, some in different form,
in *The New Rupublic* as "Ass Backward," "What's the Big Idea?,"
"Unholy Alliance," and "Fat and Sassy." © 1985, 1986, 1987,
The New Republic, Inc. By permission of *The New Republic.*

Excerpt from the lyrics of "Wernher von Braun" by Tom Lehrer
is reprinted by permission. © 1965 Tom Lehrer.

LIBRARY OF CONGRESS CATALOGING IN PUBLICATION DATA
Kuttner, Robert.   The life of the party.
Bibliography: p.
Includes index.
1. Democratic Party (U.S.)   2. Liberalism—United
States.   3. Populism—United States.   4. United States—
Politics and government—1981–   .   I. Title.
JK2316.K87   1988   324.2736   88–2412
ISBN 0 14 00.9877 1

Printed in the United States of America by
R. R. Donnelley & Sons, Harrisonburg, Virginia
Set in Baskerville
Designed by Beth Tondreau

For my mother,
a great democrat

The Democratic party of the nation ain't dead, though it's been givin' a lifelike imitation of a corpse for several years.

—GEORGE WASHINGTON PLUNKITT
OF TAMMANY HALL, 1905

FOREWORD

During the Reagan years, I wrote several articles for *The New Republic* which had a common, if not widely shared, theme. Too many influential Democrats seemed to have forgotten the basic source of their party's strength. They were moving away from the practical economic populism that had made Democrats the majority party for much of this century. They were becoming a technocratic, managerial party at best, and a *laissez-faire* imitation-Republican party at worst. Neither model was attracting voters.

It seemed worthwhile to examine in greater depth the several political and ideological forces pushing Democrats in this self-defeating direction, and to seek an alternative. Hence this book. The argument seems less eccentric today than when I first advanced it, for after November 1986 the party began to recover something of its historic voice. The Democrats now have the prospect of returning to power not just as lucky beneficiaries of an incumbent's stumble, but as resurgent progressives. But if they do regain the White House in 1988, the process of rebuilding their links to the voters will have only begun.

A further stimulus to writing this book came from my earlier book on the political conditions of economic equity, *The Economic Illusion,* published in 1984. There I argued that it was simply wrong, as a matter of empirical fact, to regard economic efficiency and social equality as adversary goals, as most conservatives and nearly all professional economists do. Quite a few nations manage to maximize "growth with equity" by having a different social contract undergirded by a different politics, and different policy blueprints. I concluded that book with the words: ". . . injustice is not necessary economics; the economics of equality can work, and often has worked, when the constituency for it is animated. The *politics* of equality—that is a little harder."

This book attempts to find that politics.

FOREWORD TO THE
PENGUIN EDITION

I completed writing the first edition of *The Life of the Party* in late 1986, just after the Democrats recaptured control of the Senate. It was published in October 1987, as the country was gearing up for the 1988 election. The book's argument can be summarized as follows:

As the party of the common people in a business-oriented society, Democrats have done best when they have stood for a philosophy of "progressive populism." Populism, in my definition, articulates the economic self-interest of voters who live paycheck to paycheck and who are vulnerable to the uncertainties of a market economy. Populism generally requires the use of the state to temper the extremes of the market. Politically, it is the one philosophy that unites the diverse ethnic and regional coalition that makes up the Democratic party, overcomes the social conservatism of many working-class voters, and motivates them to vote for Democrats.

The successful modern Democratic presidents—Roosevelt, Truman, Kennedy, and Johnson—all recognized that the Party's strong suit was its ability to champion the economic self-interest of workaday Americans. The party got into trouble when it lost that capacity—when the New Deal coalition divided, first over race and then over war, and finally over cultural schisms; when the New Deal–Fair Deal–Great Society ceased to be something for the broad working middle class, and was truncated into a self-isolating safety net for the dependent poor; and when the economy became mired in "stagflation" on Democrat Jimmy Carter's watch.

For a decade, Democrats have seemed unable to return to those successful roots. Instead, most party leaders concluded that the decline of the Democrats in the 1970s and 1980s must have resulted from the party being too left-wing for the country, even though Jimmy Carter was probably the most conservative Democratic president since Grover Cleveland. Undoubtedly, the voters were in one of their periodic conservative moods in the 1970s and 80s, but the Democrats were offering them little in the way of a credible alternative. The self-defeating impulse to move away from the legacy of progressive populism, toward the managerial center, was compounded by several other forces.

First, the old demographic base of the Democratic party had unmistakably dwindled. Blue-collar voters had become a diminished fraction of the electorate, and trade unionists were a reduced fraction of blue collar workers. The urban Northeast and Midwest controlled less than half the electoral college. The South was no longer solid. Voters were no longer so partisan. All of the emerging regions and social groups seemed to be less inclined to vote for a Democrat. And voting participation, especially among those groups that did vote reliably Democratic (when they bothered to vote), was in seemingly irreversible decline.

Secondly, money was becoming an increasing influence in politics. To be at all competitive, a Democrat had to raise heaps of money—often from people who might be fairly liberal on such social issues as abortion or gay rights, or on foreign policy issues like U.S. aid to the Nicaraguan Contras, but who had little use for the sort of economic populism that rallied working-class voters. To the extent that money talked, it counseled Democrats to seek the safe, managerial center.

The more that Democrats repaired to the political center, the less they excited their potential base.

The popularity of Ronald Reagan only intensified the problem. With Democrats offering little in the way of convincing alternatives, Reagan's optimism and patriotism attracted many voters who might have voted Democratic. Walter Mondale, persuaded that Democrats had to demonstrate their moderation, ran virtually as an austerity candidate. He proposed to raise taxes—but instead of articulating a populist demand to cut the federal deficit by taxing those few who had benefitted from Reagan's lopsided program, Mondale offered austerity for everybody. And in his effort to shake off the big-spender label, he did not propose to appropriate the new revenues, but only to use them for budget balance. In the wake of Mondale's defeat running as a Democratic Hoover, many Democratic insiders nonetheless concluded that Mondale had been defeated as a big-spending liberal. In 1985, a new organization was formed, the Democratic Leadership Council, in the hope of pushing the party to the center-right.

Fiscal deadlock completed the hamstringing of the Democrats. Even as the popular mood began to swing in a more progressive direction after 1986, the budgetary paralysis prevented most Democrats from advancing any sort of program that would cost public money. Polls showed that wide majorities supported measures to address long-term health care, to deal with a widely acknowledged housing crisis, to meet the needs of the working family, to reform welfare, to reinvest in rotting public infrastructure, and to upgrade education and training. But virtually all of these were mooted by the fiscal stalemate and the reluctance of most Democrats to embrace new taxes, even on the wealthy. Reagan's program may have failed as supply-side economics, but it succeeded brilliantly as politics by distancing the Democrats from their own tradition.

At this writing, Michael Dukakis seems assured of the Democratic nomination. Against the backdrop of recent Democratic party history, Dukakis is an ambiguous figure. Throughout his political life, he has sometimes seemed a progressive, and sometimes more of a centrist. He won early prominence as a good-government type—a procedural reformer with essentially liberal values. But in his first term as Massachusetts governor, a recession forced Dukakis to preside over both a tax increase and spending cuts, which alienated both the left and the right. He was then defeated in the 1978 Democratic primary. When Dukakis won a rematch in 1982, after four years in exile at Harvard, he had trimmed his sails. He was less of a "big spending liberal"; he no longer appointed Ralph Nader-style regulators to tweak the business establishment; he was far more respectful of party regulars, whom he had disdained during his first term; and he was fanatic about prudent fiscal management.

Some of Dukakis's most successful programs as governor of Massachusetts have a latent populist appeal: offering welfare recipients decent jobs rather than a dole; demanding that tax cheats pay their fair share of taxes; using a deft combination of carrots and sticks to diffuse the benefits of economic development. Yet by temperament, Dukakis is more comfortable emphasizing administration than advocacy. State programs that might have been sold as progressive are more often sold as merely sound management. Much of Dukakis's second term was spent repairing his ties to the Massachusetts business establishment. Rarely did Dukakis go out on a political limb in order to press a principle. The Michael Dukakis of "The Massachusetts miracle" is known as a consensus builder and a risk avoider, not as a rabble rouser.

His challenge as presidential candidate, therefore, will be to maximize his diverse strengths. He needs to continue to shine as a man of integrity and competence, but as an advocate for America's work-a-day wage earners as well. Dukakis can draw on his background as a steady, reassuring figure, a man of real intellect and a very competent manager—qualities that contrast instructively with the giddy remoteness that characterized the Reagan White House. After the escalating revelations of Reagan's detachment, the voters will welcome a presidential candidate who is truly in charge. George Bush may not be quite as remote as Ronald Reagan, but much of the belated voter dismay about Reagan rubs off on Bush, too. In its own way, The Vice President's persona also seems oddly detached. The controversies about Bush's knowledge of

Panamanian strongman Manuel Noriega's drug dealing and of the Iran-Contra affair make the Vice President seem even further out of touch, if only to exculpate himself. Dukakis's strengths beautifully highlight George Bush's weaknesses.

What remains to be seen is whether Dukakis can also find a compelling, populist voice. In his home state, he has always engendered more enthusiasm in suburban, socially liberal areas than in traditional working class precincts. His early campaign for the nomination was in grave danger of falling flat for lack of clear a message. As the campaign wore on, however, other contenders expired first. When better known national figures like New York Governor Mario Cuomo and New Jersey Senator Bill Bradley declined to run, Dukakis became the most prudent choice for party regulars. He was the best financed, and best organized. He survived the early loss of his campaign manager and closest aide, John Sasso, following damaging revelations that Sasso had leaked a videotape that destroyed the candidacy of Sen. Joseph Biden. But as he has so often done throughout his political life, Dukakis hung in, and recovered. He managed to stay alive through lackluster showings in the Iowa caucuses and in much of the Super-Tuesday South. And following a humiliating defeats in Illinois and Michigan, Dukakis finally embraced a more vigorous sort of rhetoric and won a string of impressive victories beginning with the April 5 Wisconsin primary. At last, he seemed to generate a flicker of real enthusiasm, and not merely inevitability.

Beginning with Wisconsin, everything broke right for Dukakis. By then, others had fallen by the wayside and the effective choice was between Dukakis and Jackson. In slaying an opponent who briefly captured the national conscience but who was never a serious prospect for nomination, Dukakis seemed a giant-killer. A primary season that seemed in real danger of obliterating everybody instead produced a clear winner. The only remaining challenge to party unity was the challenge of accommodating the legitimate demands of Jackson and his supporters without seeming captive to them. Yet there is also the more serious risk that if Dukakis runs a low key, centrist campaign for the White House he will fail to arouse sufficient excitement among the party's dormant base, and lose a race that ought to be winnable. A closer look at the primary season is instructive here.

As the presidential year dawned, the Democratic field was widely described as the "Seven Dwarfs". Polls revealed that the Republican candidates, to a man, were seen as stronger potential leaders than their Democratic counterparts. Possibly this had something to do with the plain fact that the Republicans were clearer about what they believed. It is difficult to come across as a leader when you are hesitant about what you stand for. While Republican candidates were clear that they espoused Reaganism—a strong national defense and a weak domestic government—the Democrats (with the exception of Jackson and sometimes Gephardt) fudged their positions on most issues.

Democratic strategists sought to appropriate another finding of numerous public opinion polls, which revealed that Americans had a vague unease about "the future." Yet because of the wide belief that the Party had to reposition itself in the political center, the future remained an amorphous theme articulated purely in symbolic terms, rather than as a concrete conviction to fight for working men and women. The candidates who embraced the future proved as ephemeral as the theme. Gary Hart was ruined by a sex scandal, and Joseph Biden was abruptly derailed by a far less consequential peccadillo involving purloined rhetoric. But neither man had established durable bonds with constituents.

As the primary season began, candidates who articulated populist themes did better than predicted. Illinois' Paul Simon started out with unexpected strength, but Simon failed to transcend his own idiosyncrasies. And his populism was truncated by fiscal eccentricities reminiscent of Reagan's own "voodoo economics." Simon kept insisting that it was somehow possible to balance the budget and increase public spending without raising taxes. The voters didn't buy it.

Richard Gephardt showed surprising strength in the early contests, running on a frank program of economic nationalism. He demonstrated just what the vague worries about the future really meant. People were concerned that their living standards were declining. Wagering most of his campaign chest on Iowa, Gephardt won that state's January precinct caucuses. Exit polls showed that Gephardt did best among just those Democrats who had defected to vote for Ronald Reagan—socially conservative working-class voters. Most impressively, Gephardt managed to attract these voters not by moving right on military or social questions, but by standing up for their pocketbook concerns. But Gephardt could not overcome two disadvantages. First, as a middle-of-the-road leader of the House Democratic Caucus, he was not entirely credible as a born-again populist. The editorial writers savaged his economic nationalism, while the columnists ridiculed his incongruous stance as "outsider." Secondly, Gephardt had severe money problems. He raised just enough corporate PAC money to impeach his claim to populism, but not nearly enough to run a financially competitive campaign. Having bet the farm on Iowa, he never raised enough additional money to compete throughout the South on Super Tuesday, and he dropped out soon after.

Bruce Babbitt, the former governor of Arizona, ran perhaps the most intellectually serious of the campaigns. He won wide praise for his willingness to propose higher taxes and spending cuts. But he won almost no electoral support. Albert Gore, a young senator of great intelligence and promise, badly muddled his strategy. At first, he ran as a son of the South, where he did well enough in the Super Tuesday contest to displace Gephardt. Then Gore tried to appropriate the role of party hawk, a role which has been repeatedly commended by Democratic neo-conservatives. Ultimately, he allied himself with the most conservative wing of the Israel lobby, and sought to portray himself as the stop-Jackson candidate. But the strategy failed on three counts. First, Gore never fit the role. A moderate liberal raised and educated largely in the North, Gore was neither as Southern nor as hawkish as the part demanded.

Second, the supposed appeal of a Democratic hawk to disaffected blue collar voters and Southerners is grossly overstated. In the 1970s, the strategy failed to ignite the presidential quest of the original neo-Conservative Democrat, Henry ("Scoop") Jackson. It failed even more dismally for Ohio Senator John Glenn. Finally, by the New York primary, Gore seemed to be merely pandering, and anyone who was serious about stopping Jackson knew to vote for Dukakis. Gore, ironically, enabled Dukakis to take the high road against Jackson.

Jackson himself provides some important lessons for Dukakis and for the Democrats. It was Jackson who demonstrated the latent power of economic populism. For a time, he collected surprisingly large fractions of white votes, demonstrating that populism can be a force stronger even than racism. Which suggests that it must be strong indeed. Jackson was of course a master rhetorician. But he also had a very clear message. And it was a message directed squarely at the Party's long-ignored working-class base. Starting with very little money and a chaotic organization, Jackson astounded the political establishment by winning an increasing fraction of white votes. In state after state, white working-class voters declared that of all the candidates, only Jackson seemed to be speaking for them. When Jackson won back-to-back victories in Illinois and Michigan, the political universe shuddered.

The abrupt rise of Jackson sowed panic among party insiders. It utterly upset the script. "What does Jesse want?" was the cliché of early spring. Few party leaders grasped that he wanted to be president.

Jackson's ascendance created a crisis for the Party. Fittingly, many of the very devices intended to move the party to the right backfired. Super Tuesday, designed by Southerners and conservatives to nominate a center-right son of the South, instead catapulted Jackson. Some leaders saw in Jackson's popularity a long-deferred source of grass roots excitement. Others feared that Jackson would turn out to be a black George McGovern—a candidate with a fanatic following who could perhaps force nomination, but never win election, and who might well lose so disastrously that other Democrats would be brought down with him. But Jackson's popularity gave the lie, perhaps once and for all, to the idea that Democrats had to repair to the safe center. He became the first Democrat since Robert Kennedy to win the hearts of both black and white working people, many of whom profoundly distrusted each other.

Pollster Pat Caddell, the theorist of outsider politics who gave the Democrats George McGovern, Jimmy Carter, and Gary Hart, and who had been unable to find a viable horse for 1988, wrote in a bitter I-told-you-so piece for *The New York Times:*

> What the elite can't seem to comprehend is that *they* might be the problem. . . . The voters were expected to ratify a result neatly fashioned by party leaders and widely heralded in the national media. Instead, the voters again rose up with a thunderous "No!" Still the leadership just doesn't get it. . . . Failing an alternative, the voters have turned to Mr. Jackson out of a sense of electoral desperation and personal fairness. Only Mr. Jackson has spoken to the substantive discontent of voters.

Jackson demonstrated the power of populism. Unfortunately, Jackson brought with him other baggage as well. His foreign-policy stands were to the left of many Democrats and most Americans. He had no experience as an elected official, let alone a manager. His one stint as chief executive—of Operation Push—was scandal-ridden. His unwillingness to disavow the openly anti-Semitic Black Muslim Louis Farrakhan and his now-famous "Hymietown" characterization of New York alienated most of the influential Jewish political establishment, which reciprocated by refusing Jackson's repeated olive branches and denying his evident political maturation. It all made the prospect of an actual Jackson administration a frighteningly unknown quantity, even for those who admired Jackson's moral leadership and liked his program.

Yet all the insiders' qualms about Jesse Jackson seemed mocked by the current White House incumbent. Any deprecating comment about the plain unsuitability of Jackson the man for the job of president also fit Ronald Reagan. Like Jackson, Reagan was careless with detail, turned aside potential gaffes with disarming quips, remained infectiously popular despite controversial stands on the issues. Jackson, like Reagan, seemed a logical creature for the age of politics-as-entertainment. He alone among the Democrats had telegenic star quality. It seemed only fair that the left should have a turn at electing someone who on his merits seemed a little farfetched as president, but who was perfect for media politics; and that blacks—having contributed such TV phenoms as Bill Cosby, Bryant Gumbel, and Kareem Abdul-Jabbar—should get a shot at the ultimate TV superstar job. Cartoonist Jules Feiffer sketched a senescent Ronald Reagan, aghast that his legacy should turn out to be "the first Teflon Black."

And then, suddenly, Jackson's moment was over. In the late states, beginning with New York, Dukakis seemed more and more like the eventual nominee. Jackson failed to retain the remarkable inroads among white voters that he had demonstrated early on. For the Democrats, the intriguing question is whether Dukakis as nominee can tap the power of economic populism demonstrated so powerfully among alienated constituencies by far less attractive candidates than Dukakis. The also rans—Simon, Gephardt, Jackson—showed that disaffected Democrats will turn out to support candidates who articulate their economic self interest, and may be unenthusiastic about candidates who don't. Dukakis needs to marry his own steadiness to their sense of commitment and passion.

A related danger is that as Dukakis transforms himself from relatively unknown governor into national standard bearer, he will become captive of the usual suspects—the same party elite, the same relatively conservative policy intellectuals who counselled Walter Mondale that austerity was necessary economics and sound politics. It is neither. There is a dreadful consensus among orthodox macro-economists that all America needs to do to salvage its precarious economy is to balance the federal budget, let the U.S. dollar keep sinking in value against other currencies, and increase the domestic rate of savings. Each of those recommendations contains a grain of truth, but taken to an extreme they would put Dukakis in an even worse version of the Mondale bind, where he would have nothing to propose to economically vulnerable voters but higher taxes and reduced help from government. Dukakis, who helped revive an ailing regional economy through activist policies, needs to follow his own lights, and find more venturesome advisors.

Not long ago, political insiders were saying that only a deep recession could prevent the continuation of Republican presidential dominance. But 1988 is turning out to be rather a more promising year for the Democrats. The Republicans have nominated perhaps their weakest candidate. The value of the Reagan legacy diminishes daily. There is a desire for change. The personal steadiness that Dukakis radiates is a more substantial asset than usual. After eight years of bad government, the good government that Dukakis champions looks attractive. But neither steadiness nor good government, by themselves, are quite enough, any more than similar virtues were sufficient for Jimmy Carter to have a successful presidency in the wake of Watergate.

The Democrats need to win back America's non-wealthy voters—not by being tougher on the Russians or by speaking with a Southern accent or by reverting to social conservatism—but by standing up for the well being of ordinary Americans. Seeming more steady and competent than George Bush is a very good and necessary beginning, but barring an economic calamity before November, it is not sufficient. Bush's persona reminds voters why they don't like Republicans. Dukakis needs to remind votes why they like Democrats. When elections are won by default, they are usually won by incumbents and by Republicans. 1988 offers a real opportunity. As usual, the election is the Democrats' to win—or lose.

Robert Kuttner
April 1988

ACKNOWLEDGMENTS

M y family should be acknowledged first. My children knew when their father had a bad day at the word processor and made allowances beyond their tender years. My wife didn't edit every word this time—she was waist-deep in her own work—but she was a model of tolerance.

Thanks to my several editors, for allowing me to take some risks and continuing to print my stuff nonetheless: to Tom Gagen, Irving Howe, Michael Kinsley, Martin Nolan, Jack Patterson, Martin Peretz, Steven Shepard, William Whitworth, Dorothy Wickenden; and especially to Elisabeth Sifton, who recognized back in 1985 that somebody just might want to read a book on liberalism and the Democrats, when most editors thought both were dead as the dodo. She is also the rare editor who edits. An acknowledgment to Dick Pollak, who more than anyone else taught me to write, is also long overdue.

Others who helped include: Ira Arlook, Sidney Blumenthal, John

Brockman, Pat Caddell, Tad Cantril, Crocker Coulson, Paul Erickson, Jeff Faux, Kathy Frankovic, Stanley Greenberg, Frank Greer, Hendrik Hertzberg, Al Jackson, Brooks Jackson, Marc Landy, Ann Lewis, Dotty Lynch, Eddie Mahe, Milton Morris, Richard Neustadt, Frank O'Brien, Gary Orren, Karen Paget, Dan Payne, Lynn Pounian, Robert Reich, John Sasso, Kay Schlozman, William Schneider, David Smith, Paul Starr, Sidney Verba, Ralph Whitehead, and Richard Wirthlin.

Thanks also to Harvard University's Institute of Politics, which, for the third time, invited me to teach a seminar that helped enrich a pending book; and to the Guggenheim Foundation, which gave me a fellowship to research another book, due in 1989, on global economic shifts. Completing this book has begun eating into that fellowship.

Two people deserve special acknowledgment: Professor Walter Dean Burnham of MIT, and Thomas Byrne Edsall of the *Washington Post*. Burnham and Edsall have each done pioneering work on political participation, social class, moneyed influence, and the resulting limits upon the seemingly possible. Both combine a technical virtuosity with an intuitive feel for politics. Both demonstrate that you needn't be marxist to appreciate that social class and money matter immensely in politics. I gratefully acknowledge the use of their lens, which often yields bad news for progressives; in this case it discerns some cause for optimism.

CONTENTS

THE LIFE
OF THE PARTY

CHAPTER ONE

DEMOCRATIC DILEMMA

I.

This is a book about the prospects of political democracy and the Democratic Party, in 1988 and beyond. In the twentieth century the expansion of political democracy, the promotion of economic opportunity, the active use of the state, and the health of the Democratic Party have been closely linked. But since the late 1970s, many Democrats and most political commentators have concluded that the party can be rebuilt only by abandoning its historic commitment to activist government and economic populism. The prevailing view has held that cautious, centrist politics are indicated by several distinct and unavoidable realities—by the popular mood, the electoral demographics, the fiscal constraints, the economic requirements of restored growth, and the financial imperatives of partisan competition.

My own view is that this counsel is self-defeating. The abrupt collapse of ideologically strident conservatism under Ronald Reagan offers Democrats a choice of seeking office either as better centrists or as resolute progressives. This book argues that Democrats need to rebuild by reclaiming the vision of progressive populism. This is the view, admittedly, of one whose own convictions are in the progressive tradition. But more pertinently it seems clear as a matter of strategy and electoral logic that a durable Democratic resurgence requires a reconnection to the progressive vision. This book will explore just what that entails.

Recent political history has not been kind to Democrats or to progressives. Americans last voted overwhelmingly for a Democratic president a generation ago, in 1964. That president, Lyndon B. Johnson, was a Southerner and sometime conservative made over into a liberal by the demands of his times. He stood for election as an accidental incumbent and a consummate insider, a year after the assassination of a beloved president. He had the further good fortune to run against an opponent whom most voters considered extremist, during a time when the public mood was one of national reconciliation, which allowed Johnson to combine the cultural appeal of a Dixie conservative, the programmatic reach of a liberal, and the contextual posture of a moderate. Johnson used his landslide victory, his big Democratic majority in the Congress, and his astute knowledge of the levers of power, to pursue the unfinished agenda of the liberal consensus. Early in his term he played to the Democratic Party's great unifying strength—the use of government to advance the economic condition of broad numbers of ordinary Americans. But he soon stumbled, on the two great issues that have often been destroyers of American liberalism—war and race. The economic populism that had united Democrats since Franklin D. Roosevelt soon gave way to bitter dissension, which widened the party's latent social and foreign-policy schisms.

Assessing the condition of American progressivism and the Democratic Party today, nearly a quarter century later, one must begin with the top rather than the base, albeit uneasily. The agony of the Democrats, of course, reflects the decay of mass politics and political participation, and the slow decline of the New Deal coalition and its loyalties. But presidential elections dominate American politics, realign voting blocs, send ideological signals, and shape ensuing assumptions of voters and leaders. Any discussion of party politics is framed by the outcome of the last presidential election, expectations about the coming one, and the behavior of the current incumbent.

The history of the modern Democratic Party begins with Roosevelt and with his use of government to capture the partisan allegiance of two generations of wage-earning voters. It peaks with Johnson—and his failure to carry that allegiance forward. It sinks to three calamitous low points thereafter, in 1972, 1980, and 1984. Presidential politics have been particularly disastrous for Democrats lately. In the past nine presidential elections, from 1952 on, thirty-two states have been carried by the Republican nominee at least six times. Only Minnesota and the District of Columbia have voted Democratic as many as six times. The crucial turning point in Democrats' presidential fortunes was 1968. In the five presidential elections since that year, the "normal" presidential vote of most states has been Republican. In March 1968, only three and a half years after Johnson's historic landslide, he stepped aside for Hubert Humphrey in a virtual abdication. Since then, Democrats have seemed unable to recover their role as the great unifier. By the early 1970s, the commodious "big tent" that Johnson liked to call the Democratic Party had become a disorderly camp of nasty little tents. The party of all the people, which made room for factory workers, urban bosses, uptown reformers, Southern racists, socialist intellectuals, rural populists, diverse ethnic minorities, and more, was bitterly divided over ideology, class, cultural style, and party rules. The fault lines in a coalition party had become open chasms. Its sprawling strength had become brawling weakness.

The next Democratic president, Jimmy Carter, was a consummate outsider, the least partisan president in Democratic Party history. He won the Democratic nomination as a dark-horse novelty and an ideological moderate, with few links to the usual party apparatus. His own past offered a kind of Rorschach to the beholder. He was liberal by Georgia standards, a racial moderate, but also a businessman-farmer and a onetime nuclear engineer. He had "good government" and technocratic overtones, not unlike the previous engineer-president, Herbert Hoover. Outsiders of various leanings found his ambiguity congenial. His ground troops and strategists included volunteers who had supported the presidential campaigns of Eugene McCarthy and George McGovern; his electorate included voters who had once cast presidential ballots for former Alabama Governor George Wallace. Carter won the presidency by running against Washington—in both senses: the expansive Washington of the Roosevelt and Kennedy Democratic past, as well as the more recent, corrupt Republican Washington symbolized by Watergate. The first recent president to declare that government is not the solution but the problem was not Ronald Reagan, but Jimmy Carter.

Despite the national revulsion against Watergate and despite Carter's appeal as a Southern moderate, a racial healer, and a force for morality in government, he could barely eke out a victory over a wooden Republican opponent who had been appointed by, and had pardoned, Richard Nixon. Carter came to Washington with the cultural trappings of a populist, but he squandered what remained of the Democrats' legacy as economic populists. He neither liked affirmative government nor led it well. His moral style was dour and prissy rather than inspirational. Four years later, Carter, with all the powers of incumbency, was trounced by Ronald Reagan, a man even more convincingly anti-Washington than he. And four years after that, Walter Mondale, a man who party insiders hoped would personify the strengths of the old-style Democratic Party coalition, suffered a record Democratic defeat. He lost forty-nine states.

Since 1968, Democrats have lost the White House running insiders, outsiders, liberals, and moderates. These losses occurred while popular participation in politics declined and the influence of political action committees (PACs) representing organized business grew, while Democratic Party institutions decayed and Republican ones were rebuilt.

No wonder the prospect of Democratic progressivism seems bleak. Geography, demography, ideology, economics, and the political economy of influence all seem tilted against Democrats in general and liberals in particular. Indeed, it has become almost obligatory to conclude that progressivism—the active use of the public sector to offset the inequalities and anomalies of a *laissez-faire* market economy—is fatally out of harmony with the wishes of the electoral majority, is instrumentally flawed, philosophically spent, and in any case is fiscally moot. Looking at the demographic and electoral map, the corollary seems to follow that the Democratic Party should move to the managerial center, away from its historic egalitarian values, away from meddling interest groups, away from government as an instrument of public purpose, if it is to regain its former status as the governing party. This has been the theme of dozens of books, movements, journals, think-tanks, and candidacies.

This book argues the opposite case. Democrats do not do well when they offer bloodless technical solutions, or when they try to compete with Republicans as advocates of Adam Smith's invisible hand. Harry Truman said it best: When the voters have a choice between a Republican and a Republican, they'll pick the Republican every time. Democrats do best when they develop broad, embracing, expansive visions combining national purpose with economic advancement, and rally masses of nonrich voters. Democrats can regain their status as majority party only by rebuilding a majority coalition of ordinary, wage- and salary-earning people, whose political and economic interests are not identical to those of the wealthy. Politically this is possible only by rebuilding popular institutions of participation and by linking them to the creative use of government as democracy's instrument of common purpose. Ideologically this requires Democrats to reassert the honorable principle that in a democratic society, citizenship values must have at least equal authority with marketplace values. As Republicans have built a temporary alliance of middle-class voters with the upper class, an alliance nourished by visions of *laissez-faire* riches, Democrats need to champion opportunity and security for ordinary people and thus restore a broad coalition of voters. Instead of appealing only to the increasingly narrow and affluent stratum that now votes (often unenthusiastically), Democrats need to become again the kind of party that will rally alienated voters and nonvoters.

Which is to say Democrats need to rebuild American progressivism. That does not mean the same old programs or the same cast of Washington insiders. In the 1930s it was easy to identify the Depression's mass unemployment as a populist cause, and industrial unionism as a popular constituency. In the 1960s it was evident that blacks were clamoring for full citizenship and that old people could not pay their medical bills. In the 1980s and 1990s the most pressing economic problems do not have self-evident remedies with simple links to the usual political interest groups. Yet they urgently require public remediation.

It is time, early in this discussion, to be explicit about labels, because words like "liberal," "progressive," "populist," and "social democratic" have had very different (and even contradictory) meanings at different times. To be liberal in the nineteenth century was to be committed to both political liberty and *laissez-faire* economics, which were then seen as logically inseparable. In this century, political and economic liberty have come to require a mixed economy, both to manage macroeconomic stability and to temper the extremes of the marketplace. Liberalism, since FDR, has meant participatory politics, popular rights, but also interventionist economics. Since the 1960s, the term "liberal" has lost some of its economic appeal and taken on overtones of "limousine liberal." In areas of social policy where idealistic economic elites inflicted well-intentioned social reforms on the working class—such as school integration and tough anti-pollution regulations—the elites (whose children were in suburban or private schools and who didn't have factory jobs to lose) seldom suffered the adverse side effects of the policies. "Liberal" has not been a good word lately among white, blue-collar Democratic voters. Liberalism has also connoted an overload of demands made on the state, and a politics of giving to have-nots out of a sense of charity rather than providing basic entitlements to everyone as citizens.

Populism usually refers to the native American radicalism of the late nineteenth century, which demanded a greater share of both political and economic power for have-nots. The term also suggests a tinge of nativism, isolationism, and even racism. Lately, it has implied a renewed emphasis on economic issues. Progressivism originally described the turn-of-the-century impulse to clean up both government and private economic abuse by enlarging popular sovereignty and by harnessing the market's energy to public purpose through regulation. Unlike populism, early progressivism was only occasionally an explicit movement of have-nots. The label "progressive" has also been used by various breakaway third parties. Lately, it has been used by left-of-center Democrats who don't like the recent connotations of the word "liberal."

In this book, I use the term "progressive-populist" to describe the modern Democratic Party philosophy that began with the New Deal, which also incorporated several antecedents and resonated with the intuitively egalitarian strain in the American character. It appropriated the demand for economic justice from the populists; it embraced and enlarged several regulatory inventions from the Progressive Era. It defined the modern mixed economy. It added the idea of macroeconomic management by the federal government, as well as direct federal spending in a variety of areas dedicated to the betterment of the common American. It included a social-democratic welfare state, and a dose of economic planning. It contained a salutary whiff of class warfare whenever "economic royalists" sought to resist its forward momentum.

The political genius of the New Deal and of subsequent approaches that carried forward the "progressive-populist" tradition was that it provided redistribution and social justice *via inclusion.* Social security and medicare, public schools and college loans, starter homes for families and low-rent housing for the elderly were never programs described as taking from the haves to give to the have-nots, though they have sometimes had that result. They defined needs—secure retirement, decent medical care, opportunity for home ownership or for good education—that applied to a substantial majority of the electorate. They engendered a sense of egalitarianism and empathy and political cohesion without being terribly radical about it. This brand of progressive populism built both civic and political community. Without saying so in as many words, it made very clear that there was more to civic life than a giant marketplace in which buyers and sellers were free to choose and free to lose. It was this conception of the society, market, state, and polity that made Democrats the majority party.

Progressive populism uses the apparatus of government to build an inclusionary politics and a social conception of citizenship. To understand this as merely "interest group liberalism"—a coalition of out-groups with their palms extended—crudely captures some of its electoral dynamics, but it leaves out the community-building aspect. Progressive populism has been our homegrown version of social democracy.

Most commentators who commend resolute centrism as the cure for the Democratic dilemma draw an oversimplified equation between interest-group politics, big government spending, and Democratic unpopularity. Their remedy is a "me too" politics, which is very unlikely to rebuild a party, to inspire voters, or to solve problems. They accept as immutable what Walter Dean Burnham calls a "politics of excluded alternatives," in which PAC money talks, alienated wage-earners do not vote, television and direct mail replace political organizing, federal deficits preclude activism, and Democrats retreat.

But this view poorly comprehends the forces that have weakened the Democrats. The assumptions that have dominated politics for the past decade compel Democrats to compete on Republican territory. In succeeding chapters, I will treat the conservatizing influence of money on both parties, the resulting asymmetry of partisan institutions, the deepening alienation of ordinary voters from the electoral process, the reinforcing failure of political leaders to animate them, the intellectual imbalance created by recent heavy business investment in ideological assets, and the currency this has given the various "neo" movements seeking to neuter the Democratic Party. There are, nonetheless, encouraging signs of new progressive life, and an emerging brand of economic populism that can marry sensible policies with effective politics, to restore the alliance between citizen, polity, and majority party. After two decades of internal division, Democrats are enjoying a measure of party unity, which has led some to counsel that the party need only avoid controversy. But Democrats need to direct that unity toward a progressive politics if they are to do more than back into office in the wake of another failed presidency, and fail to govern.

II.

Several contextual factors underlie the recent history of liberal and Democratic Party decline, and the current misleading remedies. The most obvious—and often oversimplified—is demographic.

The groups and regions that made Democrats the natural majority party between 1932 and 1968 have declined. The urban industrial states of the Northeast and Midwest no longer make up a majority in the electoral college. The West, in presidential elections, is almost solidly Republican. The South is no longer solidly Democratic. Old electoral machines are moribund. In senate and presidential elections, Democratic politics is infused with eager volunteers, but between elections the party machinery has little presence or staying power. Industrial workers in general and members of trade unions in particular form a shrinking fraction of the electorate; and in 1984 even unionists gave 44 percent of their votes to Reagan.

The Democratic base is both smaller and less faithful. In 1952 registered Democrats outnumbered registered Republicans by nearly two to one. By 1984 equal fractions of voters considered themselves Democrats and Republicans. Among the youngest voters, Reagan won by landslide proportions, which suggested an impending realignment. But the influence of these demographic shifts can be overstated. The oft-noticed and oft-misunderstood "baby-boom generation" is not firmly in either political camp. But what is undeniable, even after a surprising Democratic comeback in 1986, is that the core Democratic vote, in a normal, noncrisis election, is far less reliable than it once was.

It has also become commonplace to add, almost unreflectingly, that as American society has grown more affluent, the electorate's taste for public remedies of private ills must have declined apace; public works and public pensions were fine for a generation of proletarian voters; the postwar generation, it is argued, prefers private amenities and privatized IRAs. However, it is noteworthy that real wages have been declining since 1973, that average living standards have been maintained only by means of the two-income household, and that distribution of income has been growing more unequal for a decade. Despite the gadgetry of affluence, middle-class life in the 1980s is a struggle. It is not at all clear that declining living standards and widening inequality should generate enthusiasm for more *laissez-faire*. But when little is offered by Democrats as an alternative, the voters tend to support candidates who seem to know their way around the prevailing system.

A second factor closely related to the demographic one is the decline of the political formula known as interest-group liberalism, in which Democratic administrations deliver benefits to organized constituencies and the constituents deliver votes to the Democratic Party. "Tax and tax, spend and spend" is a scornful description of the Democrats popularized by Ronald Reagan. But the original version of the phrase, attributed to FDR's aide Harry Hopkins, went: "Tax and tax, spend and spend, *elect and elect.*" Between 1932 and 1968 progressivism was defined operationally as a twin commitment to economic opportunity and economic security. The state was the instrument of the commitment. The Democrats, as the party that championed the benign state, were the natural custodians of the policy.

Two generations of voters looked to affirmative government for economic security and opportunity—first through the work relief of the New Deal, later through the private-sector jobs that were sustained by the growth miracle of Democratic Keynesian economics. They became homeowners thanks to the FHA and VA, with mortgage loans anchored in the Federal Home Loan bank system and sold in a federally sponsored secondary mortgage market. Their education opportunities were underwritten by the GI Bill and the college loan program; their secure retirement was assured by social security and, later, medicare. Although the older local Democratic Party machine—of the much sentimentalized bucket of coal and Christmas turkey—was quite moribund by the 1960s, the newer federal programs served just as well to cement party allegiances. The Democratic hold on the electorate based on the affirmative state was so potent that only the greatest of war heroes, a man so above party loyalties that the Democrats had seriously considered nominating him before the Republicans did, could produce a Republican interlude. And even General Dwight Eisenhower's presidency was less a rejection of the New Deal formula than a pause in its ascendancy.

In the heyday of Democratic progressivism, these programs articulated and delivered economic opportunity and social fairness for a broad working and middle class—for a broad "us." They signaled that the older Lockean ideals of liberty and democratic citizenship now required more than a passive state that merely restrained leaders or majorities from imposing tyranny. They created a philosophy of social community and a sense that economic fate was not entirely the prerogative of the invisible hand. Yet the last major program to serve the economic interests and hence reinforce the loyalty of a large, mainstream voting block was the medicare program, enacted in 1965. The welfare state, after the mid-1960s, became a welfare state for "them"—the dependent poor. Today a thirty-five-year-old voter of moderate means contemplating the effect of government on his or her own life doesn't see a GI Bill, or an FHA loan, or government-guaranteed health insurance, or policies that help him cope with the realities of juggling family and work in the imperfectly liberated 1980s. His experience with public school, if he thinks of that as a service of government, is remote. His anticipation of social security and medicare is even more remote. His daily experience with the motor vehicle bureau is frustrating. The main evidence he sees of affirmative government is his tax bill.

As the broad progressivism of the 1930s and 1940s evolved into the interest-group liberalism of the 1960s and 1970s, something of its inclusionary character was sacrificed. It also became more accepting of the basic economic status quo, redistributing to outgroups around the margins. The formula of interest-group liberalism worked best during a period of steady economic growth, which was a necessary condition in two distinct respects. Government, as manager of a successful mixed economy, gained prestige and authority. And growth meant that the demands of the Democratic Party's diverse constituency groups could be met without the groups seeming to compete with each other. But if the interest-group articulation of economic needs and government response to them became the midcentury form of Lockean liberalism, by the last quarter of the century Locke had become grid-lock—or so it was widely believed. Jimmy Carter, a president who came to Washington opposed to many aspects of the liberal formula, had the bad luck to preside at a time of stagnation. When growth collapsed, the groups representing the Democratic Party constituencies understandably clamored for help from the state: public service jobs; urban aid; cost-of-living raises for social security; newly identified entitlements like special education for learning-disabled children, environmental clean up, and daycare. Although the New Deal/ Great Society agenda was still uncompleted, it became fashionable to blame both stagflation and government paralysis on "overload" induced by interest groups.

In reality the logic of inefficiency and imperfection in the American version of the welfare state more often reflects an excess of market than an excess of state. For example, medicare could not pay the health bills of elderly Americans except at an intolerable cost, because too many private-sector palms had to be greased to buy continuing support for the program. Social housing, American-style, is a bonanza more for developers than for tenants. These fatal compromises in the design of programs reflected underlying imbalances of economic power. Most of the time in America, business retains enough residual influence to demand its substantial private involvement in public programs. Likewise, taxpayers resent more the maldistribution of the tax load than the appetite of the state, but as a matter of ideological understanding, burgeoning government programs were widely blamed for the taxpayer revolts that spread in the late 1970s. In this climate, many Democrats whose values were weak and whose immediate goals were instrumental soon turned against the populist Roosevelt formula.

Early in his term Carter could sometimes resemble a truncated Great Society liberal. But as his budgetary problems and the broader inflationary pressures intensified, so did the disillusion of the constituent groups of the party base. As they grew disillusioned with government, Carter grew annoyed with them. His bonds with them had been weak to begin with, and he lacked the means of winning them back. Instead, he took refuge in a rhetoric that disparaged both government and constituent politics. Later, with Reagan's deliberately contrived budget crisis, the strategy of cementing the loyalty of the nonrich electorate by using affirmative government programs to address their economic needs became fiscally inconceivable as well as politically unfashionable. The nexus of benign state, common citizen, and Democratic Party was something for the old, the poor, and the national memory. And, anyway, it was something we could no longer afford.

Yet if the social realities and economic needs of today's electorate are markedly different from those of the 1930s and 1960s, the political logic of social community is unchanged. In a political democracy which is also a market economy, it remains the case that the left-of-center party must rally ordinary voters to offset the disproportionate residual influence of the well-off. To mobilize voters, that party must deliver things that voters need, using the common instrument of political democracy—the state. In a modern industrial society, it is impossible to imagine any other viable strategy for the party of the common people. (It is perhaps possible to imagine two conservative parties, but why bother?)

Today's practical problems are indeed altered ones. They include radical changes in the structure of the family, and a turbulent economy, which causes settled social compromises to come unstuck and produces opportunities for some at a cost of great dislocation to others. They include a bizarre housing market, which produced windfall gains for people positioned to buy homes before the great real estate inflation of the late 1970s—and astronomically costly tickets of admission for younger families belatedly chasing the escalator. During our parents' generation, the polity addressed the economic needs of the time. But for a decade or so, the polity has been mired in an earlier set of social assumptions and has failed to renew connections with voters. Today's problems are not insoluble, but they require a redirection of policy objectives, to fit actual needs and restore electoral links. Democrats can accomplish that, but not if they reject the logic of social community altogether. In this respect Democrats require a rededication to core values and goals before they can effectively assess the necessary means and policy instruments.

Thus the third crisis of the Democratic Party is ideological, and it is closely related to the collapse of interest-group liberalism. Most of the ideological principles of the post-1933 Democratic Party have been implicit rather than explicit. The overt rhetoric is a rhetoric of hope, of opportunity, of inclusion, not a rhetoric of state counterbalancing market. As public opinion analysts Lloyd Free and Hadley Cantril explained two decades ago, in a famous study called *The Political Beliefs of Americans,* most Americans remain operational liberals and ideological conservatives. They like government programs, but distrust government as an abstraction. This is hardly surprising, since the essence of the American Constitution

is a series of ingenious restraints on government, and liberalism in
the American experience has been as much a rejection of radicalism
as an alternative to feudalism. The United States, as a liberal society, has often turned to social-democratic remedies, but rarely to
a social-democratic ideology.

In nations with more ideologically explicit politics, social democracy emerged as the great middle way of the twentieth century.
Instead of demanding worker uplift via socialization of production
and dictatorship of the proletariat, social democracy recognized
that personal liberty and parliamentary democracy had their own
substantial value. It recognized that capitalism could be a great
engine of growth, but one that had to be tempered by substantial
public intervention, both to create a stable stage on which the
capitalist drama could play, and to temper the extremes of wealth
and poverty that *laissez-faire* engenders. Contrary to the conservative dictum that government interference cripples the invisible
hand, the social-democratic experience of the past half century
proved that government stabilization more often keeps the private
economy on an even keel and helps purchase the necessary social
peace that pure capitalism keeps undermining.

In the social-democratic compromise, whole spheres of economic and social life are removed from the *laissez-faire* criterion of
"to each according to his purse" and structured according to the
socialist criterion of need, even though the basic engine of production remains capitalist and investment remains substantially private. Even in libertarian America, basic education, retirement
income, and health care are substantially socialized. The social
democratic conception of society blends, albeit imperfectly, elements of capitalism with a leavening dose of socialism. The difficulty, of course, is that this remains a very difficult balancing act
over time, because in a capitalist economy to a substantial degree
money is still power. In theory the political realm is supposed to
be based on one citizen, one vote; the principle of the economic
sphere—one dollar, one vote—is not supposed to slop over into
the civic sphere, but of course it does. Far from government intervention hobbling capitalism, market imperatives and business
influence keep undermining the mixed economy. The social demo-

cratic balancing act can be maintained politically only when masses of nonrich voters remain in a high state of political mobilization, and institutions of mass participation and social democratic values remain in good working order. When that logic falters, the market overwhelms the state, the benefits dry up, the participatory machinery rusts, the ideals seem quaint, and the voters stay home. And that is what has befallen the Democrats.

The modern Democratic Party's implicit ideology is clearly a social democratic one. It counterposes citizenship values against market values. Certain economic freedoms have become concomitants of democratic citizenship, via *entitlements,* a word that lately has taken on ironic connotations of interest-group overload. As operational social democrats, Democratic progressives were not hesitant to demand that the state be the guarantor of certain economic prerogatives hitherto left to the private market—retirement income for old age and medical care for the entire population, housing for the middle class, as well as safety-net guarantees for the poor. The state also took responsibility for macroeconomic management, to assure high levels of growth and private employment. This was a giant step away from nineteenth-century economic liberalism, toward a mixed economy and frankly socialistic principles of entitlement according to need in several key areas of economic life. But although the Democratic Party implicitly proposes that populism in the twentieth century must necessarily be social democratic, our national icons remain those of liberal capitalism. Social solidarity, as a civic goal, never quite became part of the party credo or the national mythology. Nor did a frank critique of the free market ideal. Moreover, Democrats retreated fairly quickly from more interventionist economic strategies and enforceable commitments to full employment, instead coasting along on American dominance during the flush years of the postwar boom, and leaving the embryonic welfare state to pick up the residue. And most Americans, at a philosophical level, remained intuitive nineteenth-century liberals.

Paradoxically, just as Free and Cantril suggested, public-opinion polls show that affirmative uses of government to address economic problems of ordinary people remain highly popular. This has been true in the seemingly conservative 1980s as well as the liberal 1960s. Even as they re-elected Reagan by landslide proportions, most Americans believed that his administration had cut social programs too much, favored retaining most regulations on business and finance, backed substantial cuts in military spending, and wanted more public outlays for many public needs. Ironically one of the unintended consequences of Ronald Reagan's presidency, at least prior to the Iran-Contra affair, was to restore the public's faith in government. Republican strategist David Gergen, in a sober assessment for the American Enterprise Institute's journal *Public Opinion,* reported that more Americans considered themselves liberals in 1985 than in 1981, that trust in government to do the right thing most of the time had climbed from 25 percent in 1980 back to 45 percent in 1984, that the majority of Americans opposed to further cuts in social spending had grown from 51 percent in February 1982 to a solid 66 percent in March 1985.

But the ideological implications of these public-opinion findings are murky indeed. Try to distill a one-paragraph credo out of the modern Democratic Party experience, and it goes something like this: The freedoms of the marketplace are dandy, but they are not enough. Freedom also includes the economic freedoms of Franklin Roosevelt's (nearly forgotten) 1944 Economic Bill of Rights: the freedom to hold a job, to live in a decent home, to get an education, to not suffer want of medical care. The only agency that can underwrite those freedoms is the state. Even in the nineteenth century, when the populist position was usually skeptical of central government, government served as an agency of common purpose far more often than is usually recognized.

Put explicitly social-democratic themes into a political speech, and you will perplex or embarrass a Democratic Party audience. Democratic politicians today are reduced to groping for metaphors like "the family," which figured so prominently in Mario Cuomo's popular keynote address to the 1984 Democratic Convention. The family metaphor is an honorable attempt to temper the crude individualism of the *laissez-faire* creed—to find some new basis for civic empathy and social solidarity that Americans will instinctively view as legitimate. But it is a very tricky image, because most Americans don't like either the implicit confinement of their own family of origin, or the implication that a national family must take care of other people's bastard children.

The Democratic Party's embrace of operationally socialistic measures like social security and medicare was a bit like the amorous embrace of eager but inhibited fifteen-year-olds, who find the activity satisfying but cannot quite admit what they are doing. Social security was sold as "insurance," medicare as a "partnership" with profit-driven insurance companies, hospitals, and medical combines. Louis Hartz, remarking in 1955 on the pervasiveness of individualist liberal values in American politics, observed that FDR, lacking either a European-style socialist challenge on the left, or a serious conservative challenge on the right, sold his reforms as merely pragmatic: "He did not need to spell out any real philosophy at all." Albert O. Hirschman, embellishing Hartz's insight, added ruefully in 1982, "Today, of course, we can appreciate the high cost of [Roosevelt's] maneuver. The New Deal reforms, as well as the welfare state schemes that were added later, were never truly consolidated as an integral part of a new economic order or ideology."

The social-democratic state faltered first in America because support for it was always almost entirely operational rather than philosophical. Even trade unionists, who in America are the closest thing we have to institutional social democrats, have a deeply conservative economic and cultural streak. Where social solidarity is concerned, we Americans are summer soldiers. The most radical of us are radically individualist in our egalitarianism, not socialist. In a culture that celebrates swashbucklers, socially negligent ultra-free-marketeers like T. Boone Pickens seem part of our radically populist tradition, which makes for ideological confusion. As cultural radicals, we imagine a society where everyone is equally free to be outrageous, not duty-bound to our fellows, least of all duty-bound via the state. The more culturally conservative among us cherish institutional tradition and social conformism, but few conservatives regard that as any of the state's business either. In its eighteenth-century roots, the American experiment was radically egalitarian. But the engine of that egalitarian creed was fierce individualism, notwithstanding a persistent communitarian under-current.

In practice the use of collective resources to further individual ends has been part of our history since long before the New Deal. The Homestead Acts, the colonial public school, the early bond-supported economic development projects, agricultural extension, land-grant colleges—these nineteenth-century initiatives were surprisingly socialistic for their day. But our most powerful national myths continue to celebrate individual pluck far more than collaborative endeavor. Americans continue to be intuitively skeptical of any large accretions of power, with the possible exception of the military. As the political scientist William Schneider likes to observe, our most pervasive popular cultural transmitters, like television and rock 'n' roll, thrive by poking fun at big shots. Big business, big labor, big government, and big politics are disapproved almost equally—yet voters approve of social security and medicare by margins exceeding ten to one.

It is permissible in mainstream Democratic circles to bait big corporations but not to advocate things like public ownership or national economic planning as remedies. Antitrust, consumerism, profit sharing, mandated social insurance may resonate with the popular mood of economic populism; but notions like countervailing power or yardstick competition or "industrial policy" have intrigued only the party's intellectuals, not its base. Farmers have long demanded parity schemes, price supports, soil banks, loan programs, import restrictions, extension services, and the other paraphernalia of a government-managed farm economy, yet they remain cultural conservatives, antistatists, and vote Republican more often than Democratic. In America government programs that serve economic needs are popular. The state is not.

The best Democratic politicians have understood that paradox and rolled with it. When John F. Kennedy declared, "I'm not satisfied that steel is operating at 70 percent of capacity—we can do better," the "we" he referred to was not explicitly the government. He meant we as a people, we as a nation, we as a common economy. "We" also signified the link between Kennedy and his constituents, with him leading and us assenting. Presumably, with Kennedy in charge, steel somehow would operate at more than 70 percent of capacity. In this alchemy, of course, it was tacitly understood that the instrument of the "we" had to be something that government under the Democrats might do that government under the Republicans had failed to do. Kennedy, after all, was running for president of the United States, the chief of the *government*. But because of the national ambivalence about government, Democratic rhetoric has never been a rhetoric of statism, even when Democrats and voters were in a more expansive mood about the public sector than they have been in the 1980s. Industrial policy would have no more played politically as a successful slogan in the 1960 campaign than it did in the 1980 campaign.

This use of government without the advocacy of government was a delicate, if intuitive, high-wire act for Democrats. Although an ideological defense of the state has not generally been part of the Democratic repertoire, the pragmatic, constructive use of the state is its essence. When Democrats lose the bonds linking state, constituency, and party, they lose everything. The ideology may be more implicit than explicit. But it is essential, and in the past decade it has been laid aside.

The philosophical vacuity of the current Democratic Party reflects not only the disarray of interest-group liberalism and the disrepute of the public sector, it also reflects the almost complete failure of Democrats and liberals to reproduce the cultural institutions of modern progressivism, at either the elite or mass levels. The Reagan era has not brought about an end of ideology. On the contrary, it has produced a one-sided resurgence of ideological zeal. Older American progressivism was often an alliance of genuinely populist institutions, such as trade unions, cooperatives, farmers' organizations, with university-based intellectuals and reformist newspapers and journals. Since the collapse of Bull Moose Republicanism and the failure of such third-party movements as Norman Thomas's Socialism or Robert La Follette's or Henry Wallace's Progressivism, the Democratic Party has been the umbrella electoral vehicle of progressive ideas. During the New Deal, radically liberal intellectuals united with authentic working-class movements to produce a generation of activists, scholars, and practitioners who were idealistic, practical, resolute, and competent. The domestic policymakers of that generation were well to the left of their counterparts today.

By contrast, the intellectual dialogue of the 1970s and 1980s has been between a resurgent, yeasty new right and a defensive center, with a mainstream progressive populist left almost totally absent. The two most visible liberal journals are the *New Republic* and the *Washington Monthly*. The *Monthly*, primarily a voice of neo-liberalism, is idealistic and iconoclastic, skeptical of affirmative government and coalition politics, and equally critical of big business. The *New Republic* is a feisty blend of neo-liberal, neo-conservative, and New Deal progressive—a diversity that produces lively journalism, but not necessarily a consistent politics or public philosophy. More left-wing journals, such as the *Nation*, the *Progressive*, or *Dissent*, though heroic, often seem hermetic, as if they are speaking for and to "the left" rather than attempting to influence the mainstream debate *from* the left.

There are no prominent left-of-center policy quarterlies doing what *The Public Interest* and its many conservative clones do so well. Two that attempted to do so in the early 1980s, *Working Papers* and *Democracy,* folded when their sole financial backers pulled the plug. Such are the vagaries of the political economy of influence. There is plenty of money around for the celebration of a business-oriented society and far less available to criticize it. Young scholars of conservative leanings have no shortage of mentors, networks, journals, and well-paid research posts. The presence of such resources breeds more resources. Its absence breeds isolation, demoralization, and the temptation to join or at least emulate the other side. Those Democratic, or quasi-Democratic research institutions, such as Brookings, which do command resources, have come to share many of the intellectual premises of conservatism. This is congenial to the business interests that help finance them. Most economists advising Democratic politicians are reverential advocates of free markets, with little sympathy for the political and social logic that underpins the policies of a mixed economy. It takes time for a political culture of progressivism to mature, and a close reading of journals, speeches, and policy papers indicates that ours had become perilously close to extinct. However, as we shall see, after a decade of near paralysis there are again some heartening signs of genuine renewal, as Democratic progressives begin to recover their voice.

III.

Beyond the demographic, coalitional, and ideological problems besetting the party, a further source of Democratic crisis is rooted in the abrupt recent changes in the world economy. One of the great hallmarks of the Democratic era (1933–68) was that institutions in the global economy tended to stay put. There were no great speculative flows of capital. Enterprise and technology tended to be national. Wartime controls in Europe were dismantled very gradually, and a truly *laissez-faire* world economy only emerged in the 1970s. The United States was insulated from global pressures, and domestic economic change could occur at a socially manageable pace. This was a superb context for a party whose political appeal was premised on some kind of implicit social contract.

The Democrats of the Roosevelt-Truman-Kennedy era were great internationalists and great institution builders. They conceived and built the foundations of the mixed international economy, which served the postwar quarter-century of unprecedented prosperity: the Marshall Plan, the Bretton Woods system of stable currencies, the World Bank, the GATT system of liberal trade. They sponsored the Atlantic Alliance and cheered on European economic union. But what is often overlooked is that the internationalism of the 1940s under Democratic auspices was an economic globalism that valued stability along with free markets and produced a good blend of the two. It provided a complementary international counterpart to a domestic mixed economy. In contrast, the ultra-*laissez-faire* internationalism of the Republican 1980s cherishes turbulence and makes domestic economic stabilization all but impossible.

During the three postwar decades, it was taken for granted that nations had the right, and the running room, to pursue national economic policies. If the U.S. government wanted to pursue a particular mix of fiscal and monetary policies, to keep the right

balance between unemployment and inflation, this was both ideologically and operationally possible. In theory, "Keynesian" management of the economy manipulated public spending to stabilize
total demand. In truth, the demand management of the sort practiced between, say, 1946 and 1973, was far less Keynesian than its
sponsors claimed. Government budget deficits and surpluses rarely
oscillated by more than a percentage point or two of the gross
national product. The real flywheel that kept the economy moving
ahead at a steady speed was the immense inertial push of defense
spending, which bulled its way across the valleys and peaks of the
business cycle. The other countercyclical stabilizer that kept purchasing power more or less homeostatic was the impact of union-
driven three-year, industry-wide master contracts, which assured
that periodic business recessions did not produce self-deepening
cycles of wage reduction and depression of demand. This was not
quite the sort of Keynesianism that was advertised, but as long as
the United States was more or less insulated from the global economy, it worked.

By the same token, if the government thought that banking stability required regulations keeping commercial banks out of the
brokerage business, limiting interest on passbook accounts, creating specialized savings institutions to finance housing, and limiting
cross-national flows of currency, that was also permissible. There
were no multinational pressures demanding a lowest common de-
nominator of the freest possible financial market. If a government
wanted to subsidize development of, say, a military jet transport,
and that work spilled over into a commercially marketable Boeing
707, this was no problem. There was no global excess of production capacity, no global interpenetration of national markets compelling nations to mutually swear off industrial strategies. If
government wanted to anchor the American farm economy in a
system of price supports and import quotas, that was praised as
clever management and astute politics rather than an evil recipe for
inflation, protection, and glut. And if social peace required a genteel toleration of oligopoly, whose slightly illicit fruits could be
shared with unionized workers, nobody minded too much. The
ruthless pressures of global competition still lay ahead.

All of these *de facto* elements of stability served the Democratic

Party, which was in effect the guarantor of the social contract. But how do you deliver assurances of job security and living standards to an American factory worker when the interdependence of the world economy creates continuous pressures to lower his wages to meet those of a worker in Manila? How do you guarantee workers that their productivity efforts will be reciprocated when the company may be restructured tomorrow through a leveraged buyout and the new executives were not party to the deal? How do you fine-tune fiscal and monetary policy in Washington when the most important lever of macroeconomic management is a floating exchange rate that influences the willingness of a pension fund in Tokyo to buy U.S. Treasury bonds? How do you defend a farm program, or an industrial-development subsidy, or a housing loan scheme, when both the reality and the prevailing ideology call for totally free international trade, giddy institutional restructurings, undifferentiated global financial markets, and competitive deregulation, across corporate and national boundaries? The modern Democratic Party is advertised as the great manager, broker, equalizer, and tamer of the raw, often brutal energy of the marketplace. But how, in such a world, does the Democratic Party *deliver*? As a market researcher might put it, what remains of the party's Unique Selling Proposition?

An integrated global market economy leaves little if any room for national *policy*. It serves as a relentless engine of *laissez-faire*. It also creates the image as well as the reality of government paralysis and incompetence—which is very handy if you happen to be the conservative party whose doctrine is that governments are seldom competent anyway. This is why conservative parties are now ascendant throughout the Western democracies. This conundrum has been noticed and studied intensely by the democratic left parties of Europe. It has been all but ignored in the United States.

For the American Democratic Party, the integration of the global market economy presents special ideological and practical dilemmas, because our Democratic Party was always more reluctant about interfering with free markets than its explicitly social democratic European counterparts. "Pragmatic" interventions in the economy were accepted, as long as the postwar U.S. economy existed in splendid, towering isolation. Planning was never explicitly sanctioned. Integration of the global market economy forces the issue, in an ideological fashion that Democrats would just as soon not confront.

Global *laissez-faire* drives a wedge between the Democratic Party and its ability to deliver populist remedies to its natural base of nonrich wage earners who are vulnerable to the vagaries of the market. In the Depression and in the postwar context of a malleable national economy, the Democrats figured out some rough formulas for delivering that security domestically via a "mixed economy," though they were reluctant to peer too deeply into what that meant ideologically. They have yet to even consider what a mixed economy means or requires, practically or ideologically, in a globalized market.

Many aspects of the Democratic Party's confusion today can be understood as a refusal to consider or define the limits of *laissez-faire* capitalism, as it operates globally. In an individualistic, market-oriented America, Democrats are in the habit of bending over backwards to assure voters, business executives, investors, editorialists, and themselves that they believe in free markets, "too." In moments when the electoral mood seems conservative, too many Democrats rush to assure the voters that they don't much like big government either. Thus the Democratic uncertainty about how to address the agony of the farmer, the factory worker, the semiconductor industry, or the savings-and-loan business without transgressing the sacred doctrine of resurgent free markets. Seemingly, it would make sense to restrict overproduction of farm products, and to stabilize prices, as Democratic administrations have effectively done in the past. But in a global economy where cheap wheat, meat, butter, and fiber are all available for purchase abroad, a farm-stabilization scheme seemingly would just raise prices, annoy allies, and restrict consumer choice. Ditto steel, autos, and semiconductors. Why pander to Democratic constituencies just because they vote?

Because of their ambivalence about interfering with the free market, most Democrats are reluctant to acknowledge that steering the national economy through a period when the world economy is being radically restructured will require a substantial measure of planning if the costs of transition are not to come at the expense of Democratic voters. In practice, major sectors of the economy have experienced a degree of planning: the farm economy, the aerospace industry, and defense-driven advanced technology have been intimately tied to public policy decisions—but only in practice and not in theory. Explicit planning lacks legitimacy. In 1984 poor Walter Mondale oscillated between proclaiming his support for American industrial workers, defending himself against editorials proclaiming him a xenophobe, contemplating industrial strategies for industry, and assuring his business supporters that he believed in the free market. Pressed by a "Meet the Press" interrogator on his "protectionist" leanings, Mondale sighed guiltily, "I've come to the point where I don't know what other defense there is." No wonder the same trade union constituency that was condemned for delivering Mondale the nomination failed to arouse great enthusiasm for him among its own rank and file.

IV.

The 1984 Mondale campaign epitomized the Democrats' confusion about what they stood for. The only things worse than the campaign itself were some of the lessons drawn from its failure. The Mondale campaign managed to present interest-group liberalism in its worst possible incarnation—serving the lobbies without rousing the voters. Mondale, seeking to lock up the nomination early, pursued an endorsement strategy not unlike the one that worked so badly for Edmund Muskie in 1972. He solicited the endorsements of the entire party elite. The only thing he offered was his supposed inevitability. Mondale appeared as the candidate not of the broad populist coalition that benefits from activist government, but of the party insiders. Though Mondale himself was a man of decency and moderately progressive instincts, his candidacy reeked of smoke-filled rooms. That Mondale was almost eliminated in the primaries by the nearly unknown Gary Hart demonstrated the hollowness of his appeal. Recognizing that he had an image problem, Mondale wrongly concluded that what was unpopular was his liberalism. Taking his advice from orthodox economists and from fiscally conservative former Carter administration officials, Mon-

dale was persuaded that the Democrats' primary electoral liability
was their image as big spenders, and that his primary task was to
offer a platform of budget balance. Just as Ronald Reagan was at
last liberating the Republican Party from its austerity complex and
spending like a sailor, Walter Mondale was discovering the maso-
chistic pleasures of the tight fisc. He ended up with all the political
liabilities of interest-group liberalism and none of its ample assets.

Since the logic of budget balancing means that you must raise
taxes but not increase spending, Mondale managed to get the least
marketable rump end of the New Deal formula—the taxing without
the spending. Budget constraints and the fear of seeming too liberal meant that genuinely popular, long-standing Democratic commitments, such as jobs programs or national health insurance, were
jettisoned as both too expensive and too liberal. In tax policy,
Mondale's desire to ingratiate himself with the business community, both for fund-raising and ideological purposes, drove him to
distance himself from the most populist Democratic proposal then
in circulation, the Bradley-Gephardt tax reform bill, which proposed to lower taxes on ordinary working voters by closing loopholes used by the rich and by increasing taxes on business.
Ironically, when something very like the original Bradley-Gephardt
bill became law in 1986, it was Ronald Reagan who appropriated
much of the political credit. Finally, Mondale's campaign was constrained from using the public sector to serve popular economic
needs by the advice that to further distance himself from the party's
bad, liberal past, Mondale had to seem hawkish on defense. This
meant that military spending, which had been increased by over 60
percent in just four years, was not to be cut. Mondale thought
himself bold to advocate reductions in the rate of its increase.

So when Mondale triumphantly announced in his nomination-
acceptance speech that he would raise taxes and restrain the usual
profligate liberal instinct to spend money, he got himself hanged
for both a sheep and a lamb. The pledge alienated many voters
opposed to a tax increase, and it gave other voters no affirmative
reason to support Mondale. The odor of interest-group politics
lingered, without the beneficial substance. And with the evils of
interest-group pandering serving as the 1984 media cliché about

what ailed the Democratic Party, even Mondale's truly bold choice of a woman as running mate was seen less as a nervy initiative than as another capitulation. Worst of all, Mondale's acceptance speech virtually endorsed the Republican claim that Democrats were big-spending wimps. "I want to say something to those of you across our country who voted for Mr. Reagan—to Republicans, to independents, and, yes, to some Democrats: I heard you. And our party heard you. After we lost, we didn't tell the American people that they were wrong. Instead, we began asking what our mistakes had been," Mondale declared.

Democrats, Mondale boasted, had learned what *not* to do. "Look at our platform. There are no defense cuts that weaken our security; no business taxes that weaken our economy; no laundry lists that raid our treasury. We are wiser, stronger, and focused on the future." This had to be one of the most self-defeating passages in the annals of American political rhetoric. Imagine Eisenhower, or Nixon, or Reagan declaring in an acceptance speech that, yes, the Republicans used to be cold-hearted and bellicose and inept at managing the economy, but that they had recently and belatedly learned—from the Democrats!—to mend their ways. To hear Mondale, one might have thought that Jimmy Carter had gone down fighting for pacifism or socialism. In a stroke, Mondale gave away the entire post-1932 Democratic tradition. And if Mondale failed to appreciate the political asset that the Democratic past represented, Ronald Reagan was quick to recover the fumble. The recent presidents who Reagan most often invoked were Kennedy, Truman, and Roosevelt.

Astonishingly, Mondale's weak showing was held by many party regulars to be the fault of his liberalism. Though Mondale had done his level best to expunge the vital substance of liberalism, he couldn't escape its onus. In reality the liberalism of the 1984 Democratic campaign was so faint that it roused few voters. Mondale's own issues director, a political scientist named William Galston, saw the party's 1980 and 1984 defeats this way:

> . . . the concept of the national interest advocated by Democrats
> for half a century was dissolved into a myriad of benefits for

specific groups—the so-called special interests. Citizens who did
not regard themselves primarily as members of such groups felt
left out entirely. Small wonder that one out of five Americans who
had voted for Carter in 1976 deserted him four years later.

By 1980, according to Galston, a majority of Americans "wanted
to get government off their backs. Ronald Reagan's simple message
was that their wish was his command, and it carried him to two
overwhelming victories." Now, if this were truly the import of the
Reagan popularity, what could a Democrat do but attempt to emulate Reagan? The budget-deficit dilemma, according to Galston,
further constrained Mondale to run a campaign, however reluctantly, somewhat at odds with his own activist convictions. "But for
lack of any other credible alternative, Mondale ran as a conservative. . . . His message was sober and responsible. But it lacked
inspiration and hope." So, not surprisingly, Mondale got clob-
bered. And Galston concluded with the depressing observation
that the Democrats will remain in the political wilderness until they
"offer a compelling diagnosis of our national needs and a persuasive prescription for dealing with them," but offered neither the
diagnosis nor the prescription. Thus did the issues director of the
Mondale campaign confess the barren state of his own cupboard.

Other Monday-morning quarterbacks had no such modesty.
Most of them thought that the problem of the Mondale-Carter
administration and the Mondale candidacy was that neither man
moved the party rightward compellingly enough, and that this was
the fault of those damned interest groups spawned by the Roosevelt coalition. In early 1985 several conservative and moderate
Democratic officials from the South and West organized a Democratic Leadership Council, with the express purpose of pushing the
party to the center, out of the clutches of liberal interest groups,
most notably organized labor. DLC, according to one jibe, stood
for Democratic Leisure Class. Also in 1985, in a closely fought
election, the Democratic National Committee made Paul Kirk its
new chairman. Kirk had once been a political aide to Senator Edward Kennedy, and he was the candidate of organized labor for
party chair. Kirk's election as party chair seemed to set up an epic
factional contest. However, Kirk accommodated much of the DLC's

tactical view and used his influence to rid the party of official caucuses and other McGovern-era machinery that emphasized special-
interest politics, but without joining the DLC in abandoning the
party's progressive message.

The DLC, in a sense, represented a new phase in the long, stormy
shotgun marriage between the national party and its once solid
Southern wing. Before 1968 many racist Southern Democrats had
been populist on economic issues; their populism simply had excluded blacks. Most of the Roosevelt program received Southern
support because loopholes were written into social legislation making sure that it wouldn't alter race relations in the South. The
Democratic South of the Roosevelt era produced a large number
of economic populists, a few of whom were moderate and occasionally even liberal on race. The Southern tail, however, did not wag
the Democratic donkey. The national party remained resolutely
liberal on race, even to the point of forcing a Dixiecrat walkout in
1948 and the George Wallace splinter in 1968. The three landmark
Civil Rights Acts of the 1960s, passed by Democratic administrations and Congresses over white Southern protest, at last gave
blacks full citizenship. In the process, the Democratic Party traded
the solid regional vote that had been once assured in the white
South with a smaller solid black vote throughout the country.

After the completion of the civil rights agenda of the 1960s,
however, most regular Southern Democrats became racial moderates. They accepted, however reluctantly, the broad reforms of
desegregation. They competed for black votes. They also became
far more business-oriented than many of their populist Southern
predecessors. By 1980 the Southern wing of the party was less a
force for racial conservatism than for economic conservatism. And
with the arrival of the DLC, the white Southern tail indeed began
pinning the whole donkey to the economic status quo.

In the DLC view, Democrats had to move to the economic center
and away from interest groups, in order to win, especially in the
South and the West. Yet the 1986 election, in which the Democrats
regained control of the Senate, seemed to suggest something else.
Several of the Democrats who won in 1986 ran as economic populists. So did other Democrats who had recaptured once-Republican
seats earlier during the Reagan presidency: Paul Simon of Illinois,

Tom Harkin of Iowa, and Albert Gore, Jr., of Tennessee. In 1986, Wyche Fowler, in Georgia, became the most progressive Democrat elected to the Senate from the Deep South since the young Claude Pepper of Florida (then known as "Red" Pepper) graced that chamber in the 1930s and 1940s. Two other freshmen, Bob Graham of Florida and Terry Sanford of North Carolina, were well to the left of the average Southern Democrat. Sanford had come to prominence in 1960, when he was John Kennedy's North Carolina campaign manager. In that year, Sanford was elected governor, and he promptly devised what today would be called an industrial policy, when he upgraded North Carolina's educational system as the bait to attract high-technology industry to Research Triangle Park.

Elsewhere, out-and-out populists took back Republican seats won in the two Dakotas and in Maryland; liberals beat conservatives in Colorado, Nevada, and Washington state, and held on to seats in such conservative places as Vermont and California. In the sixth year of a presidential term, it was a good year to represent the opposition party. But it also didn't hurt to run as a progressive.

Still, Democrats and liberals should not draw too much comfort from the new Democratic majority in Congress, or the party's continuing majority among governorships and in state legislatures. Much of this hold is merely inertial. In the South, voters are now willing to send Republican senators, congressmen, and presidents to Washington, and GOP governors to their statehouses, even though county courthouse politics remain Democratic. Almost nowhere does the persistence of Democratic voting habits express party renewal or increased popular participation.

The Senate went from a peak in Democratic strength of sixty-eight in 1965 and sixty-six in 1975, to six years of narrow Republican control under Reagan, and is now back to fifty-four Democratic seats, about the average of the Eisenhower years. But what Senate Democrats lack is a critical mass of resolute liberals, of the sort who dominated the 1958–80 generation. The loss in 1980 of twelve prominent liberal senators, of committee chairs, and of a Democratic majority reinforced the impression that liberalism was finished and left the Senate with neither the votes nor the convictions to oppose Reaganism effectively.

During the last two decades, the U.S. House of Representatives has remained only slightly less stubbornly Democratic than during the previous two decades. Some of this reflects the immense advantage that House incumbents enjoy in hanging on to their seats. The ratio of incumbents re-elected in 1986 was a record 98.4 percent. However, between 1968 and 1986, eighty-four Republicans ousted Democratic incumbents, but during the same period, eighty-six Democrats beat Republican incumbents. Similarly, Republicans picked up fifty-five open seats formerly held by Democrats, while Democrats picked up fifty-eight open seats previously held by Republicans. What is noteworthy in these competitive races is that despite the presumed declining appeal of liberalism, the vast majority of Democrats outside the Deep South who picked up open seats were liberals. Indeed, of the forty-eight Democrats who picked off Republican seats in the Watergate election of 1974, thirty were still in Congress ten years later. And from such unlikely Republican corners as Peoria, Illinois, eastern Idaho, North Dakota, and suburban Long Island, freshman Democratic liberals or populists got elected to Congress during the Reagan years, ousting Republicans. Yet even as Democrats retained control of the House, they did so against a backdrop of declining voter participation and the decay of party loyalty and partisan institutions.

For nearly a decade in Congress, the main legislative tasks confronting Democratic liberals have been defensive and fiscal. Given the politics of depressed expectations under Carter and the politics of fiscal impossibility under Reagan, it is striking to appreciate that no Democrat newly elected to Congress since 1978 has had either the votes, the appropriations, or the will, to use government affirmatively; no Democrat with less than eight years seniority has first-hand experience with the innovative use of government to deal with practical problems. That dreary, daily reality tends to stifle the liberal imagination. Yet at the same time, the Republicans' hoped-for realignment has failed to materialize. So 1986, despite the Senate victory, heralded only narrowly hopeful news for Democrats. No realignment in their favor occurred, either. Turnout was at the lowest level since 1942. In effect, the pool of voters dropped to such a low level that the topography of the ocean floor became visible, a base topography that remained slightly Democratic.

V.

Notwithstanding heartening gains in 1986 and improved prospects looming in 1988, the Democrats have only just begun to move beyond the clichés of 1984. At this writing, the accumulated flaws of the Reagan administration have burst onto center stage, seemingly sparing Democrats the need to ask hard questions. There are two sorts of dangers for the Democrats in 1988: The first is that the Democrats will fail to rouse popular excitement and will lose. The second is that they will win a lame, unsustainable victory because an improbable second Watergate crippled a sitting Republican President, not because the Democrats rebuilt their message, philosophy, or base. The Reagan presidency, scandals and all, offers contradictory lessons for Democrats. Reagan's politics of genial symbolism nonetheless conceals a politics of real substance, based on fierce, systematic activism by those with a self-interest in seeing his policies prevail. Reagan's persona and his presidency are the capstone of more than a decade of party rebuilding and ideological work, not a substitute for it. In contrast, much of the recent Democratic search for "themes" has been only a quest for a competing set of symbols, with neither the philosophical substance nor the political linkages even of a Reagan. In 1988 there is a danger that some neo-liberal novelty will break out of the Democratic pack, based on the usual vagaries of the campaign, propelled more by gimmickry than vision. Things will break right. He will be undervalued at first, then will gain unexpected momentum and win the nomination. But if such a Democrat is elected in 1988 on a smile and a shoeshine, he is likely neither to solve America's accumulated problems, nor to rebuild the Democratic Party base. A further danger is that a widely predicted economic crisis will fall in on the next Democratic president, much as the stagflation of the 1970s fell in on Jimmy Carter. And if the next Democratic president is another Carter—an antiparty figure with faint convictions—the Democratic Party and the progressive tradition will stagger into the twenty-first century even weaker than today.

This grim prospect, of course, is not inevitable. Reagan's personal fall usefully exploded the myth that voters had been attracted by conservative ideology. The Democratic challenge is to restore the link between citizen, polity, and party by addressing the actual economic needs of ordinary voters. Many Democratic politicians seem far more willing to entertain that approach than seemed possible after Reagan's 1984 triumph. The voters seem ready for such initiatives.

However, the political undertow of big money and the low political participation of wage-earning voters will continue to tempt good Democrats to believe that the party needs only to keep moving right, in order to appeal to the elite portion of the electorate. Low voter interest, a disconnection between people's economic needs and the political process, and the political cynicism of economically distressed people are the logical outcome of that sort of politics. The impression in 1986 that there were "no issues" was not a passing fluke, but a chronic condition of recent American politics. The seeming absence of political issues and the seeming inevitability of *laissez-faire* economics reinforce each other.

Before considering new policies to articulate old values, we need to understand more of the politics: why popular participation has declined, how the two parties compete as institutions, the way money influences the boundaries of the politically possible, and the struggle for a viable progressive ideology. It is to these dynamics that we now turn.

CHAPTER TWO

MONEY

I.

The corrupting effect of money upon politics has complicated political life since the dawn of organized society. It is a particular problem for modern democracies, where there is no sacred, monarchic, or aristocratic basis for political authority, and the explicit first principle is one citizen, one vote. But in a world of PAC-dominated politics, money talks much louder than votes. This wholesaling of influence short-circuits the premise of political democracy. More specifically, it corrodes the fundamental compromise of *capitalist* political democracy, according to which the unequal influence of the economic realm is supposed to operate in a sphere separate from the equal influence of the polity. The more that money equals political influence, the more the polity is for sale and the less power the principle of equal citizenship has.

The problem is not that votes are literally for sale—defenders of PACs have an easy time demolishing that straw man. Rather the problem is that the political logic of raising campaign money is often at odds with the logic of effective populism. Thus the ascendancy of political money is not just a civic blight, but a phenomenon that especially undermines the left-of-center party. PAC politics forces a "heads-I-win-tails-you-lose" choice upon progressives and the Democratic Party. By competing for PAC money and other business-inspired contributions, progressives are contradicting their own political base and ideological agenda. By *failing* to compete for PAC money, they often deprive themselves of the means to run competitive campaigns.

Campaign-finance reformers of recent seasons have been all but oblivious to the ideological assymetry of the corrupting influence of modern political fund raising. The presumption has been that money corrupts in a more or less even-handed manner; if Republicans are on the take from business, Democrats are taking from labor, and somehow it all comes out in the wash. The political scientist Larry J. Sabato, in a sophisticated and well-reviewed 1984 book, *PAC Power,* declared, "PACs are misrepresented and maligned as the embodiment of corrupt special interests." Invoking James Madison's maxim that if men were angels, no government would be necessary, Sabato shrugs, "There is no heaven on earth, and both government and PACs are here to stay."

In reality, campaign-finance politics tends to confound Democrats more than Republicans, liberals more than conservatives, populists more than neo-liberals. Organized business groups, who have plenty of money, invest in *laissez-faire* Republicans to do what comes naturally—keep the government out of their hair, and champion a minimalist "night watchman state." They invest in Democrats in the hope of encouraging them to do what comes *unnaturally*—to abandon their commitment to affirmative government and break their historic alliance with the nonrich, which was originally intended to redress market inequities. In other words, Republican campaign finance tends to reinforce a natural ideological affinity, while Democratic campaign finance operates at cross purposes with the natural Democratic function as the party of the little guy. To the extent that business money talks to Democrats, it talks more comfortably with Democratic conservatives and increases their influence in the party. When it talks to Democratic liberals, it usually does so because they are incumbents and because it hopes to wean them from their liberalism.

As a consequence, the Democratic Party's poignant quest to rediscover and secure its philosophical moorings is complicated and compromised by its more immediate need for money. It is one thing for Democrats to conclude rationally that they must abandon old themes and values because the voters seem weary of government programs, labor unions, and needy people. It is another thing altogether for the party to move rightward because that is where the money is. The Democrats' identity crisis and their cash crisis are happening simultaneously, and they are hard to disentangle. The risk is that the Democrats' natural identity as the party of the non-rich will be fatally undermined by the imperatives of campaign financing, leaving little basis for mobilizing masses of currently disaffected voters.

As we shall see, alternatives exist, but they require a substantial revision of prevailing assumptions. One alternative is a much greater effort to raise a huge number of small donations. Democrats have begun this, with some success. (Small donors tend to respond to ideological appeals, but much conventional wisdom today holds that Democrats need to become *less* ideological. If the Democrats follow that counsel, they won't raise much small money.) Another alternative is to seriously reform the campaign-finance laws so as to neutralize the effect of big money. Many party insiders look at the post-1974 history of campaign-finance reform as a naive cure that turned out to be worse than the disease. As we shall see, the story is rather more complicated than that, but it is true that the present system has the unintended consequence of leaving money more influential than ever. The party's self-styled realists argue that since reformers only made things worse, the system should be left alone now that Democrats are finally learning to play the PAC game. But with Democrats back in control of the Senate, there is real opportunity to reform the system properly. Increasing numbers of Democratic incumbents are at last sick of the domination of PACs and recognize that a total overhaul of campaign finance is not naive good-government reformism but shrewd, essential partisan politics.

When Gary Hart dropped out of the presidential campaign after it was revealed that he had spent the night with a young woman, having already taken a cruise with her to Bimini, most observers concluded from this that Hart must have had a kind of political death wish. That may well be so. But Hart's downfall also suggests broader lessons about the corrupting effect of the ubiquitous culture of political fund raising. The reason Hart got to be friends with William Broadhurst, his yachting companion, was that Broadhurst was a pipeline to other rich people, and incidentally to such campaign perquisites as the yacht *Monkey Business* and model Donna Rice. In the era of permanent presidential campaigns, candidates spend an amazing amount of time courting very wealthy people, not a few of whom are influence-seeking or sleazy, and many of whom are quite conservative. At best, this crowd is culturally and financially light-years away from the base Democratic voter. Even if a corporate campaign contribution does not literally buy a single vote, presidential campaigns are insatiable money-consuming machines, and the perpetual quest for money puts good Democrats figuratively if not literally in bed with the very rich, only a few of whom are in politics for innocent or civic reasons. Too few Democratic elected officials hold on to their progressive values after years in this fund-raising milieu. Perhaps the Kennedys, born to wealth yet always remembering their father's relatively humble origins, could cavort on yachts and still inspire factory workers. But as fund raising becomes the main preoccupation of Democratic candidates, that balancing act becomes ever harder to sustain.

II.

The Democrats' money problems boil down to three. First, Republicans ordinarily have a lot more money. Second, Democrats have to tie themselves into ideological knots to raise what they can. Third, money politics tends to drive out mass-participation politics, which is the one hope Democrats have.

The first of these problems is the more straightforward, and it is a fairly recent development. A century ago, money corrupted politics, but it mattered less because politics then was a more labor-intensive affair. In the 1880s, according to one history, more than two million people were personally involved in electioneering. In 1896, an estimated five million people listened to one of William Jennings Bryan's six hundred speeches, in the flesh. But the Republican candidate, of course, won the election that year; the Republican national chairman, Mark Hanna, had systematically assessed banks and business firms at a specific fraction of their capital, raising a then-astronomical $3.5 million, about five times what Bryan could raise. Hanna was the first serious Republican broker of business campaign finance, and it might be said in his defense that he was only acting to offset the Democratic advantage of patronage workers. Unfortunately for Hanna and his allies, McKinley was assassinated and succeeded by the reformer Teddy Roosevelt, and this first era of business-led campaign finance ultimately ended with the 1907 Tillman Act, prohibiting corporate political donations.

That act was poorly enforced, and large contributions from wealthy individuals remained legal. But between the late 1920s and the late 1960s, at least, the two parties were roughly at financial parity. As late as 1956, the entire presidential campaign cost under $13 million, of which Eisenhower spent $7.8 million and Adlai Stevenson $5.1. If the Mark Hanna era anticipated the tight alliance between business groups and the GOP, the 1920s heralded a period not unlike the present one, in that business influence then also bought into the Democratic Party. With the Republican electoral ascendance after 1920, many prominent Democrats concluded that "New Era" politics and "permanent prosperity" were indeed at hand, swamping the idealistic visions and social concerns of the progressives, and that Democrats had better effect a rapprochement with organized business. In this climate, the 1924 Democratic nominee, a conservative called John W. Davis, led the party to its all-time low fraction of the popular vote, 28.8 percent.

During this first flowering of Democratic neo-conservatism, John J. Raskob, former chairman of General Motors' finance committee, became the Democratic National Committee chairman. By 1932, he was donating on the order of $500,000 annually out of his own pocket to keep the national party solvent. After the 1932 election, Franklin Roosevelt replaced him with his own man, James Farley. Raskob went on to found the right-wing Liberty League, and systematic business influence in the Democratic Party went into a period of welcome eclipse. Prior to the 1970s, Democratic campaign finance was largely the province of individual big donors, and far less formalized contributions from businesses and trade unions. Thanks to the continuing inertial momentum of the New Deal period and the anomalous tendency of just enough millionaires to have liberal politics, the Democratic Party had its share of financiers.

By 1968, however, a partisan financial imbalance was returning. In the presidential election that year, Richard Nixon raised a reported $25.4 million to Hubert Humphrey's $11.9 million. Then, as an incumbent president, Nixon sought to put his campaign finance on a systematic basis unknown since Mark Hanna. The financial excesses and organized shakedowns of the 1972 Republican campaign became an important aspect of Watergate, leading to rare prosecutions of dozens of corporate executives and, ultimately, to the 1974 reforms.

The saga of how attempted reform backfired has been widely recounted. To make a very long story short, the first modern campaign-finance reform was the Federal Election Campaign Act of 1971, commonly known by its initials, FECA, which are usefully connotative of filthy lucre. The 1971 FECA tightened disclosure requirements and explicitly gave legal recognition to what were then a handful of corporate and trade-union political fund-raising committees, generally known as political action committees. By making PACs an officially sanctioned vehicle for political finance, the 1971 law stimulated their proliferation.

The 1974 amendments, after Watergate, set limits on how much money individuals and PACs could contribute to any one candidate or party (but not on how much candidates or parties could spend). They also created public financing of presidential election campaigns, though not of House or Senate ones. They succeeded in eliminating most illegal cash bribes, but in a manner unimagined by its sponsors, the 1974 law further promoted the systematic organization of campaign finance. Not surprisingly, the groups best positioned to take advantage of the new system were businesses. A 1975 advisory opinion by the newly formed Federal Election Commission made it clear that corporations could solicit contributions from employees and stockholders, as long as these were not "coercive." This led to a geometrical growth in PACs, overwhelmingly representing business groups, from just 11 business PACs in 1964, to more than 100 in 1974, to more than 2,000 by 1983. Labor PACs increased moderately from 201 in 1974 to 389 by 1986, but the labor share of total PAC money dropped dramatically. In 1972, business and labor PACs had each spent about $8.5 million. By 1980, business and ideologically conservative PACs were outspending liberal and labor PACs by at least three to one. By 1984, the disparity was better than four to one. (These PAC statistics understate the proportion of money raised by organized interest groups, for when a PAC gets serious about backing a candidate, it not only donates its own money, to a maximum of $5,000 per candidate, but also orchestrates fund-raising events that permit other individuals to give donations to the candidate directly.)

A 1976 Supreme Court ruling, *Buckley* v. *Valeo,* struck down the limits on contributions by ostensibly independent committees, as contrary to the First Amendment guarantee of freedom of speech. It held that they could spend unlimited sums to support or oppose particular candidates, as long as they were not organizationally linked to a campaign. This led to the growth of yet another form of special-interest financing, which again went overwhelmingly to conservative and Republican candidates, by a margin of at least four to one. In the 1981–82 cycle, for example, negative campaigns by independent committees spent more than $4 million to defeat Democrats, but only $550,000 against Republicans. A further, innocent-seeming amendment, in 1979, permitted unlimited contributions for state and local "party building" activities, which also worked to the systematic advantage of the GOP.

That the legislative scheme backfired as a *civic* reform has been widely acknowledged; instead of money being contained, money was unleashed. What should be equally unambiguous was the partisan result—an extraordinary financial tilt in favor of Republicans and conservatives. The new campaign-finance era coincided with an unparalleled period of party building and ideological consciousness raising—but only on the Republican side. The RNC chairman in the late 1970s, William Brock, took full advantage of the fund-raising climate not just to steer money to GOP candidates but to build a modern, ongoing party infrastructure.

Meanwhile, despite the incumbency of a Democratic president, the Democratic National Committee remained chronically broke. To help heal the wounds of the 1968 rupture between the nominee Hubert Humphrey and his antiwar rivals, Eugene McCarthy and Robert Kennedy, the Democratic National Committee agreed to assume responsibility for all 1968 campaign debts, and in 1984, it was still paying off the last of these. Carter likewise was not adept at party building. Rather than using his incumbency to fatten the Democratic Party, his White House political operation was a substantial drain on scarce party funds. His pollster, Patrick Caddell, charged his services to the DNC, and relations were so frayed that by 1978 the DNC was refusing to pay his bills.

This impasse was partly due to Carter's own political innocence and disdain for party, and partly to Caddell's volcanic personality. But in a more profound fashion it reflected scarcity economics. With not nearly enough campaign money to go around (and the Republicans raising money by the bushel), every dollar that went to Caddell was, it seemed, one less dollar for a deserving congressman or senator. Because Carter was a personalist politician rather than a party loyalist, other Democrats could not see the logic of underwriting his White House political operation at the expense of other Democratic politicians. The contrast between the penury and bickering among Democrats during the Carter period and the well-financed synergy between party and White House under Reagan could hardly be more dramatic.

While Republicans rebuilt, Democrats squabbled. The greater Republican productivity and gentility was less the product of superior temperament than the predictable consequence of financial well-being. Yet circumstances nicely reinforced the image of Democrats as querulous, factionalized incompetents.

The gap between Republican and Democratic money widened each year. In 1976, according to the Federal Election Commission, the Republican National Committee and the GOP House and Senate campaign committees spent a total of $40.1 million; the counterpart Democratic committees spent $17.6 million—for a gap of slightly over two to one. In 1978, this widened to more than three to one; in 1980, to more than four to one; and in 1982, when the Democrats spent $40 million, the Republicans spent over $214 million or almost five and a half times what Democrats did, a ratio that has more or less held since then. (It declined very slightly in 1986, when Republican Party committees raised a total of $185 million, to the Democrats' $35 million—a ratio of about 5.3 to one.)

The average Democratic candidate is not outspent five to one, but that is primarily because the average Democratic incumbent can raise money from special interests, most of which represent organized business. By the same token, the two Democratic House and Senate fund-raising committees can redress some of the imbalance by selling the power of incumbent candidates. As Representative Tony Coelho, then head of the Democratic Congressional Campaign Committee, bluntly explained his pitch to business PACs, "I tell them, 'You're going to need to work with us. Do you want to be able to talk to all of the parties that make the decisions, or only some of them?' " The not-so-subtle implication is that it costs money to gain access to legislators, and those who won't or can't pay will have less access. That is perhaps a credible threat to make to Republican-oriented interest groups, who may need to be addressed in an idiom that will get their attention. But a further implication is that important elements in the Democratic voter base who don't engage in the campaign-finance game lose access and influence, too. Coelho's operation won grudging praise in most Democratic quarters; he was able to cut the gap in party financing of congressional candidates from about eight to one to four to one. But this awkward muscling-in on business groups by ostensible liberals should not be mistaken for anything close to institutional, financial, or ideological parity.

The Republicans' superior partisan financial strength, year in and year out, builds coherence, loyalty, and linkage in a fashion that crude numbers understate. In the 1981–82 cycle, Republican Party committees gave GOP Senate candidates some 15 percent of all the money they raised; in the case of Republican challengers, the party total was over 21 percent. Democratic candidates got just 4 percent of their money from the party. With the exception of well-entrenched Democratic incumbents who have systematically (and anomalously) built alliances with business PACs, Democratic candidates in competitive campaigns, not to mention long-shot campaigns, spend a disproportionate amount of time on the phone, or at fund-raisers, asking rich people to part with their money. Some Democrats, like Senator Joseph Biden, are said to relish this fund-raising ritual; it gets the adrenaline flowing and brings hard proof that the candidate is loved. Others find fund-raising calls a demeaning chore, and must be coaxed by their staff to make so many calls during a set period every day. But either way, the need to raise money makes it hard to concentrate on other things, and leads to mistaken and misleading surmises about who and what is important in politics. Ann Lewis, former political director of the DNC, says, "If you have access to money, you can spend your waking hours figuring out how best to spend it. If you have to spend 99 percent of your time raising the money, there's no way you can be smart and thoughtful about deploying it."

III.

By and large, the Democratic effort to catch up with Republican financial supremacy has intensified the strains in the Democratic coalition. Tactically, it has caused the party's technicians to emphasize money over participation and big money over small money. It has given the people who raise money disproportionate influence within the party. Philosophically, it has caused Democratic insiders to cultivate a commonality with organized business interests that is not otherwise indicated by the party's roots or goals. The ascendance of money has exacerbated the chronic strain of being the left-of-center party in a fiercely capitalist economy. To debate whether PAC money does or does not pull the strings on roll-call votes, as many political scientists do, is to miss these several layers of meaning.

In the 1933–1968 period, most Democratic money was not ideologically at odds with most of the Democratic program. Labor unions loomed much larger, and they were successful at turning lots of small donations into serious money. John Perkins, head of the AFL-CIO political operation, estimates that in the 1940s and

1950s, labor money contributed 20 percent of Democratic campaign finances, and of course a great many ground troops. One estimate placed the cash value of labor's phone banks and semi-official volunteer hours at $8 million.

But labor's influence within the party and its ability to single-handedly offset business money have both been steadily declining. In addition, the generation that reached affluent maturity in the first two decades after World War II included many well-to-do people whose pocketbooks bespoke the 1950s but whose social values and political attitudes still reflected the harsh lessons of the 1930s. Traditionally, most Democratic money brokers tended to be slightly apart from the mainstream Republican corporate establishment. They were often social outsiders, Jewish or Catholic rather than Protestant, representing new entrepreneurial money rather than inherited wealth, investment bankers rather than commercial bankers, oil wildcatters rather than oil majors, real-estate developers rather than industrialists. And there was a good sampling of plain class traitors, after Franklin Roosevelt: millionaires with either left-wing convictions or a serious sense of *noblesse oblige.*

It is possible to put a marxian fine point on this phenomenon by divining "splits in the ruling class." After 1933, arguably, one wing of the elite needed government to save capitalism or, after 1945, to advance empire. These business leaders included industrial managers and Wall Street internationalists who valued labor peace and stability more than volatile innovation. They tended to look to alliance with the state rather than to the ultra-*laissez-faire* so fashionable in the 1920s and 1980s. By the same token, some very wealthy people, notably real estate developers dependent on decisions of government, needed liaisons with municipal officials to advance their business interests at the local level. During the long period of Democratic majority, this wing of the business elite found it convenient to bankroll the Democratic Party as the party of internationalism and industrial collaboration. When class interests changed, the faithless capitalists dropped the Democrats like a bad habit.

In this view, the Democratic ascendancy heavily depended on temporary divisions in the business class. It is certainly true, as the political scientists Joel Rogers and Thomas Ferguson argue in their provocative book *Right Turn,* that a larger fraction of the business community today embraces the *laissez-faire* school rather than the mixed-economy school, and that may have something to do with the changed circumstances of American capital. But the essence of the post-1968 phenomenon is less a matter of business uniting against Democrats than of Democrats frantically trying to ingratiate themselves with business, during a period when business is far better mobilized, more ideologically self-conscious, and more explicit about its own political goals.

There are still plenty of internationalists in the business community, but they are more right-wing about their internationalism than they once were. There are also fewer reliably left-wing millionaires today. Business as a whole is exercising much more systematic influence on both parties, via campaign finance. In the "end-of-ideology" years, there was more slack in the system, as well as more residual partisan allegiance to the Democratic Party, which offset the generally conservatizing role that money did play.

A related factor in the contradictory effect of campaign finance on Democrats has been the shift in the articulated interests of the organized Jewish community. Jews, it has been said, are the only people "who live like Episcopalians and vote like Puerto Ricans." Since the New Deal, Jewish voters have overwhelmingly supported liberal Democrats. Jewish philanthropists, both disinterested and self-interested, have contributed a disproportionate share of liberal political money. Though there is no precise accounting available, political insiders place the Jewish fraction of Democratic campaign finance at about one-third. The liberal propensity of Jews has been the subject of much debate. It may have roots in the Biblical and Talmudic traditions of compassion and community-mindedness, or in the political history of Jews' own oppression, or the Jews' need, as what Felix Frankfurter called a "despised minority," to work hard for a society of tolerance and liberal values and to make common cause with other minority groups. But for whatever reason, liberal Jewish campaign finance of Democrats has helped to offset the conservatizing tendency of money generally. During most of the 1932–1968 period, Jewish campaign donors were more often expressing the interests of social conscience than of purse.

In the past decade or so, however, Jewish campaign giving has become less of a force for liberalism. One popular explanation for this is that as Jews have become more affluent they have become more like other Americans and have increasingly voted their straight pocketbook interests. Though that is certainly a fair description of some Jewish political leaders, Jewish *voters* have continued to support liberal causes and progressive Democratic candidates by lopsided margins (the only major exception being the 1980 presidential election, when Jewish voters were notably unenthusiastic about Carter). A more important factor seems to be the Israel issue.

Israel, not very long ago, was a left-wing cause. The state of Israel was governed by labor Zionists whose ideology was social democratic. Since the 1973 war with Egypt, however, Israel has gradually become a far more closely integrated and supported strategic ally of the United States, and rather more vulnerable geopolitically. The organized Jewish political leadership has given a far higher priority to the very survival of Israel and its close military alliance with the United States. The Israel lobby, led by the American Israel Public Affairs Committee (AIPAC) and one hundred or so political action committees that follow its lead, has become disproportionately visible and vocal among domestic Jewish political organizations.

At the same time, political power in Israel has shifted to the right-wing Likud coalition, making Israel a more natural ally of American conservatives. While many domestic causes dear to American Jews have suffered under the Reagan administration, aid to Israel more than trebled. For the first time, there is a practical alliance between American Zionists and Republican conservatives, in which a common conservative geopolitical agenda overcomes deep divisions over domestic social policy. Leaders of Jewish PACs have generally argued that Israel dwarfs other issues of interest to American Jews.

The effects on the Democratic Party of this ideological and political shift have been profound. First, one important traditional source of financing is now frequently denied to many Democratic challengers. Conservative Republicans, so long as they voted "right" on Middle East issues, could generally be assured that little of the usual organized Jewish campaign finance would flow to their opponents. In the 1986 Senate campaign, for example, this had a significant effect in several key states. In Wisconsin, the Republican incumbent, Robert Kasten, voted with the right-wing Jesse Helms on most social issues. Other things being equal, his liberal Democratic challenger, Ed Garvey, might have expected to get a good deal of Jewish financial support. But Kasten also voted down the line in favor of Israel and was chair of the crucial Foreign Appropriations Subcommittee, which doles out Israel's five billion dollars of U.S. foreign aid. So Garvey's effort to raise money from the big Jewish donors in New York and Los Angeles failed miserably. In fact, when he tried simply to meet an influential Jewish PAC director, Morris Amitay, he was rebuffed. Amitay, who had sent PAC members a newsletter describing Garvey as "not good on our issues," later explained to an incredulous aide that he didn't like the fact that Garvey, while executive director of the Professional Football Players Association, had refused to sign a letter opposing sale of the AWACS reconnaissance system to Saudi Arabia. (Not surprisingly, the Players Association takes no foreign-policy positions.) Outspent by better than three to one, Garvey lost narrowly (though he apparently won a wide majority among Wisconsin's Jewish voters).

Money influences who gets into a race. If a Republican is seen as financially secure, the strongest potential Democratic candidate may decide not to give up his present job for a long-shot challenge. This was dramatically demonstrated in New York, where the Republican incumbent, Alfonse D'Amato, had several vulnerabilities but an immense war chest. The press, the established politicians, and the interest groups convinced each other that he was unbeatable. Governor Cuomo handpicked an independently wealthy but lackluster Democrat, John Dyson, to make the race. Dyson, he hoped, would spend enough of his own fortune to make a presentable showing, and would have the additional virtue of not competing with Cuomo's own prodigious fund-raising appetite. But Dyson proved to be such a lame candidate that the primary was won by Mark Green, who conventional opinion considered an even longer shot. Yet even though he was heavily outfinanced, Green ran a quite respectable race, holding D'Amato to about 54 percent of the vote in a low-turnout election. Had he gotten adequate funds and had his effort been taken seriously by party pros and the press, the turnout would have been higher and Green might have won an upset. But because of his strong support for Israel, Jewish political groups actively worked to discourage any strong challenger from taking on D'Amato. In the jockeying before the primaries, Jewish leaders passed the word to several prospective Democratic candidates that D'Amato would have a virtual lock on Jewish PAC money.

One prospective candidate, Arthur Levitt, Jr., told a meeting of the Democratic Senate Campaign Committee that he had been advised by prominent Jewish leaders, including Howard Squadron and Kenneth Bialkin, recent chiefs of the Conference of Presidents of Major Jewish Organizations, not to run against D'Amato and that if he did he would not get the substantial Jewish financial backing that usually goes to New York Democrats. Former Congresswoman Elizabeth Holtzman, another Democrat who expressed interest in taking on D'Amato, got similar advice. Malcolm Hoenlein, the very influential head of the Jewish Community Relations Council of New York and a close friend of D'Amato, recalls, "The Jewish community was a very significant factor in their decision not to take D'Amato on." Ultimately when the nomination went to Mark Green, he raised almost no money from the New York Jewish political establishment, which had convinced itself that D'Amato spoke for Jewish interests. Outfinanced by better than four to one, Green lost. But he had one satisfaction: he carried 69 percent of the Jewish vote. Once again, the views of the money elite were not in harmony with those of Democratic voters.

By the same token, in both Oregon and Kansas, Jewish PACs actively worked to dissuade potential Jewish Senate candidates from challenging the well-entrenched Republican incumbents Robert Packwood and Robert Dole, who were considered good friends of Israel. In Pennsylvania, Robert Edgar, a liberal with a down-the-line pro-Israel voting record in his twelve years in the House, nonetheless raised little Jewish PAC money in his challenge to Republican Arlen Spector.

Not all Jewish campaign finance has become conservative. Many individual Jews continue to donate money, as liberal Democrats, not as loyalists to the organized pro-Israel lobby. Two small Jewish PACs, MIPAC (standing for Multi-Issue PAC) and JAC, a women's

Joint Action Committee, were formed explicitly to challenge the Israel-above-all-else mentality, and demand that candidates asking their support have good records not only on the Middle East, but on other issues, such as separation of church and state, school prayer, etc. In some states, Jewish PAC financing helped Democratic allies, such as Alan Cranston in California, fend off Republican challengers. In at least one state, Florida, a governor who was close to the local Jewish community was able to prevail against a pro-Israel right-wing Republican. But on balance, the ascendance of the Israel issue has meant that Jewish campaign finance has been substantially divorced from domestic liberal politics. As Max Palevsky, the Los Angeles financier who was George McGovern's early backer, says, "That intense instinct that Jews have about what is good for them used to mean that Jews backed liberal candidates intuitively; what was good for the Jews meant civil rights and a society without intense social warfare. In Southern California today, a lot of the money that used to be normal Jewish do-gooder money has a string."

This brief account of how one notable group of fund raisers has influenced which candidates got several Senate nominations suggests yet another way that money influences campaign strategy: the importance of money as a factor in candidate recruitment. The vicious circle of needing money to be taken seriously and needing to seem serious in order to raise money tends to weaken Democrats generally and economic progressives in particular.

Given the logic of needing money in order to be taken seriously, an independently wealthy Democrat or one with close ties to business often seems to fill the bill better than a progressive one who is anathema to business groups but more appealing to voters. In the 1986 Senate race, money helped to keep potentially strong Democrats out of Senate races in Wisconsin, New York, Indiana, Iowa, Kansas, Oregon, and Alaska and in countless House races as well. Several other Democratic victories, such as Kent Conrad's upset in North Dakota, were much narrower than they should have been because the candidates had such difficulty persuading the money men to take them seriously.

Research on candidate recruitment, by the political scientists Gary Jacobsen and Samuel Kernell, suggests both primary and secondary effects of campaign-finance disparities. Their statistical work confirms the widely recognized truth that money is especially important for challengers. Since an incumbent begins with a widely recognized name and a history of delivering services to constituents, a challenger by definition is playing catch-up ball. In the 1982 election, they found that an extra hundred thousand dollars produced an average increase of 3.5 percent in a challenger's vote. The ability of Republican challengers to raise far more money than Democratic challengers is a noteworthy factor in the systematic tilt to the GOP.

The most obvious thing that money gives a challenger is the ability to finance the usual campaign machinery. Radio and TV advertising, staff expenses, direct mail, and get-out-the-vote drives. But looking behind that well-known effect at the more subtle dynamics of how money creates influence, Jacobsen and Kernell found that money helped Republicans to recruit "a much stronger set of challengers than political conditions would normally have produced" in a predictably strong Democratic year like 1982, and helped hold Republican House losses to twenty-six, far more favorable than historical patterns or current economic conditions would have suggested. Conversely, the relative absence of money on the Democratic side kept many attractive candidates out of the race.

IV.

Given these several financial imbalances, what is a good Democrat to do? Recent history offers illustrations of several different kinds of response, each with its own special peril. The most dangerous has been a redoubled effort to persuade business groups that Democrats really aren't all that liberal, and to shake loose more money. The limitations on individual giving have placed a premium on collective money raising, which tends to mean business-oriented PACs and well-to-do individuals who are adept at shaking down their friends and colleagues. Herbert Alexander, the author of several books on campaign finance, observes, "We've exchanged the big giver for the big solicitor."

More systematic fund raising has produced more explicitly self-interested donors. The Democrats' financiers come in essentially three varieties: wealthy idealists who raise money out of ethnic habit, civic obligation, or ideological conviction; newly rich entrepreneurs seeking political influence or social cachet; and rising Washington-based lawyers who can invest a few years laboring for the party, making contacts, distributing funds, collecting IOUs—and then cash in handsomely via an enlarged law/lobby practice that serves mostly Republican-oriented business interests.

Some of the Democrats' money men are looking for nothing more sinister than a bigger stage to play on. Someone newly rich from a business success can transform himself into a minor public figure by volunteering to raise money for the party. Many are satisfied with merely the appearance of influence, which can be useful in their business and social life. When a list of the Democrats' hundred-thousand-dollar "soft money" donors was discovered by a reporter, it included a man named Stuart Moldaw, for example, who was hardly known in political circles outside the San Francisco Bay area. He turned out to be a venture capitalist, "whose worst self-seeking motive," according to an associate, "is the desire to sit at the elbow of the most important person in the room." There was also Nathan Landow, a hitherto obscure Washington real estate developer, who emerged as one of Walter Mondale's early financiers. Landow paid an uninvited call on Mondale only a few days after the Carter-Mondale 1980 defeat to offer him his full support for 1984. Landow placed his private jet at Mondale's disposal, and he personally raised more than $2 million for the campaign.

Unlike more passive money raisers, Landow considers himself something of a king-maker. During the 1984 campaign, he took to calling the party's thirty-seven-member national finance board "the board of directors," almost as if it were the campaign's final authority. Landow says that money people are tired of being asked for support and then having their advice ignored. After Mondale's campaign ended, Landow organized several of the biggest money raisers into his own PAC, called IMPAC-88, to interview candidates and, he hoped, to influence the choice of its nominee. The Democratic Party, Landow believes, "needs to move in a more moderate, centrist direction." At a grand strategy meeting of the IMPAC group, in Tucson, in January 1987, the group failed to agree on a candidate. (Those whom Landow invited to address the group included Reagan's former political director, Ed Rollins.)

Why does a Nate Landow get involved in party affairs? "Nate already has his $60 million and his Learjet," says an associate. "He's looking for respect." Landow himself says, "I just enjoy politics. It's a great experience for me, having friends all over the country, meeting new people. It's a hobby."

Irvin Kipnes, a defense contractor from California and large party donor, insists that the Democratic Business Council, which he then headed, was instrumental in pushing the 1984 party platform to adopt a more aggressive posture on defense spending. "For the first time in twenty years," he says, "the Democrats were not beaten over the head on the defense issue. I take some pride in that. The defense contractor members of our Business Council worked very hard on that. So we had some real insider knowledge and input on the defense issue." Most party insiders scoff at that claim. A number of factors helped to push Walter Mondale to adopt a conservative position on defense issues in 1984, and only a conspiracy theorist would attribute the main influence to the party's defense contractors. But the fact that this attitude pleased the party's money men helped to make the impulse seem like grown-up, sensible politics.

The role of individual millionaires, like a Landow or a Moldaw, though far from ideal, is probably less insidious than the role played by "access brokers." A Landow may have rather grandiose conceptions of what he is doing, but he ultimately has only limited influence on what the party stands for. Far more damaging is the brokering by Washington insiders who are hoping to trade their fund-raising gifts for legislative access and policy influence on behalf of conservative business clients. Robert Strauss may be the grand champion of this brand of political entrepreneurship. After serving the party as DNC chairman and then as treasurer, and the government as U.S. Trade Representative under Carter, he became one of the capital's premier power brokers: the Washington office staff of his law firm grew from two lawyers in 1971 to ninety in 1982.

Strauss serves as a compelling if troubling role model. The corpse of the Mondale campaign was not yet cold when several top campaign aides sought to emulate him. Mondale lieutenants Timothy Finchem, the campaign's chief fund raiser, and Robert Beckel, its deputy chairman, formed a new Washington lobbying firm called National Strategies, with a clientele made up of companies with regulatory problems. One of the first men they hired was David K. Aylward, staff director of the House Subcommittee on Telecommunications, Consumer Protection, and Finance, which has jurisdiction over such lucrative issues as telephone deregulation and tender-offer rules. The firm readily signed up several junk-bond dealers as clients.

The Democratic Party's 1981–85 finance chairman, Peter Kelly, a Connecticut-based lawyer, joined forces with one of Washington's most visible Republican lobbying firms—Black, Manafort and Stone. Roger Stone was one of the architects of the National Conservative Political Action Committee (NCPAC). As part of the firm's new bipartisan look, it also took on top former aides to Senator Russell Long and Representative Dan Rostenkowski, the chief Democratic tax legislators in the Senate and House. And after the 1986 election, David Johnson, chief of staff of the Democratic Senatorial Campaign Committee, formed a lobbying firm with a top aide to Senate Democratic Leader Robert Byrd, also aiming at corporate and trade association clients. Anne Wexler, once a McCarthy and McGovern lieutenant, as well as public liaison chief in the Carter White House, also made the transition from liberal party activist to corporate lobbyist.

One could go on and on. If people like Kelly, Aylward, Finchem, Beckel, and Wexler were simply joining the Republican side, they would be following a well-beaten American path of upward mobility and personal embourgeoisement. But the logic of crossing campaign finance with business lobbying in order to gain access to lawmakers on behalf of corporate clients requires one to keep one's Democratic Party connections intact. Wexler served as a senior advisor to Geraldine Ferraro. Kelly continued to raise funds for Democratic House and Senate candidates, which keeps current the legislative contacts and the IOUs that attract the corporate clientele. With former DNC chairman Charles Manatt, Kelly also created a National Democratic Institute of International Affairs, of which he became treasurer. The institute is said to be in the business of helping Democrats think through trade and foreign-policy issues, and of course it gives Kelly's firm one more avenue of access. Here again consider the partisan asymmetry: it is hard to imagine a top official of the Republican Party or the Reagan campaign graduating to the AFL-CIO.

The stock in trade of men like Kelly is the modern equivalent of what George Washington Plunkitt of Tammany Hall called "honest graft." Just as there was nothing illegal about Tammany delivering contracts to its allies, or about individual party leaders like Plunkitt profiting personally from being positioned to see opportunities and take them, Kelly is not breaking the law when he markets the access to legislators that he enjoys as a party fund raiser. So let us be very clear about our qualms. Honest graft of the modern sort is troubling not on grounds of civics-book morality but on *partisan* grounds.

For Democrats, the political problem with the new money brokers is not that they are personally corrupt but that they are politically androgynous. It is that they are unreliable allies. Their personal agendas and loyalties are more careerist than ideological or partisan. Their self-interest rarely suggests a bold straightforward liberalism, let alone economic populism. It suggests ambiguity and accommodation. It suggests governmental episodes like the 1981 tax act, in which Democrats outbid Republicans to deliver corporate favors. By contrast, Reagan could turn around on a dime and sponsor a populist tax-reform bill over the objections of his corporate allies, knowing that they ultimately would remain good Republicans.

As the capacity of the money brokers to influence the Democratic Party grows, the party's message loses its clarity. Their influence tends to make it less the party of egalitarianism and more a fuzzy-headed, second business party. When an elected official speculates that perhaps the time has come for Democrats to move rightward, the money brokers can be counted to declare, "Right on!" The faint stench of decay that emanated from the Mondale campaign in 1984 had far more to do with professional money mechanics than with the supposed obsolescence of the professed idea that Democrats should continue to serve America's dispossessed.

To be sure, the Democrats' uneasy financial relationship with organized business has been an incipient problem ever since ex-

New Dealers of the Paul Porter and Tommy "The Cork" Corcoran generation set up law practices and switched sides but neglected to switch parties. The slippery slope from the SEC, the FTC, or the antitrust division of the Justice Department to the pro-trust divisions of Washington's K Street law firms is well worn. But that circuit lately has acquired new significance. Though business-oriented Washington lawyers like Porter, Clark Clifford, and Lloyd Cutler have long been party insiders, shunting money to Democratic candidates was only a minor part of their activity. Even in the 1970s, the lawyer-lobbyists had only a very limited function in party finance, and in any event it was offset by the balancing influence of labor, civil rights groups, public-minded individuals, and the rest of the old Democratic coalition. But today, unlike in the days of a Clifford or a Cutler, influence is brokered increasingly in the coin of campaign finance.

V.

In late August 1984, about seventy of Mondale's big financial backers got him to sit still for a meeting in St. Paul, Minnesota. The money men were unhappy. They were annoyed that their phone calls were not being returned, and that Mondale's rhetoric, if not his program, was occasionally taking on a disturbingly populist tone. As Irvin Kipnes recalls the Democratic Party's "Business Council" meeting, "Several of us said, 'Fritz, quit knocking the rich; they're financing your campaign.' " According to Kipnes and others present, Mondale replied, "Oh my goodness, I'm so sorry. There's nothing wrong with wanting to be rich. I want to be rich."

It would be a gross oversimplification to conclude from this ironic anecdote that the party's money men dictate the party's message, but they surely confuse it. As noted, throughout 1984 numerous Democrats urged Mondale to support the Bradley-Gephardt tax reform bill. Bradley-Gephardt turned a clever technical reform into ingenious politics: it proposed to close most tax loopholes and to use the revenue savings to cut tax rates drastically. Most of the loopholes were the province of the Republican upper class; most of the savings would go to the Democratic wage-earning class. The bill astutely combined populist substance with good-government procedure, and delivered something tangible to the hard-pressed Democratic base—lower taxes.

Eventually, the Reagan administration perceived the sagacity of the approach, and began to support a proposal that looked very like Bradley-Gephardt, taking the political credit when the bill was finally signed into law in 1986. But in 1984, Mondale, taking the advice of his financial people, never did back Bradley-Gephardt; instead of tax relief, the centerpiece of his campaign was a call for a tax increase. And because his economic advice was coming from the party's fiscal conservatives, that tax increase was not linked to much in the way of government programs that might appeal to Democratic voters. Its purpose was mainly to reduce the deficit. This was the tax-and-spend formula minus the spend. As Harry Hopkins might have warned, minus the elect, too.

The same tension shows up in the legislative branch. In the mid-1970s, I worked as an investigator for the U.S. Senate Committee on Banking, Housing, and Urban Affairs, chaired by Senator William Proxmire of Wisconsin. Proxmire was an intriguing combination—a tight-money populist. He did not like expensive government programs, but he liked private economic concentration even less. He often voted to pare social appropriations, but he saw great virtue in careful economic regulation. From Proxmire flowed the Truth in Lending, Fair Credit Reporting, Community Reinvestment, and other landmark consumer-protection bills. He was fiercely skeptical of big Pentagon programs, money center banks, and other loci of economic power. Proxmire not only refused PAC money; he was so popular in Wisconsin that he took no contributions at all and campaigned only in person or on the nightly news. As a result, the lobbyists had no special leverage or access with Proxmire, because he owed them nothing. He was very attentive to his Wisconsin constituents, but lobbyists' telephone calls were returned in the same order as anyone else's.

In those years, the committee progressives had a narrow working majority of one or two votes, which shifted among the swing members. There were five Republican conservatives and six Democratic liberals; the swing group included liberal Republican Ed Brooke of Massachusetts, who was usually dependable on social issues, and

John Sparkman of Alabama, an aging Dixiecrat with a vaguely populist streak who fancied himself Mr. Housing. The two most instructive swing votes were the liberal Democrats Harrison Williams and Alan Cranston. Williams was chairman of the powerful subcommittee on securities. He was later caught by an FBI investigator posing as a wealthy Arab, in the famous Abscam case. Williams was videotaped in the act of offering the "businessman" a bribe, was convicted, and served time in prison. A prison sentence was surely too harsh a remedy for such an entrapment, but Williams's taking of the Abscam bait was in character. He prized his subcommittee chairmanship, which he used systematically to solicit Wall Street brokerage houses for big campaign contributions. Not surprisingly, he was seldom a tough or independent-minded regulator. Cranston, also a good liberal, was one of the Senate masters of campaign finance. He worked the business PACs even more astutely than Williams, and he was invariably the first liberal vote to go to the other side on a regulatory matter. His staff tended to take its cues from the big trade associations that monitored our committee—the Realtors, the Savings and Loan League, the American Bankers' Association, all of whose clients were big contributors to Cranston's campaigns.

My point here is not to posit a simple, linear relationship between millionaire campaign finance and neutered Democratic Party behavior. The more subtle problem is that the imperatives of campaign finance tend to reinforce the disastrously mistaken view that what Democrats most need is a rapprochement with business leaders and with *laissez-faire* capitalism. When Democrats go all out to reassure the business establishment, the occasional populist is as welcome as the picnic skunk. As one of a handful of Democrats who reject PAC money, Proxmire could vote the public interest because he did not have to worry about keeping the business lobbies happy. He remained democratically accountable in the manner that the founding fathers intended—to the voters of Wisconsin.

The thesis of this book is that it is economic populism that unites Democrats and allows them to be the natural majority party. Campaign finance corrodes that populism in one more respect. To the extent that some big Democratic donors still consider themselves liberals, their liberalism tends to take the form of everything *but*

economic populism. Most of the ideologically motivated big givers
tend to be liberal on social or foreign-policy issues (such as the
nuclear freeze, environmentalism, gay rights, and so on) but then
reflect their own natural class interests on economic issues. Stanley
Sheinbaum, one of the mainstays of Los Angeles left-liberal philan-
thropy, observes, "My Beverly Hills liberal friends think the Republican tax reform plan is too left-wing." It is the fragmentation
over social and foreign-policy issues that has splintered the post-
1968 Democratic Party. The last thing that will rebuild the party is
culturally avant-garde and economically conservative millionaires.
When Alan Cranston mounted a brief run at the 1984 Democratic
nomination, he did so by finding a niche on the party's foreign-
policy left. He continued to vote with the business trade associations on economic issues, but he ran to the left as the darling of the
nuclear freeze movement. He lost badly. In 1986, Cranston could
be seen presiding over a large Los Angeles fund-raising event
starring Barbra Streisand, which brought in several million dollars
the party badly needed. Looking out over the jewel-spangled
crowd, Cranston praised them lavishly as "the very best of the
Democratic Party."

In fairness, some of the money raised at Barbra Streisand's
Malibu ranch that September evening ended up helping to finance
the campaign of genuine populists in the Dakotas. But the dependence of the party of the common American on the partying of the
elite has to be troubling, for it is ultimately corrosive of the Democrats' identity.

VI.

One antidote to big money is small money. Since the early 1970s,
as the Democratic Party has been hopelessly outfinanced by the
Republicans, most of its leaders have chosen the easier (but self-
defeating) course of "hunting where the ducks are"—going after
big money. During the same period, Republicans became the
anomalous wizards of small-donor direct-mail money raising,
though, ironically, it was a Democrat, George McGovern, who first
used direct mail effectively to become financially competitive. In his

1972 insurgent campaign for the Democratic nomination, and later, for the presidency, McGovern built a list of 600,000 loyal donors, relying on the ingenuity of a liberal direct-mail expert from Alabama named Morris Dees. By early 1972 he had a core list of some 10,000 "sustainers," who each contributed $10 a month. During the nominating process, the direct-mail effort brought in a gross income of $4,850,000, of which only $650,000 went for mailing expenses. Incredibly, so much money poured in during the fall campaign's final weeks that McGovern became the only Democrat in recent memory to end the campaign with a surplus.

Of course, McGovern also lost the election, and he lost it as the candidate of what many leaders considered a dangerous fringe of the Democratic Party. As a result, his populist device of raising a lot of money in small contributions from many donors gained little currency in Democratic Party circles. And his list itself was somewhat tainted with the reputation of being a list of left-wingers. When Robert Strauss, a moderately conservative Texan, became party chairman in late 1972, he did not make direct mail the centerpiece of the DNC's fund-raising effort: he concentrated on raising business money.

Instead of the liberal Morris Dees going down in political history as the modern guru of direct-mail finance, that title fell to the arch-conservative Richard Viguerie, whose use of starkly ideological appeals to rouse millions of small donors has bankrolled a whole range of conservative causes. The Republican National Committee caught on fast. It used big-donor money to pay the start-up costs of a massive direct-mail program, while the Democrats had a far more modest program and were continually compelled to eat their seed corn. In the early 1980s the RNC had a total donor list of 1.8 million, compared with less than half a million on the Democratic side. Even worse, Democratic direct-mail appeals did best in the wealthy Zip Codes of Manhattan, Cambridge, and Beverly Hills. Thanks to a "party building" loophole in the 1979 FECA amendments, fund-raisers could raise money from well-to-do people who had reached their contribution limits ("maxed out") and could give no more money to federal candidates. This money given to "nonfederal accounts" soon came to be known as "soft money," meaning that it did not have to be disclosed under the federal laws.

According to most rough tallies, the Democrats in 1984 raised more soft money than the Republicans, most of it from the party's wealthiest donors. Thus the Republicans had the best of both worlds—a business-oriented party with a mass financial base—while the Democrats, a party ostensibly dedicated to the common citizen, remained deeply in hock to organized business.

Lately, party leaders have tried to refill the Democrats' coffers with both small, direct-mail money and big money from PACs and wealthy donors. Charles Manatt, a California lawyer-businessman who served as party national chairman from 1980 to 1984, launched initiatives on both tracks. He hired a very talented young direct-mail expert, Frank O'Brien, and Manatt was willing even to borrow money to finance the starting costs of O'Brien's small-donor project. Unlike most of the party professionals who float through the DNC, O'Brien stayed for six years, and he continues to operate its direct-mail program as a consultant. Under O'Brien, the Democrats' list grew from under 60,000 to over 500,000, and direct mail began breaking even and showing a small profit some time in 1983.

On the other track, Manatt redoubled the party's efforts to reach out to business. He encouraged young entrepreneurs to run for Congress and created a Democratic Business Council, 350 members strong, headed by his friend and fellow Californian Irvin Kipnes. For a contribution of $10,000, a businessman could join the council and presumably influence party thinking. Manatt was playing the old game of separating fat cats from their money, but with a subtle new wrinkle. Rich people were being asked to involve themselves, not just as financially successful individuals who happened to be Democrats, but as business leaders hoping to educate the party on the business viewpoint.

This two-track strategy seems to make tactical sense, but it also intensifies the contradictions in the party's message. Direct mail uses frankly ideological appeals to the party's most militant core—such as scare letters to senior citizens warning that Republicans are unreliable defenders of social security. Fat-cat financing tends to emphasize mushy ambiguity and rapprochement with business. Doing both simultaneously reinforces the party's schizophrenia, which so plagued the Mondale campaign. The Republican Party has doctrinal splits, but it has no such schism at its core. There are important differences between Representative Jack Kemp's version of an opportunity society and tax lobbyist Charls Walker's, but the GOP's direct-mail appeals and its PAC appeals share a coherent ideological theme.

Admittedly, the Democrats' big-money donors are a diverse group, covering a wide part of the ideological spectrum, but their cumulative message is that the party, to revive, must have friendlier relations with the business community and should generally move rightward, particularly on economics. The Democrats today have fewer money men motivated by *noblesse oblige* and more who express the self-interests of business as an economic class. In the jousting over the 1982 tax bill, Manatt himself used his party position to lobby Democratic members of Congress to retain one of the most economically indefensible gimmicks in the 1981 Reagan tax cut, something called "safe harbor leasing," which allowed companies to buy and sell tax deductions.

VII.

There are those who insist that a stout-hearted Democrat can squeeze money out of businessmen without corrupting the party's populist soul. Their favorite quotation is a pungent line that I have heard attributed both to California's "Big Daddy" of Democratic politics, Jesse Unruh, and to the late House Majority Whip, Hale Boggs: "If you can't eat their food and drink their liquor and take their money and screw their women and still look them in the eye and vote against them, then you don't belong in Congress." Their favorite exhibit is the prodigious former chairman of the Democratic Congressional Campaign Committee, Representative Tony Coelho, now the House Democratic Whip. Coelho is a sort of Milo Minderbinder of campaign finance, with something to sell just about anyone if it will raise money for the Democratic Party. He once introduced a New York Zionist activist, Jay Zises, to a group of Texas oil wildcatters interested in more liberal tax breaks for domestic oil drilling. The two groups agreed to join forces in a new PAC called The Council for a Secure America, based on the dubious premise that freer-flowing domestic petroleum would punish the Arabs.

Coelho became head of the Democratic Congressional Campaign Committee in 1981, when the DCCC was barely raising enough money to pay its own bills. In the 1979–80 election cycle, the DCCC raised $1.8 million, about one-tenth of its Republican counterpart. Coelho, then a relatively obscure Congressman from Fresno, California, resolved to get serious about campaign finance. He abolished a small influential House advisory body created by his predecessor, James Corman, and replaced it with a *pro forma* fifty-member group, assuring that most of the decisions would revert to Coelho himself. And he got very serious about raising money.

The DCCC had for some time held an annual fund-raising dinner. Lobbyists would buy tables at a thousand dollars a plate; Democratic congressmen, who were in the habit of asking for free tickets, sometimes brought their wives and children. Carter administration officials also got complimentary tickets. The meal itself cost fifty or sixty thousand dollars to put on, and sometimes the dinners produced an embarrassingly small net. "Coelho was the first to insist that members of Congress pay for their own tickets," recalls Marta David, the DCCC's former field director. "It caused a hell of a furor. He was asking these guys to take a thousand dollars out of their own campaign and give it to the D-triple-C. They had been getting free tickets forever."

Coelho's real target, however, was the business PAC community. He worked hard to raise money from the PACs directly and to introduce PAC men to Democratic congressional candidates he hoped they would find ideologically compatible. He hired a staff person whose sole job was liaison with PACs. Coelho says, "We provide the PACs with information on our candidates. We say, 'Here's a candidate who's reasonable, a candidate who's taken a position that X PAC should be comfortable with.'" A favorite Coelho phrase is "the business of politics." He told me, in early 1985, "A lot of the PACs are contributing to us as a committee because they like our businesslike approach." Other PACs did not particularly like what Democrats stood for, but according to Coelho, "Business has to deal with us whether they like it or not, because we're the majority."

This new approach brought in a lot of money, about half of it from PACs. DCCC income went from $1.8 million in 1979–80 to $6.5 million in 1981–82, to $11 million in 1983–84, to nearly $15 million in 1985–86. Coelho increased the committee's contributions to candidates and—this aroused great opposition—shifted them to Democratic challengers and away from incumbents, who until then had been hogging most of the DCCC budget. So effective was Coelho's pressure on business PACs that in the 1983–84 cycle, business PACs actually gave slightly more than half their total money to Democrats, almost entirely to incumbents, up from about one-third to Democrats in 1981–82.

To Coelho's admirers he is a hero for getting the Democrats back into the game. Even his detractors agree that the party faced a terrible choice of "being virtuous and losing, or playing the game and compromising our soul," in the phrase of populist Congressman Pat Williams of Montana, a rare, on-the-record Coelho critic. "It's a genuine dilemma," Williams says. "We have to have the dollars to be competitive, and Tony figured out how to get them. But if we think we can out-special-interest Republicans, we're in for a big surprise at both the bank and the ballot box. Ultimately the votes are more important than the dollars."

According to Williams, House roll-call votes have occasionally been delayed at Coelho's request because they coincided with DCCC fund-raising events, lest members be put in the awkward position of voting on the interests of businesses that Coelho was shaking down for campaign money. "I've been on the House floor," says Williams, "when people have said, 'Pull that. We can't have a vote on that yet. We're having a fund-raiser Wednesday, and we're calling PACs.' " Perhaps the nadir of this sort of politics was the famous 1981 "bidding war," in which Democrats decided to ingratiate themselves with business groups by adding new special-interest preferences to the already overloaded Republican tax bill. "The deficit," says Williams, "is largely the responsibility of Democrats because we didn't have the courage to say no, and the campaign dollars were there to say yes." The *Atlantic Monthly*'s Gregg Easterbrook, in an otherwise admiring profile of Coelho, termed the 1981 tax debate the time "the party tried to sell its soul and failed."

But in a sense, Coelho did a very effective job of marketing the party's soul. And even his critics concede that he was able to run an astute money laundry. In 1981 and 1982. Coelho used a substantial portion of the income to finance the start-up of a direct-mail drive. By 1984, direct mail was a net source of income. In 1985–86, direct mail produced over $15 million. Through this alchemy, business money provided the seed capital to raise small contributions from good grass-roots Democrats responding to good Democratic themes. Even as he was counseling something of a tactical alliance with business PACs, Coelho remained a sturdy partisan Democrat, so that when polls began showing that the greatest Republican weakness was that the public thought the GOP stood for economic unfairness, he urged Democrats to campaign as economic populists.

In 1987, Coelho moved up from DCCC chairman to Democratic whip. To be fair, his money laundry did raise more money from business groups for Democratic liberals than they could raise individually, and at slightly less ideological peril. His own role as the party's Doctor Faustus, unseemly as it was, perhaps ran interference for other liberals. They could keep business lobbyists at arm's length and still take money from the DCCC. However, the bargain, like most faustian deals, is a very tricky one. On balance, the tight alliance between Coelho and the business PACs has been one more factor contributing to the conventional view that Democrats need to become economic centrists. Coelho himself is a charter member of the neo-liberal Democratic Leadership Conference.

VIII.

As the 1988 election approaches, there is good news as well as bad on the money front. The bad news, as noted, is that Republicans still are far richer than Democrats, and that the Democrats' effort to raise big money induces schizophrenia. The good news is that Democrats are becoming serious about the two strategies that offer a natural avenue to party growth—small-money direct mail and campaign-finance reform.

According to Frank O'Brien, the party's direct-mail chief, the first big breakthrough came when Manatt allowed him to plow the proceeds of a direct-mail campaign back into further direct-mail prospecting, rather than siphoning it off for other party expenses. Until then, Democratic direct mail had been stuck in first gear. Lately, the Democrats have become ingenious at developing new techniques, such as using free, public-record voter lists, which are then demographically targeted through census data. The idea is to pick a group of probable Democratic voters—say, moderate-income homeowners approaching retirement age—and reach them with a suitable "Democratic" theme such as defense of social security or medicare.

The DNC's hot mailing piece in the 1983–84 cycle was a letter from Representative Claude Pepper, the party's grand senior citizen, explaining that Reagan's budget cutters were mounting yet another assault on medicare and social security, and concluding, "Right now, millions of older Americans are counting on you and the Democratic Party as their defenders against Medicare cuts." The mailer included a photocopy of an authentic tearjerker of a letter that Pepper's office had received from one Arthur M. Nottingham of Mt. Meigs, Alabama, complete with spindly handwriting, recounting, "Recently, I had surgery to replace clogged arteries," and warning that "too many elderly people like me (70) without adequate insurance may die if Medicare benefits are cut any more."

The Pepper mailing piece was ideological, issue-oriented, constituency-rousing, slightly demogogic—and highly effective. Unlike much that the Democratic Party does, it had the further virtue of taking a clear position. Not surprisingly, mail of this sort is closely linked to the party's still-visible role as deliverer of tangible benefits to ordinary people, via public policy—that old nexus of party, state, and constituency.

According to Ralph Whitehead, a professor of public policy at the University of Massachusetts and a student and practitioner of political mail, "Direct mail is the grass-roots organizing tool of the information society. Whether you sit at someone's kitchen table or reach them through the mail, both are forms of political participation." Admittedly, direct mail by itself is a very limited form of communication. It lacks the rich back-and-forth of a political meeting or a campaign. But Whitehead is surely right when he adds that direct mail is a superb point of initial contact. Many people whose first political act is writing a check soon graduate to become volunteers and then activists.

Governor Michael Dukakis of Massachusetts has effectively used a direct-mail strategy together with a volunteer strategy to build what once would have been called a machine, but one that is entirely free of reliance on either PAC money or patronage. Instead of discovering potential contributors through mass mailings to lists of Democrats, Dukakis began with a core of known supporters, whom he asked to sponsor small, local fund-raising events, slowly building up a base of proven small donors through personal contacts. At the state level, most candidates do not bother with events that charge ten or twenty dollars at the door, but Dukakis adroitly used them to build a computer bank of 40,000 proven supporters, seven thousand of whom were newly recruited in 1986. This equals about 2 percent of the entire Massachusetts electorate. About half of them have personally attended some campaign event. Most of then donate more than once.

"They are our gold," says John Sasso, the governor's chief political aide. "We keep in touch with them through newsletters; we tell them when the governor is going to be in their area. They feel a real involvement." Dukakis uses a custom-designed computer system to keep track of his activists, coding them by address, occupation, precinct, how much money they have contributed, which events they attended, whether they have done other volunteer work, and so on. If the campaign wanted to send a letter to every pro-environment carpenter named Brian who was also a caucus delegate, the computer could do so on command.

With this approach, little money is wasted on mass mailings soliciting prospective donors, since nearly every contributor has been recruited the old-fashioned way, by some other supporter. The Dukakis campaign raised about $2.5 million in 1986; the process nets not only money but a proven organization. Ordinarily with direct mail, you have to spend money to make money. Since mass mailings are costly and produce a low response rate, something like half of the proceeds go for expenses. But in the Dukakis method, using only an already proven list, the net almost equals the gross. "Dukakis really pioneered this," says Frank O'Brien. "His success at building a base of small donors and activists is the best I've seen."

Dukakis has astutely tapped the base membership that PACs on the Democratic side profess to represent. Normally, labor unions finance Democratic candidates by having their PACs raise the money. Rank-and-file members are encouraged to give money to the union PAC; the PAC treasurer writes a check; the candidate gets some money; the union acquires a political IOU. But something is missing: the process of brokering money, wholesale, does little to rebuild the Democratic Party's flagging mass base. Dukakis won't accept that sort of money. Instead, he urges unions to organize mass meetings, where members will turn out and each fork over ten or twenty dollars, one member at a time.

In July 1986, for example, the carpenters' union organized a fund-raising event for Governor Dukakis at the IBEW union hall in Dorchester. Some six hundred carpenters from several union locals paid ten dollars each to hear the governor. Each month in his re-election campaign, Dukakis held several such events, across the state, at places like the Dorchester IBEW Hall, the Knights of Columbus Hall in Charlestown, or the Lynnfield armory. True, the union rank and file showed up mainly because the leadership urged them to. But nonetheless this approach is certainly more authentic and base-restoring than collecting money from a union PAC, not to mention relying on a big-business PAC. Dukakis's strategy accomplishes several goals simultaneously: it allows him to avoid PACs; it creates a secure, diverse financial base; and it builds organization and mobilizes activists. As a side effect, it compels better communication between union leaders and members. This approach could be a model for Democrats nationally.

By disdaining PACs, Dukakis converts good government into smart politics. He is happy to take money from unions—or service workers, or other groups of workers—he simply insists that the money involve voters directly. "We are not running away from unions," says one of his strategists. "Far from it. We are running away from money that doesn't have personal commitment behind it."

The Dukakis strategy disproves a couple of false dichotomies that tend to paralyze liberal Democrats. Many observers and strategists have assumed that the party has a choice of either practicing the old-time religion of liberal interest-group politics, or becoming centrist and high-tech. Militant centrists, like the party's former executive director, Brian Lunde, gained political influence because they were good technicians. Some consultants think that computerized mass mailings and clever TV commercials can substitute for old-fashioned, one-on-one activist politics, that if you have the money to buy the technology, you can dispense with personal politicking. In the 1986 California Senate race, the candidates used technology to raise money, which they spent on television and radio ads. In California, the joke went, a political meeting was defined as three people watching a TV commercial. But Dukakis has used a high-tech tool—the computer—to rebuild a mass base of involved voters. His computer is not a substitute for but a more efficient version of a precinct captain's file of index cards. Dukakis's approach also disproves the claim by some political scientists that issue activists and reformers are a fair-weather army whose primary loyalty to a single issue rarely carries over into party or even candidate loyalty. Dukakis reaches supporters on the basis of issues, but they become part of his general political apparatus. To be sure, he also has his share of big donors and big fund raisers, but the small-money strategy helps to keep them in their place.

It is sad that it has taken the Democratic Party more than a decade to find its way back to McGovern's all-but-discredited insight that small money and issue-oriented volunteers can compensate for a lot of big money. At the Democratic National Committee, Frank O'Brien is now attempting to use direct mail for party building as well as fund raising. Typically, he notes, Democrats in any given area are so protective of their own lists that they seldom pool resources, and the DNC itself was reluctant to let specific Democrats "prospect" from its own list. Often, says O'Brien, one Democrat rents a mailing list from another Democrat, uses it, and then only breaks even or makes a very modest return. "If two Democratic fund-raising groups have 50,000 names, and each one mails to the other's list, 100,000 names switch computer files, but no new money is raised for the party. It amazed me how much money circulates, and how little spins off into useful new resources,"

O'Brien says. So O'Brien has organized a project to have the DNC share lists and resources with the state parties.

The DNC now can operate direct-mail programs for state candidates and parties, design the packages, and keep the computerized files of the lists of names. Names are traded rather than bought and sold. The first mailings sent out under this new program, in March 1986, netted about $300,000. O'Brien observes that because of the faint ties between individual candidacies and institutional Democratic parties, "much candidate activity is wasted activity for the long term. We hope to have the party invest in candidate efforts in exchange for party control of those lists over the long term. If the party doesn't bring anything to the table, the party can't come away from the table with anything. That's the big challenge—to find ways to marry short-term candidate activity with long-term party-building activity."

O'Brien also argues that a fund-raising strategy built around direct mail has the further virtue of identifying issues that are popular with voters. "Short of an election, there is no better way to test-market political ideas. Direct mail can rebuild the party around populist themes and neutralize the influence of the money people," he says.

But can it? In the 1985–86 cycle, approximately 60 percent of total Democratic Party money came from small-donor direct-mail solicitations. That fraction had been dropping until the 1983–84 cycle, when it began turning up modestly, but it is still growing too slowly. Direct mail has enormous potential for developing linkages and rebuilding a party base, but all by itself it can't make the Democrats financially competitive with the Republicans under the present system of campaign financing. PACs simply have too much money.

IX.

Until 1986, most Democratic Party professionals thought the last thing the party needed was another round of campaign-finance reform. The party had been more competitive *before* the 1974 reform. It was politically naive professional reformers, of the sort who belonged to Common Cause, who had badgered Congress into enacting the misconceived 1974 reforms, which neutralized big Democratic donors without providing offsetting public financing, and loosed business PACs on the world. Now that Democrats were finally learning to exploit PACs, in the manner of Congressman Tony Coelho, it was time to leave the damned system alone. Those who still talked about reforming the reforms were regarded as hopelessly naive. This view was reinforced by some political scientists like Larry Sabato, who argued that big money had always been influential in politics and always would be.

But after the 1984 election, a number of prominent and worldly Democrats began talking serious reform again. Once again, campaign costs exceeded previous records. There was widespread revulsion that the whole political system was being driven by the demands of campaign money. Senator David Boren, a moderately conservative Democrat from Oklahoma, gave an influential speech declaring war on the whole PAC system. In 1985 and 1986, officials like Dukakis, who refused PAC support, were raising a lot of money. Gary Hart nearly won the party's 1984 nomination without taking any PAC donations.

Designing an effective reform is difficult, however, not only because incumbents generally tend to profit from the existing system, but because successive Supreme Court rulings have narrowed the options. While the courts have upheld limits on PAC giving, they have struck down limits on candidate spending. And candidates are permitted to spend unlimited amounts of their own money to get elected.

There are nonetheless numerous ways of limiting the power of big, self-interested money in politics. Given that a great deal of campaign money today is spent on television, Congress could forbid television stations from selling commercial time to candidates, and could require them to give all candidates for major office free air time. This would perhaps not be feasible in large metropolitan areas where there are numerous contests, but free mail privileges might be an alternative. Another approach, devised by Richard Conlon, Director of the Democratic Study Group, would give 100 percent tax credits for small donors, provided that they lived in the district or state of the candidate. This would not put PACs out of business, but would dilute their influence.

Perhaps the most ingenious proposal, set forth in a bill sponsored by Senators Boren, Kennedy, and others, would provide public financing for House and Senate races. The Supreme Court has held that public-financing schemes must be voluntary—candidates may opt out of them—but if they choose to accept the money, they are bound by the rules. The Boren-Kennedy bill creates a devilishly clever incentive to opt for the public funds. It provides that if candidate *A* takes the public financing, but candidate *B* chooses to raise private money and exceeds the total financing limit, then *A* gets a bonus of double the usual public subsidy. This would put immense pressure on both candidates to accept public funding, and to abide by the limits.

Obviously there are plenty of technical pitfalls in designing a public-financing system that will pass both constitutional and political muster. But the impulse that led Congress to try to fashion a serious campaign-finance reform after the Watergate excesses was a good impulse, and it got the presidential aspects more or less right, even if it got the rest of the system wrong. If a Democrat wins in 1988, there will be an opportunity again, though cynics will argue that Democrats should savor their moment of incumbency to really shake the bastards down. But, as Pat Williams suggests, Republicans will always win that game in the long run. Democrats in the Senate during the period of Republican control (1981–86) got a chilling taste of what life is like when Republicans can market not only ideological affinity, but incumbency as well. During those years, the Republican Senate Campaign Committee outraised its Democratic counterpart by something like ten to one.

Notwithstanding the cynics' view that money will always find a way to talk, the reformist enterprise is worthwhile. If structural solutions to human frailties never did any good, the American Constitution would be a grand fraud. The need for a carefully thought-out reform of campaign-finance law has something to do with good government, but it has everything to do with partisan parity. Democrats ought to limit the role of big money in politics, for good partisan reasons. And this time, they had better do it right.

CHAPTER THREE

PARTY

I.

In Chapter Two, we saw that the quest for money buys Republicans at least double the political resources available to Democrats, cements a liaison between the GOP and its natural business allies, and tends to confuse the Democratic Party's message. Now we need to take a closer look at exactly what money buys for the two parties; how much difference it makes, both in the heat of an election and over the long term, in strengthening party infrastructure, strategy, and voter loyalties; whether it creates insurmountable difficulties for Democrats; and how these difficulties might be overcome.

The Democrats began rebounding from their absolute nadir after the 1984 election. Modest recoveries are evident on several fronts. The money disparity narrowed slightly in 1985–86. Direct-mail efforts began to bear fruit. The national Party began some initially modest but potentially important state party-building work. The Democrats made strides in the development of sophisticated polling and targeting techniques. Some doctrinal conflicts within the Democratic Party receded. Some new citizen activists became party volunteers. Some blue-collar Democrats came back home to the party, and a cohort of populists got elected to the Senate in 1986, helping Democrats retake control of that body not by retreating into centrism but as good economic progressives.

The Democrats also had a stroke of overdue good luck when the Reagan administration's casual management of a potentially explosive foreign strategy finally blew up in its face. So the party seems better positioned for an electoral and institutional comeback than one might have predicted just two years ago.

II.

This book is about the Democratic *Party*. It is high time to ask the not so self-evident question, what do we mean by a party? More than forty years ago, the grand scholar of American parties, the late V. O. Key, Jr., observed that people tend to use the word "party" somewhat carelessly, in three quite distinct senses. A party means, first, a set of popular allegiances. People identify themselves as Republicans, or Democrats, or independents, or something else; Key called this the "party-in-the-electorate." Once, partisan attachments were very strong. They have been eroding for at least three decades. Today there are fewer avowed partisans, many more self-described independents, more ticket-splitters, more swing voters, and more people for whom "party" is just not a useful conceptual label. As we shall see, this is particularly bad news for Democrats.

Secondly, "party" means the organizational party: the ward, township, and state committees, the regulars who inhabit that territory, the scattered local machines, the citizen activists, and the two national committees. Unlike the parliamentary democracies, the United States has traditionally had very weak national parties, which reflect the federated structure of our system of government. Ironically, it is the Republicans, who profess belief in decentralized government, who are becoming a more coherent, centralized national party. Generally, the modern institutional competitors of parties—such as PACs, lobbyists, pollsters, lone-wolf candidates, and media campaigns—are said to erode the parties. Yet the Republican Party manages to coexist very nicely with, and even to draw strength from, the separate mechanisms of what Sidney Blumenthal called the "permanent campaign."

Finally, as Key observed, "party" also means the "party-in-government." The Republican Party is the glue that binds Reagan's White House to its supporters in the Congress; it is the GOP apparatus in the House and Senate. The Democratic Party similarly functioned under a Roosevelt or a Johnson. The party-in-government helps bridge over the constitutional separation of powers, making it possible to govern, and it informs the image that successive cohorts of voters have of the two parties. In the 1930s, the Democratic Party-in-government was a party of economic recovery. In the 1970s, it was the party of stagflation. In the 1940s, the Republican Party-in-government was remembered as the party of Hoover, *laissez-faire* economics, and the Great Depression. In the mid-1980s, it was the party of Reagan, *laissez-faire,* and economic recovery.

One might add that the modern party has a fourth meaning, as a set of shared ideological principles. What is intriguing is that these various meanings of party tend to lead fairly autonomous lives of their own, and don't necessarily shift in unison. For example, the late nineteenth century was a time of strong and stable party allegiances but fairly localized and personalist party organizations. Often, a "machine" failed to survive a particular boss. Yet people were very clear about whether they were Republicans or Democrats. In Congress, the discipline of party-line voting waxes and wanes quite independent of the strength of the voters' party allegiances. Organizationally, the institutional party may be in a period of ascendance while personal party allegiance is in a period of decay.

In clarifying these different meanings of "party," we can understand better what has been occurring lately. In general, the voters' partisan allegiance and identification with party has been weakening. It has become a cliché to observe that what has happened since 1950 is less a realignment of voters than a "de-alignment"—fewer voters feel a strong attachment to either party. Yet since the mid-

1970s there has been a very strong resurgence of the Republican Party as an institution. There has also been a very effective linkage between the Republican Party-in-government and the Republican Party as an organization out in the country, as well as an ideological rebuilding on the Republican side. So while the decline in party allegiance—the party-in-the-electorate—has been fairly generalized, even in this sense of party the Democrats have lost more than the Republicans. (In 1984, about 27 percent of voters identified themselves as Republicans, virtually the same proportion as in 1952. During that period, the proportion of self-described Democrats dropped from more than 50 percent to the low 30 percent range.) But the Republicans, flush with money, have rebuilt their party organization, while Democrats have barely begun to rebuild theirs. Personal party affiliation and voting behavior don't march in lock-step with a party's organizational strength, but at some point a superior organization and a coherent ideology help to recruit voters.

Only a few of the political scientists observing this trend have called attention to this organizational imbalance. What has attracted greater attention is the more nearly symmetrical decline in stated party affiliation. One recent, well-documented book, *The Decline of Political Parties,* by Martin Wattenberg of the University of California at Irvine, uses three decades of survey data to demonstrate the multiple ways in which partisan affiliation has eroded. Not only do more voters consider themselves independents, but a closer look at the data reveals that growing numbers of voters don't find partisan party concepts relevant at all. Wattenberg astutely observes that declining partisanship and cynicism or alienation are not logically or empirically linked phenomena. "There is no evidence," he concludes, "that the rise in cynicism has been responsible for the decline in partisan identification." In fact, the young voters who were least cynical about political participation also showed the least attachment to party.

Wattenberg's study reveals sharp declines in the intensity of partisan feelings, even among voters who were interested in politics. The percentage of voters who felt positively about one party and negatively about the other declined in every election, from just over 50 percent in 1952 to 27.3 percent in 1980. In a series of questions about what domestic policy positions they liked or disliked in candidates or parties, over half the voters surveyed in 1952 mentioned substantive areas of agreement only with parties, while just 2.7 percent mentioned only candidates. By 1980, that had reversed: 27.7 percent mentioned only candidates and 11 percent mentioned parties.

In 1952, about a third of all voters said they liked the Democrats because they were the party of ordinary working people. Another third said they liked Democrats because of their position on economic issues. By 1980 voters had few strong likes or dislikes about either party. The only statement about either party that produced a like or dislike response of more than 12 percent was the statement that Democrats were for the common working person, with which 25.5 percent of the respondents agreed. Wattenberg observes, "These feelings that Democrats are the party of the common working person while the Republicans are the party of the upper class and big business represent virtually the last remnant of the images of the parties that developed during the New Deal." That perception, significantly, declined by only about eight percentage points, and it remains the one powerful, positive voter attachment that Democrats have to build on.

Wattenberg, like most observers, blames this declining partisanship on the rise of candidate-driven and media-dominated campaigns. In an analysis of newspapers and magazine articles, he finds that the ratio of candidate references to party references increased from less than two to one in 1952 to five or six to one in 1980. The more public attention is focused on candidates, the less is focused on parties. The more that candidates don't really need parties to get elected, the less attention they pay to parties.

Wattenberg, astute as he is, has almost nothing to say about the unequal implications of this shift for Republicans and Democrats. Only a handful of observers* have examined how differently things

---

*The most perceptive, in my view, are Thomas Edsall of the *Washington Post,* David Ademany of the University of Wisconsin, and David Price of Duke University, now a member of Congress.

look on the Republican and Democratic sides. Perhaps there is a subtle pressure among scholars and journalists to be civic-minded and even-handed, rather than seeming partisan in their conclusions, even when the facts suggest highly partisan, as well as civic, implications. David Broder's fine 1971 book, *The Party's Over*, lamented the decline in parties that was evident even then, as a loss for the democratic system, not for the Democratic Party. But even as the discrepancy has become more palpable, the assumption of symmetrical decline has persisted. In a much more recent (1985) book, *The Party Goes On*, written almost as a rejoinder to Broder, political scientist Xandra Kayden and former Republican National Committee executive director Eddie Mahe, Jr., claim that parties have been buried prematurely and are making a big comeback. After sifting the evidence, they proclaim, "Today's political party is stronger, not only because it is more professional and has more money, but because it is now in a relatively better position to influence the outcome of elections and the behavior of government than it was before, and more than any other actor on the political scene." That is surely a more fitting description of the Republican Party than the Democratic Party. But with a couple of notable exceptions, this is the prevailing view. The debate is about whether the decline is accelerating or slowing, not about its partisan tilt.

Another recent (1984) standard work, *American Parties in Decline*, by the political scientist William Crotty, agrees more with Broder than with Kayden and Mahe. Crotty explores the usual factors corroding party—the rise of independent voters, campaign consultants, television, PACs, interest groups, declining party-line voting in Congress, and so on. He concludes that partisan decline is likely to continue, and he hasn't a word to say about whether this decline is symmetrical. Yet another very valuable recent book, by the political scientist David Price, *Bringing Back the Parties*, makes an eloquent case for the role of parties. Price was executive director of the Democrats' Hunt Commission on Party Rules, which attempted to counterreform the earlier McGovern Commission rules in order to create a bigger role for party regulars. Besides teaching political science at Duke, Price recently got himself elected to Congress, taking back a Republican seat. Price concludes that the

Democrats desperately need to emulate the Republican's party-building success.

III.

The changing partisan landscape gives the advantage to Republicans in two distinct and reinforcing ways. First, as we have suggested, Republicans have more resources and have used them effectively to build a stronger institutional party. Second, Republicans and conservatives are able to compete more effectively when partisan affiliation is in decline. Without strong parties to offset them, influence flows to sources of power outside the electoral polity—namely, to economically dominant groups. Democrats need strong party allegiances more than Republicans do.

A well-tested rule of politics is that the fellow who seems above party is usually a conservative. The weaker party ties become, the more likely it is that such leaders will succeed. An Eisenhower or a Reagan can be simultaneously a president of all the people and a man who seems to be above party, while paving the way for a partisan Republican agenda. A political climate of disaffililated voters and media and PAC dominance serves Republicans more naturally than Democrats. Democrats, as a coalition party of have-nots, are more dependent on the party loyalty of voters. As these loyalties loosen, Democrats lose more than Republicans.

There is a long and distinguished political-science literature, once again going back to V. O. Key, arguing that parties are essential institutions for advancing the interests of ordinary citizens in a democracy. This conclusion about the function of parties goes against the advice of the founding fathers, who warned about the divisive influence of "faction," and against the instinct of many modern editorialists, who counsel citizens simply to vote for "the best man [sic]." But Key's logic is very persuasive once the argument is heard. A political party is the one institution in a democratic polity that effectively aggregates, articulates, and brokers the interests of ordinary citizens. In this respect, a party is superior to the other great mechanism of American Lockean liberalism, the "pluralist" constellation of pressure groups, because it is more accountable to voters. As E. E. Schattschneider, another advocate of strong parties, observed, "The flaw in the pluralist heaven is that the heavenly choir sings with a strong upper-class accent." The skepticism that the founding fathers expressed about party was quite in character with their economic conservatism; it was not coincidental that the great growth of popular democracy in the Jacksonian era heralded the creation of the modern Democratic Party. The party's founder, Martin van Buren, saw it as a vehicle for ordinary citizens to offset the natural influence of the aristocracy of wealth.

According to Walter Dean Burnham, a prominent disciple of Key, "The existence of parties . . . acts as a constraint on the . . . opportunism of politicians because, as institutions, parties have a permanent collective identity, a permanent core clientele, and an institutional memory." In the same manner, an ideologically consistent, institutionally effective party-in-government serves the democratic goal of political accountability, by providing partisan standards on important issues. The absence of parliamentary discipline in the United States makes party coherence that much more important, if accountability is to survive at all. When the House Democratic caucus temporarily stripped Representative Les Aspin of his Armed Services Committee chairmanship in late 1986, for the partisan heresies of supporting the MX Missile, Star Wars, and aid to the Nicaraguan contras, he was disciplined as a faithless Democrat.

Sidney Verba, a well-known student of political participation, suggests, "The present-day brand of politics moves away from public kinds of political participation like parties and voting, which are open and equally accessible, into forms that are more private and quiet, like PAC finance and insider lobbying. In that kind of politics, little guys tend to lose. People who are disadvantaged require aggregating mechanisms. Upper status people have many avenues of exerting influence. A party is a vehicle for organizing a broad mass around issues that serve broad, collective goals." Maurice Duverger, in his classic cross-cultural study *Political Parties,* concluded flatly, "A regime without parties is necessarily a conservative regime."

The history of partisan attachment in the United States and elsewhere tends to confirm this analysis. The 1920s were a period of weak partisan linkages, low voting participation, and the dominance of both parties by conservative moneyed elites. The resurgence of the Democrats coincided with a resurgence of both popular participation and partisan affiliation. The New Deal period was the modern high-water mark of partisan consciousness and loyalty. Ticket splitting peaked in the late 1920s, reached a low point in the 1930s, and gradually began creeping up again until the early 1960s, when almost half of congressional districts had greater than 10 percent divergence in their vote for president and for Congress. By 1984, 189 congressional districts cast votes one way for president and the other way for Congress. Though voting for candidates of different parties ("the best man") for different offices is often taken as a sign of a sophisticated, independent-minded electorate, it more often means only the decomposition of the party system. Historically, ticket splitting has gone hand in hand with high voter cynicism and low levels of working-class political participation.

Party serves as a shorthand guide to voters. In America, with its federal system and its "long ballot," a citizen may be asked to vote for thirty or forty separate candidates plus dozens of ballot propositions. It is inconceivable to expect the average citizen to become conversant with the views of all of these candidates as individuals, or with every ballot question. A party affiliation serves as a pretty good rough substitute. This is more important for Democrats than for Republicans: the one strong socioeconomic correlation that has refused to go away is that lower-income and lower-status people, when they vote, tend to be Democrats. Such voters need the shorthand of a party label more, because they are less inclined to bone up on electoral details.

David Price writes, " 'Candidate appeal' is often based on the most superficial, contrived kind of media image. . . . Nonpartisanship may be particularly disadvantageous to the poorer and less-educated members of the community, who tend to rely relatively heavily on the party cue to identify candidates who reflect their interests." Parties, as Burnham observes, "are the only devices yet identified by the wit of Western man which with some effectiveness can generate countervailing collective power on behalf of the many individually powerless, against the few who are individually—or organizationally—powerful."

There is a further virtue to parties, one which is of particular importance to the more egalitarian party. Political man to an extent relies on "the state" to leaven and to humanize the cold inequities of the market, but the state in its practical incarnation often presents itself as a cold, bureaucratic institution. Parties, as more social, "fraternal" creatures, in Wilson C. McWilliams's term, serve to humanize the citizen's links with the state, and make the state more responsive and accountable. Sociability, as a civic virtue, is more likely to be encountered in a party gathering or a political club than in a public agency. But political clubs are steadily losing this function to campaigns and to incumbents. As parties weaken, the state becomes more foreboding and less tractable.

Even fairly conservative commentators agree, as James Q. Wilson writes, that the Democratic Party has been "a device for the socialization of the lower classes and the excluded minority groups." In the absence of party affiliation and articulation, and a general feeling of cynicism of what the political process can deliver, a dissaffected blue-collar voter is a sitting duck for the purely symbolic and patriotic appeals of a Reagan—the circus aspect of politics without the bread. Conversely, a closely knit bond between party and voter can overcome a great deal of financial dominance on the opposing side. In 1932, when the Hoover administration was staggering to an end and Democrats were poised for a landslide win, Senator Huey Long quipped, "The great trouble with Democrats is that we have all the votes and no money. In the present situation I believe the best thing we could do is to sell President Hoover a million votes for half of what he is going to pay to try to get them. We could spare the votes and we could use the money." Would that the Democrats had such troubles today.

As the Democratic partisan machinery has decayed and collapsed, candidate machines have filled the vacuum. Individual campaigns are where volunteers are recruited, where political professionals work year in and year out, where political money is raised and spent, and where campaign expertise resides. On the Democratic side, all of this operates at the institutional expense of the Democratic Party. On the Republican side, where there is money enough for both, it operates in tandem with the party.

Similarly, most mayors and governors in office today are very weak partisans. If one compares "Republican" and "Democratic" state economic-development programs, or public-health programs, or anti-crime programs, one finds managerial government in all but the most extremely ideological local administrations, and partisan identification matters little. A Congressman who initiates a public-works project or a mayor who cuts a ribbon on a new school does so as an incumbent, not as a Democrat or a Republican. This may seem modern and conducive to good government, but as Key, Schattschneider, and Burnham have reminded us, it signals a weakened party system and a diminished ability of the non-wealthy to use the civic and political realm to counterbalance the market realm.

Thus, it isn't just just the Republicans' money that does in the Democrats. It is a combination of Republican business money and declining popular mobilization by the Democrats. Consequently, the weakening of party links to voters has special import, not just for democracy but for Democrats. The Republicans, before Reagan's fall from grace, had the best of both worlds—a personalist president, who seemed above party, and an effective party machine to build support for him and his allies. The news that Democrats are "only" suffering a dealignment, and not a full-fledged realignment, is small comfort.

IV.

Before the Iran scandal, Ronald Reagan was known as the Teflon President. Nothing stuck to him—no criticism, no bad news, no bad luck. At first, this seeming invulnerability was attributed mainly to Reagan's cheerful, optimistic personality, and his remarkable ability to distance himself from the unpleasant details of political events and to bask in the warmth of pleasant ones. It has gradually become clear, however, that Reagan was also the beneficiary of a small army of Teflon engineers. Long after Reagan goes, the Re-

publican Party and future Republican presidents will be protected
by a sort of permanent Teflon not yet fully available to Democrats.

The first ingredient in this permanent Teflon is an impressive
rebuilding of Republican Party organization. This first began after
the Goldwater debacle of 1964, under the party chairman Ray Bliss,
then took off under a later chairman, William Brock, beginning in
1977; it reached high gear after 1980, in alliance with the Reagan
White House.

Brock's four-year tenure coincided with a period of intensified
business investment in politics. RNC income went from $8.9 mil-
lion and a direct-mail base of some 300,000 donors in 1975, to $77
million and 1.2 million donors in 1979–80. In the 1983–84 presidential cycle, the RNC had 1.8 million donors and a total budget
of more than $97 million, compared to the Democrats' $39 million.
In the nonpresidential 1985–86 cycle, the disparity widened further, with the RNC raising $75.5 million to the Democrats' $15.1
million.

By the time Brock departed in 1980, the RNC had a headquarters
staff of over 350 (four times the Democrats' strength), a direct-mail
operation that provided most of the party's income, an extensive
polling operation, as well as tight links with state Republican parties and a well-developed program to build mini-RNCs in each
state. The RNC had already begun paying salaries of many Republican state party officials, and by 1985–86, it was funneling an estimated $17 million into state party building. Overall, Republican
Party resources for state and local party building have remained at
over four times those of Democratic resources.

One RNC program helps tutor state parties in fund raising, sharing the costs of development of state direct-mail programs and
paying staff salaries. In the 1983–84 cycle, the RNC hired and
placed finance directors in several key state parties. In effect, the
Republican Party has become a unified national machine. According to the RNC's national field director, Ed Brookover, "We've
been able to marry the national party, the state party, the county
party, and the campaign. We can have the three national committees (the RNC and the GOP House and Senate Campaign Committees) sit down at the same table, agree on a master plan for a state,

and allocate the cash." Brookover's field office alone has a staff of thirty-two, which nearly equals the entire professional staff of the DNC.

This infrastructure allows the Republican Party to perform a variety of political tasks more effectively than the rival Democrats, whether maintenance of voter lists, public-opinion polling, training campaign activists, or recruitment of candidates. The RNC often identifies pollsters, media advisors, and other professionals acceptable to state party officials and candidates, and then picks up the tab. Public-opinion polling ostensibly done for a state party can be shared with local candidates after a few weeks and be allocated as a contribution to their campaigns, at a steep discount of its true value. Republicans have even organized a special PAC, called GOPAC, to funnel money to state and local Republican parties.

A Local Elections Campaign Division has worked closely to train state party activists, recruit candidates, and target marginal districts. According to one account, between 1976 and 1980 some 10,000 Republicans attended training seminars sponsored by the RNC's local elections division. The party also began "institutional advertising," touting the GOP as an institution, which is permitted by the party-building provision of the 1979 campaign finance amendments, to complement explicit candidate advertising. In 1980, the RNC sponsored a $9.4-million "Vote Republican for a Change" television advertising campaign. In 1982, a series of RNC institutional ads backing Reagan around such themes as "Stay the course" and "Give the guy a chance" helped limit Republican losses in a severe recession year, with a budget of over $15 million. A counterpart Democratic ad campaign, with the effective tag line, "It isn't fair, it's Republican," spent just over $1 million.

At present, even the smallest Republican state party has a year-in, year-out professional staff of no fewer than four—an executive director, finance director, media director, field director—plus one or more support people, and many state GOP parties have staffs of several dozen. Twenty state parties have budgets in excess of a million dollars. In Pennsylvania, for example, the state Republican Party received a grant of $350,000 from the national party committee to hire telephone solicitors for the 1985–86 election cycle. They in turn produced 35,000 new donors for the Pennsylvania party.

The national party also helped the state GOP build a computerized list of Pennsylvania's 5.7 million registered voters, complete with demographic coding derived from census data and phone numbers. On the Democratic side, there is no comparable list, and only token assistance from the DNC. The state Democratic Party has a paid staff of four, compared to fourteen on the Republican side. The Pennsylvania Democratic Party began the 1985–86 cycle $159,000 in debt, and owed two years of back taxes on its headquarters building. In the 1986 election, the party managed only one get-out-the-vote mailing.

In the 1985–86 election cycle as a whole, the RNC and the affiliated House and Senate committees spent about $2.5 million to help thirty state parties develop computerized voter lists. The DNC, for the first time, launched a miniature version of the same idea, on a shoestring budget of $160,000 for the whole country. The Republicans could afford to use paid telephone solicitors. The Democrats relied on volunteers. In Missouri, where Democrats ultimately lost a very close race for an open Senate seat, the party paid a consultant to computerize the official raw list of registered voters. Telephone calls were supposed to add indispensable information about partisan inclination and demographics, but a shortage of volunteers, factional infighting, and a very tight telephone budget meant that a usable, coded list of only about 250,000 names was produced by election day. The Missouri Republicans had a complete coded list of 1.5 million Republican voters and used three sets of mailings as well as election eve phone calls. Nominally, the disparity in money resources is about three to one—a $450,000 budget for the Democrats versus $1.5 million for the Republicans. But officials of both parties concur that Republican state party resources in Missouri exceed Democratic resources by more like ten to one.

The well-financed nexus between the RNC and the state parties allows Republicans to try out a variety of sophisticated techniques, such as targeted enlistment of absentee voters. In California, for example, the law permits anyone who finds it inconvenient to vote on election day in his home precinct to request an absentee ballot. There, RNC and the state GOP devised an ingenious program to identify likely Republican voters. People in this group receive a direct-mail packet inviting the recipient to apply for an absentee ballot. Then, at the board of elections, a Republican Party worker takes note of all people who requested such ballots and sends them off the materials, along with precoded materials inviting them to vote Republican. This is followed up by at least one phone call to each Republican-leaning voter. Ordinarily, simplified registration and voting for shut-ins are considered the province of Democrats, who have advocated such devices in order to increase the voting turnout of low socioeconomic groups. But in this case the GOP, reversing that assumption via adroit targeting, turned a populist voting reform to Republican advantage. Thanks to this absentee-voter program, the California Republican ticket in 1986 enjoyed a several hundred thousand vote lead before the polls even opened. The RNC is sponsoring similar programs in the sixteen other states with simple absentee registration.

The development of strategic polling, targeting, and a well-financed national party apparatus also gave Republicans the capacity to spot shifts in public opinion, identify targets of opportunity, pour in resources, and pick off Democrats who thought they had fairly safe seats. This first bore fruit in the 1978 Senate elections, when Republicans blindsided two fairly popular Democratic incumbents, Senators Dick Clark in Iowa and Tom McIntyre in New Hampshire. Between 1978 and 1984, the heyday of the Republicans' technological lead, there were twenty-four U.S. Senate races where the winner squeaked in with 51 percent or less. Thanks to superior targeting techniques and the ability to pour in late money selectively, the Republicans won nineteen of these, or nearly 80 percent.

According to Brookover, the RNC field director, "We have much greater coordination on the Republican side because our operation is vertical. The Democrats' operation is horizontal." Democrats tend to concur. "The Democrats' great strength as a coalition party is also the Democrats' great weakness," says Pat Caddell. The Democratic state parties are still independent fiefdoms, as they were in Richard Daley's day, but with much less capacity to deliver votes. Unlike their Republican counterparts, DNC national strategists have little influence in the development of party strategy because they bring few resources to the table.

Democratic polling and Democratic voter-registration efforts, to mention two key jobs that parties perform, tend to mirror Democratic coalition politics. Everybody has his hand out, and there is never enough to go around. Whenever the Democrats sponsor a major poll, which is infrequently, there is immense pressure to give each of the major pollsters a little piece of the action. In off-years, according to Lynn Pounian, another Democratic public opinion analyst, "the supply of pollsters far exceeds the demand, and nobody can make a living." By the same token, the modest party-financed voter registration drive on the Democratic side in 1984 was badly hobbled by coalition politics. Instead of being driven by strategic considerations, the allocation of voter-registration money had to be guided by delicate coalition politics, further complicated by the fact that the party's most powerful—and most explosive—voter-registration magnet was the Rev. Jesse Jackson.

The Republicans have no such problems. They just put everybody in sight on the party payroll. The RNC's sense of the big picture and its financial ability to hire virtually the entire available pool of Republican-oriented professional campaign talent purchases a degree of harmony, loyalty, and party unity woefully lacking on the Democratic side. A careful tabulation of FEC filings in early 1987 by the *Washington Post*'s Thomas Edsall revealed that the RNC and its affiliated committees had most of the major Republican-oriented consultants on retainer.

The RNC and its affiliated House and Senate committees underwrite much of the cost of the major GOP pollsters doing work for candidates, state parties, and the White House, including Arthur Finkelstein, Lance Terrance, Linda DiVall, Richard Wirthlin, and Robert Teeter. The GOP Senate Campaign Committee pays for one statewide poll every year in every state with a Republican senator. This provides year-in, year-out income for Robert Teeter and a set of well-nurtured institutional relationships. "That's our biggest advantage," according to Eddie Mahe, former executive director of the RNC. "The full funding of the state races forces everybody under the tent." Democratic operatives, in contrast, tend to scrounge what business they can, in the heat of campaigns, and are far more competitive with each other.

Much has been made of the fact that PACs, pressure groups, and free-booting campaign mercenaries are institutional rivals to parties. But Republican-style interest groups and Republican campaign professionals seem to coexist more easily with the institutional Republican Party than their Democratic counterparts. This is partly because Republicans have more money with which to buy the allegiance of technicians. On the Democratic side, a Pat Caddell is a real threat to the institutional Democratic Party and makes no secret of his contempt for it. On the Republican side, pollsters Richard Wirthlin and Robert Teeter coexist in splendid symbiosis with the party machine. Labor's supposedly excessive influence in the Democratic Party is a subject of much debate and bitterly divisive infighting, but in the Republican camp, despite an occasional populist-sounding speech by a Richard Darman or a Jack Kemp, few Republicans find the financial alliance with Chambers of Commerce and three thousand allied PACs a serious institutional liability.

In effect, the RNC has created a national Republican Party by becoming a superb service organization. But by underwriting political services, the RNC became far more than just a dispensary of services. It has become a strategically unitary national party. "The functions of party have changed," says Richard Wirthlin, who got $2.6 million from the three national party committees, mostly to finance polling for the White House. "We no longer knock on doors. Television does that. But in the application of research and in the development of strategic techniques, the party has become a repository of political capital."

Or at least the Republican Party has.

V.

As traditional linkages between voter and party weaken, party image and symbolism become more important. Republicans at present have a significant advantage in strategic planning, in political "research and development," and in marketing—all three, not surprisingly, extensions of the natural idiom of corporate America. They didn't have to be invented by Republicans, but only borrowed from corporate marketing techniques. The circle of campaign professionals and pollsters supported year in and year out by the Republican National Committee functions as a kind of Bell Labs of American politics, refining techniques and providing intellectual discipline. This is not to say, however, that Democrats have only to emulate Republican "marketing" skills. On the contrary, the Democrats' advantages lie in delivering real benefits to ordinary voters and in mobilizing them. Historically, they were able to capture and retain durable voter allegiances. When those allegiances falter, Republican marketing superiority tends to prevail by default. The Democratic task, therefore, is not to find shortcuts to become more competitive in a "de-aligned" political environment, but to rebuild the voter allegiances.

The Republican Party's strategic use of public-opinion polling is worth special attention, because it suggests in fine detail just what advantages money and organization can buy, and where superior political technology bumps up against its natural limits—and occasionally undermines itself. The main pollster for Reagan's White House is Wirthlin's Data/Management/Information Company, which gets more than $100,000 a month from the RNC and more in election years. Wirthlin has known Reagan since the late 1960s, and did Reagan's polling in his 1976 and 1980 campaigns. Since 1980, Wirthlin has conducted polls for the White House at least monthly, and during some periods *daily*. He also polls for dozens of other GOP candidates.

By 1986, the result of all this polling was a cumulative file of nearly 100,000 separate interviews, all coded geographically and demographically. "It's a large enough file for us to target sub-sub-sub groups," according to Dee Allsop, a DMI executive. This allows the pollster to manipulate variables and examine very small clusters of voters—to find out, say, how Italian blue-collar workers of ages twenty-five to thirty-four will react to a change in the President's position on school prayer.

In contrast, Pat Caddell, Jimmy Carter's pollster, polled only four times a year during Carter's first year and less frequently after that. In 1978–79, he went a year and a half without conducting a poll for Carter. While the Reagan-Wirthlin alliance produced cumulative benefits for the White House and the Republican Party, becoming better institutionalized as time went on, the alliance between pollster, president, and party under Carter gradually became ever more frayed. Although Democratic pollster Peter Hart spent over a million dollars polling for the Mondale campaign in 1984, there was little spillover into the institutional party on the Democratic side. The party did have a director of polling, Dotty Lynch, between 1981 and 1983. She presided over exactly one national poll, in the winter of 1981–82, was laid off in 1984, and was not replaced. The DNC sponsored one additional national poll in late 1985.

Intriguingly, Wirthlin's polling company had its genesis in the ideological resurgence of organized business two decades ago. "To the extent that DMI had a godfather," Wirthlin reminiscences, "it was the American Medical Association. In 1966 and 1967, the AMA was the bridging element between the development of new techniques and their practical application in politics."

In 1966, the AMA had a problem. Liberal Democrats had a working majority in both houses of Congress for the first time since the New Deal, and national health insurance was at the center of its liberal agenda. Congress had just passed medicare and medicaid legislation over the AMA's strenuous objection. The AMA struck back, pouring millions into AMPAC, the first corporate mega-PAC. The AMA also decided to invest in long-term techniques of public persuasion. They hired Vincent Barabba, a political scientist of conservative leanings (who later became director of the Census Bureau in the Nixon administration); Barabba brought in Wirthlin, then a young economics professor. The AMA wasn't demanding overnight results, Wirthlin recalls. "They wanted us to develop advanced techniques in advertising, persuasion, and political strategy, for the long term." The AMA's ongoing support allowed Wirthlin to refine his techniques, and to underwrite what became DMI, which is today a $10-million company. Again, business-oriented interest groups, conservative campaign professionals, and the Republican Party apparatus proved mutually nurturing.

Wirthlin's brand of public-opinion technology brings three kinds of benefits to his most important client, Ronald Reagan, and to Reagan's partisan allies. It is very useful in elections, but also in long-term strategic planning and in damage control. In the 1984 presidential election, Reagan's public-opinion analysis was substantially more expensive and sophisticated than Mondale's. For example, the Republicans had a computer program, devised by Wirthlin, that allowed strategists access to an extensive data file of voting histories, sorted by demographic group and by Congressional district. With this program they could manipulate assumptions about turnout, shifts in voting preference, and response to issues by demographic subgroup and region, and could make decisions about which issues to emphasize, which rhetorical themes to sound, and how to schedule the candidate accordingly. Wirthlin's computer had not only his own polling results, but the results of all other polls, such as Gallup, Roper, Harris, as well as the three network polls. When the White House political staff wanted to know everything about what voters of different social groups thought about drugs, or teacher testing, or Contra aid, or whatever, Wirthlin's computer could respond on command. For example, women in the 1980s have tended to vote Democratic at a substantially higher rate than men. This became known as the "gender gap." While Democrats were pondering, at a fairly high level of generality, how to maximize this advantage, the Wirthlin operation had broken the gender gap down into eight subgroups, finding that the greater Democratic propensity of women was far more striking among certain subgroups, such as single working women between the ages of twenty-one and thirty-five.

Wirthlin's operation even took the trouble to input the hour-by-hour campaign schedule not only of Reagan, Bush, and all the administration "surrogates" campaigning for the Republican ticket, but Mondale, Ferraro, and their surrogates as well. Mondale's campaign had no such apparatus, nor did the Democrats even do state-by-state polling after early October, according to the campaign's chief pollster, Peter Hart. Scheduling decisions, rather than being informed by knowledge of where public opinion might be moving in the Democrats' favor, turned on such factors as which local leaders wanted the candidate in (or out), or the campaign managers' often flawed intuition.

"Frankly, we were sort of amazed that they would have Ferraro in Texas, where our tracking polls could see her dragging the Democratic ticket down, but not in Pennsylvania or New York where she might have helped," Wirthlin observed afterward. "We beat our brains out trying to figure out what kind of nefarious, convoluted campaign plan they had. We finally realized they didn't have a plan."

RNC-sponsored polling by Wirthlin's company became a capital asset that spilled over to help House and Senate candidates. A system called the Precinct Index Priority System, or PIPS, was designed under contract to the RNC, to allow strategists to analyze shifts in voting preference by demographic group down to the precinct level. Republican and Democratic pollsters agree that the GOP had about a four-year head start on the Democrats in this kind of technique and that the Democrats now have close to technical parity, but far less in the way of resources to apply what they know.

Wirthlin also uses public-opinion techniques to do long-term strategic planning for the White House and the Republican Party. One favorite graphic device is a chart showing on one axis the gap between the voters' perception of Republican and Democratic performance, issue by issue; on the other how important the issue is to voters at different times. Wirthlin has used this sort of analysis to demonstrate emerging opportunities for the President. It is possible to test which issues will produce benefits with particular target subgroups that the White House is seeking to woo, and to watch public opinion "move" in successive polls, as initiatives are launched. Candidates of both parties do "tracking" polls in elections. Only the Republicans have the funds to use them year in and year out for issue development.

Several key issues where White House strategists "repositioned" the President were the fruits of this sort of analysis. On the education issue, for examples, polls showed that the President was taking a beating for his administration's cuts in federal education aid. The White House succeeded brilliantly in redefining the issue as one of teacher competence. Teacher testing rather than public spending suddenly emerged as the issue. Wirthlin calls this an "offset issue." The ill-fated "teacher-in-space" flight of the shuttle *Challenger*, which claimed the life of schoolteacher Christa McAuliffe and six others, had its genesis in a White House public-relations effort to demonstrate that the President cared about public education. Public-opinion techniques were also central in the well-orchestrated make-over of Nancy Reagan, from an aloof figure whose main concerns were wardrobe and lavish entertainment, to a benign, caring wife and mother concerned about children and families.

Strategic planning informed by polling helped the Reagan administration identify itself with several "I care" issues, to offset the quite reasonable conclusion that its budgetary priorities indicated very little care. The administration launched belated initiatives to increase federal funding for drug-abuse education and for the enforcement of laws against drug traffickers. It sought to demonstrate symbolic concern for the quality of education, by offering special laurels and salaries for "master teachers." Over the objection of the right-wing purists in and around the administration, the White House endorsed a "catastrophic health insurance" plan, to pay some costs not covered by medicare. The White House also backed a program recommended by the Labor Department to give retraining and re-employment assistance to workers displaced by plant shutdowns and industrial transitions. These last two initiatives, late in the Reagan administration, were bitterly condemned by the right wing, all too accurately, as watered-down versions of Democratic programs. Ironically, public opinion polling had demonstrated to the Reagan White House what Democrats themselves were reluctant to appreciate—that progressive economic programs were basically popular.

A third advantage of such public opinion polling—within evident limits—is that it enables the White House to characterize an unfolding public issue in a way that the polls indicate will be favorably viewed by public opinion. In the jargon of the Reagan White House, this was known as "spin control." A striking example was the October 1986 summit meeting at Reykjavik, Iceland, between Reagan and Soviet leader Mikhail Gorbachev. The session, which was hastily convened, had no ostensible agenda other than to show the two leaders cordially meeting. But the world was electrified by reports that Reagan and Gorbachev were suddenly on the verge of an unexpected historic agreement for a radical reduction in nuclear weapons. However, the meeting ultimately broke down, apparently over Reagan's refusal to negotiate limits on his Strategic Defense Initiative, otherwise known as "Star Wars."

On Sunday, October 12, President Reagan and his top advisors came home from the summit, seemingly empty-handed. Expectations had been raised, but the President had walked out. The Monday morning newspaper stories, based on direct, on-the-scene reporting and background interviews with dejected officials, suggested that the summit was a major failure. Sunday night, however, Wirthlin was polling, and his polls showed that most people thought Reagan had shown admirable toughness in refusing to accede to Soviet conditions. Wirthlin's report was on the desks of the President's top political advisors at 7:30 Monday morning. By late Monday, reporters were puzzled that administration aides were suddenly proclaiming the summit a great success. The President had faced down Gorbachev, hadn't he? The President had been sufficiently tough-minded to refuse to trade Star Wars for Soviet concessions that were full of loopholes. That shift in the administration line was the Tuesday morning story. By late Tuesday, the network public opinion poll results were coming in, a crucial two days behind Wirthlin's. They showed what White House strategists knew Monday morning: most voters liked Reagan's resolve. By Wednesday, reporters, still a bit perplexed, were writing that Reykjavik must have been a win for the administration after all, and opposition Democrats stopped mentioning Reykjavik. The press allowed the White House to change the public issue from the substantive question of whether failing to get an arms agreement was good policy, to the cosmetic question of whether the walkout was initially popular with the voters. The polling had armed the White House with the political self-confidence to brush aside the substantive questions.

Of course, all of this technology has its natural limits. As in the case of most technological calamities, the weak link is usually the human one. On many issues, such as whether to send U.S. military aid to the Nicaraguan Contras, Wirthlin's polls made clear that the policy was not popular with public opinion, but the White House went ahead anyway, for ideological reasons. Even so, the availability of sophisticated polling results allowed the strategists to understand how to manipulate the issue, to minimize the damage it would cause to the President's personal popularity.

Reagan's personal commitment to such "social issues" as a ban on abortion and a constitutional amendment permitting prayer in public schools similarly overrode the advice of his pollsters. For major speeches, Wirthlin invites a cross section of ordinary citizens, numbering several dozen, to sit in a room with hand-held computers, watching the speech on a television monitor and pushing either a "feel good" button or a "feel bad" one. This produces a graph that looks a little like a cardiograph, which indicates seconds of elapsed time, and the positive or negative reaction to particular themes. When Reagan said, "We can take pride in twenty-five straight months of economic growth," the chart turned dramatically up. When he said, "No citizen need tremble, nor the world shudder, if a child stands in a classroom and breathes a prayer," and "The question of abortion grips our nation," the chart dipped into the red zone. The Republican pollsters, with their fingers on the pulse of public opinion, were naturally allied with the pragmatists who dominated the White House staff in the first Reagan term. But they couldn't save Reagan from his own instincts, nor from the politically naive and ideologically motivated conservatives who dominated the senior White House staff in the first two years of Reagan's second term.

Here again, political amateurs trying to use sophisticated political technology met the fate of a sorcerer's apprentice. With Reagan ever more oblivious to the nuances of his own administration's policy, and Donald Regan far less of a political creature than the first-term team of Baker, Michael Deaver, and Edward Rollins, the White House was living on borrowed time. Cut loose from practiced political hands, even astute public opinion polling can inadvertently *produce* spins. We now know that Colonel Oliver North was the brains behind several successful other high-risk military forays—the Grenada invasion, the bombing of Libya, the *Achille Lauro* rescue, among others. All of these adventures were politically popular because they succeeded. They suggested that America was, indeed, "back and standing tall." One of the things that gave North such currency around the White House was the pollsters' finding that his exploits improved the President's approval ratings. But apparently nobody thought to consider what might happen to the poll results if these adventures became public.

Another self-defeating aspect of this kind of technology is that it tends to reinforce a purely symbolic politics, which, rather like a jolt of sugar, can produce temporary gains but headaches afterward. The classic example of this variety of political empty calories was the White House response to rising public concern about drug abuse. "Drugs had been a concern at a level of about 2–4 percent," according to Tim Gohmann, Wirthlin's director of advanced applications. "All of sudden, we could see the issue taking off. By the time it peaked, at 21 percent, the White House was able to tailor a program that fit their own ideological objectives, but also fit the feelings of the coalition we were trying to assemble." In the summer of 1986, the White House launched a dramatic "war on drugs." The only problem was that fighting drugs costs money. In its antigovernment mode, the administration had been cutting funds for the war on drugs ever since 1981, and when the fiscal 1988 budget was unveiled in January 1987, funding for the war on drugs was cut once again. Editorialists pounced on the evident hypocrisy. In the end, the average voter was impressed less by the Reagan administration's professed concern about drugs than by its gross cynicism.

VI.

Ultimately, as any practicing politician is quick to tell you, the only poll that counts is the one on election day. But that conclusion says both too much and too little, for public opinion technology, used astutely, can indeed influence votes.

The events of 1986 seemed to prove that none of this fancy technology mattered all that much, after all. Partly this was because of some memorable high-tech gaffes. One device, a recorded telephone message "from President Reagan" to some 2 million targeted GOP voters ("Hi, this is Ronald Reagan, and I wanted to remind you to go out and vote on Tuesday") produced more bemusement than turnout. In one case, the dialing machine jammed and kept placing repeated calls to the wards of a Texas hospital. Human telephone banks apparently didn't do much better. Many of the women in the large telemarketing companies hired by the GOP were black. In much of the country, a telephone call to well-heeled GOP voters from a friendly black voice did almost more harm than good. Yet another seemingly sophisticated technique, a "ballot security" program intended to threaten prosecutions of improperly registered voters and reduce turnout in heavily Democratic, primarily black, precincts, backfired badly. Indignant black voters turned out in near record numbers, possibly costing the Republicans a Senate seat in Louisiana.

On Election Day, Democrats won most of the close Senate races. The Republicans' scientific campaign technology was the political counterpart of that scientifically designed dog food whose only flaw was that the dogs wouldn't eat it. And Wirthlin's spin control, clever and well-financed as it was, failed to protect Ronald Reagan from himself. But a closer look at the events of 1986, and other recent elections, suggests a more complex set of conclusions. Though the Democrats did win back the Senate, several of the races were far closer than they should have been. In the political scientist William Schneider's words, 1986 was a "normal" election, a predictable swing back from the abnormal election of 1980, where several weak Republicans picked off twelve Democratic incumbents. The Republican class of 1980, up for re-election in 1986, was an unusually undistinguished and vulnerable lot. Richard Nixon, in an unguarded moment, called them "the turkey farm." Yet very strong Democratic Senate candidates, both with previous statewide landslide victories, only barely won in the Dakotas despite depression and political disaffection among farmers; a strong Democrat lost in Missouri, where an imbalance in campaign technology clearly affected the outcome; in Iowa, Indiana, and Kansas, Democrats failed to field strong candidates. In Pennsylvania, the Democratic Senate candidate, Bob Edgar, miscalculated his financial resources and had to cancel TV advertising in the crucial final weeks. A shift in some 50,000 votes nationwide would have denied Democrats Senate control and produced a radically different post-election psychology. In the House, where Democrats gained only five seats, Republican and Democratic analysts agree that superior GOP organization, financing, and campaign technology saved ten to fifteen seats. And Republicans gained eight governors. Other things being equal, this superior Republican ability to target opportunities and to cut losses will continue until the Democrats get themselves better organized as a party.

VII.

On balance, then, the GOP's formidable party building and its technological superiority remain very useful tools in the hands of political professionals. They can make the difference in close elections, they can help parties to develop long-term plans; if the White House isn't out of control, they can help limit damage. It is very hard to imagine a Howard Baker, a Robert Dole, or even a George Bush, indulging in some of the gross blunders that led to Contragate. To this extent, the Republican Teflon will outlive Reagan. As the 1988 election approaches, however, there are two big pieces of good news for Democrats. Human foible is still capable of neutralizing even wide advantages of money, party, and technical superiority. And Democrats have begun to play serious catch-up, though with fewer resources.

On the party-building front, Democrats have in place a variety of skeletal programs. Plans to develop state voter files, for example, are progressing in twenty-six states. For the first time, lists of contributors assembled by individual candidates are not being treated as proprietary information. For example, North Carolina Governor Jim Hunt's carefully developed 30,000-name list of party activists and donors was donated to the state party after his narrow election loss to Senator Jesse Helms in 1984. The DNC, working with Frank O'Brien, is continuing to create incentives to encourage list sharing. Increasingly, candidates are sharing voter and contributor lists with state parties, and state parties are sharing them with the national party.

In the 1985–86 election cycle, the Democratic National Committee, for the first time, recruited and paid the salaries of state party officials in eighteen states. In a number of key states, the gross disparity between Democratic and Republican resources is narrowing. The national party is also working to overcome one of the great structural weaknesses of its 1984 performance—the fact that virtually no resources went into planning for the November general election until after the convention.

As the presidential election approached, the smartest operatives on the Democratic side scurried onto the staffs of candidates, while the less high-powered ones stayed on the slow track, the party organization, which was considered to be less prestigious; the party nominee usually replaced the senior party staff anyway. In 1984, the entire party establishment backed Mondale before the convention, except for the chairman, Chuck Manatt, who as an aspiring party builder announced that he would be neutral in the nomination contest. Mondale forces took this as a sign of disloyalty, and as soon as Mondale clinched the nomination, he tried to fire Manatt. This was a major blunder. The convention was held in San Francisco, in Manatt's home state, and he was popular with the delegates, who had to approve his removal. Mondale's candidate for successor, Burt Lance, was monumentally unpopular. Faced with a delegate rebellion, Mondale had to reverse course and reinstate Manatt. But because of the party organization's low repute and its chronic impoverishment, even Manatt's resolve did not allow the DNC to proceed simultaneously along two tracks. Until the convention, the jousting for the nomination had consumed all available energy, and the only pure party activity was the logistical planning for the convention itself. Despite Manatt's efforts, no serious general election planning began until after the convention.

If the present party chairman, Paul Kirk, can make good on his promise to plan for the general election campaign well in advance of the convention, he will have accomplished a great deal. The Kirk administration, which took office after the 1984 defeat, has endeavored to tread a narrow path between the Democratic Leadership Council on the right and the "interest groups" on the party left. Kirk was the candidate of the premier Democratic interest group, organized labor. But in office he has bent over backwards to accommodate the party's conservative critics, using his influence to do away with the official party caucuses (which spotlight divisiveness). He also canceled the enervating and divisive midterm party convention. This was devised by the McCarthy-McGovern reformers to encourage mass participation, but the off-year conventions of 1974 and 1978 were public-relations calamities because they created a forum for raucous factional infighting. To dampen the Democrats' fractiousness, Kirk publicly urged the AFL-CIO to refrain from making a prenomination endorsement, and called for monthly meetings of presidential candidates to discourage them from attacking each other. He also sought to ingratiate himself with party conservatives by excluding Jesse Jackson from official party functions, a move which could well prove counterproductive, given Jackson's immense appeal to black voters, whose loyalty the party needs. Kirk, like his predecessors, remains hobbled by the fact that the Democrats, as a coalition party, depend on their several factions more than the factions depend on the institutional party. Trade unionists, pacifists, feminists, environmentalists, and civil rights advocates all accord their own goals priority over party unity.

The party rules, meanwhile, have swung back from the extreme openness of the period of McCarthy-McGovern dominance, to a middle ground that tempers broad participation with more party regularity. The McGovern reforms opened all primaries and official caucuses to any registered Democrat who cared to participate and allocated most delegate seats according to popular election, either through primaries or open party caucuses. Under the "counter-reforms" recommended by the party's Hunt Commission and adopted in 1982, delegate selection rules now require that a candidate in a primary election must win at least 15 percent of the popular vote in order to be awarded delegates, and this helps discourage splinter candidacies. The earlier rules were also seen as destructive of party unity, because a local Democratic mayor or party official who ran for delegates pledged to a losing candidate got excluded from the party convention. (Before the 1970s, a great many states chose delegates by convention, or sent unpledged or "favorite son" delegations, thus assuring the attendance of key party leaders.) To solve this problem, the current party rules provide that 641 delegate seats are reserved for the party's elected leaders.

Some political scientists, such as Austin Ranney of the American Enterprise Institute and Nelson Polsby of the University of California at Berkeley, have argued that most of the Democratic Party's current troubles can be understood as the result of the McGovern-era reforms. In Polsby's view, opening the party to activists severed the necessary link with local machines, and gave the party to radicals who nominated candidates that would rather be right than be president. However, this view overlooks the fact that the old party could be very cavalier in excluding entire ethnic groups and political viewpoints. The party reforms of the 1970s were a response to the legitimate demands of self-identified Democrats to be permitted to participate in party affairs. Although party regulars, under an unreformed system, would not have nominated George McGovern in 1972, they surely would have nominated Walter Mondale in 1984, and Mondale did just as poorly as McGovern. It is hard to make a convincing case that a less democratic set of party-nominating procedures would necessarily lead to stronger candidates. It is also the case that the reforms allowed a whole new group of activists to bring their activism within the two-party system, where it belonged, rather than on the streets. Before romanticizing the old system, it is worth recalling that the heyday of machine politics, in the late nineteenth century, produced a remarkably undistinguished group of Democratic nominees—and a string of Republican presidents.

To some extent, the same people who are unhappy with the substantive views of the "New Politics" activists who swept into Democratic Party affairs on the antiwar tide also couch their criticism in procedural terms. An unreformed set of party rules would make it harder for citizen activists and leftists to win primary elections, hence delegate seats, and they would not get to write the party platform or the party rules, and they would presumably not scare off socially conservative working-class voters. But the procedural critique and the substantative criticisms are best kept separate. The whole history of the Democratic Party in the United States is a history of allowing formerly excluded groups to participate, and this has been a source of party strength. Since 1972, onetime antiwar activists have gotten much more serious about learning how to practice a majority politics, just as Republican activists of the Barry Goldwater generation learned to fashion their ideology in a manner that had mass appeal. Liberals today want to win elections.

There is of course a delicate line between leaving the party in the hands of insiders who exclude whole classes of voters (which was the case before 1972) and making the party so open that candidate-dominated primaries sweep in whole new groups of activists with no commitment to the party as an institution. On that score, the current party rules have more or less settled down to a happy medium.

As for campaign technology, the Democrats have an excellent group of professionals, but here the problems are resources and continuity. The national party's first (and only) national public opinion poll, taken during the first Reagan term in late 1981, provided hard evidence that Reagan's victory had not been an ideological repudiation of the Democratic Party. It identified the party's commitment to social justice, to "fairness," as a winning theme for Democrats.

The party's 1985–86 poll was far more sophisticated. Rather than hiring one of the party's well-known candidate pollsters, such as Peter Hart, William Hamilton, or Patrick Caddell, the DNC turned to a firm called Targeting Systems, Inc. (TSI), which uses a system called Claritas that sorts census data according to one of 105 demographic types or clusters. Claritas is used mainly in the marketing of commercial products and services. But it can also be used to test political issues and appeals according to narrowly targeted demographic variables. TSI's poll for the Democratic National Committee tested issue appeal, ideological attitudes, partisanship, party image, and fund-raising potential among each of several dozen demographic clusters. Its main finding was that economic activism remained the Democrats' strongest suit. The poll also served as a rare tool of long-term planning. Lynn Pounian, who directed the poll, urged that the Democratic Party go on to create voter lists coded according to race, sex, income, and other demographic variables, small fund-raising campaigns, and focus groups for issue development, state by state.

Though this technology exists, the DNC has not done any follow-up polling. The Democratic Congressional Campaign Committee did sponsor one major poll in the 1985–86 election cycle, and it was useful in confirming that voters were enjoying prosperity on the East and West Coasts, but felt serious economic disaffection in the Midwest. The so-called "bicoastal" economy became a key Democratic electoral theme. But the dynamics of polling again illustrates how coalition politics can be a problem for Democrats. There is very sophisticated public-opinion research going on, within the larger Democratic family, but it is underwritten in a catch-as-catch-can way. Ralph Whitehead, who teaches at the University of Massachusetts and advises Democratic candidates, has conducted an extended series of open-ended interviews, known in the political trade as "focus groups," to examine the political motivations of nonrich younger voters, whom Whitehead dubs "New Collar" voters because they are typically not in traditional blue-collar occupations but often not really white-collar either. Whitehead observes that this is not the sort of voter research most Democratic candidates are interested in buying. His own work was underwritten by Richard Dennis, a well-to-do Chicago donor to a variety of liberal causes. Whitehead says, "In the normal course of Democratic electoral politics, there is a market for TV spots and a market for polls, but no market for long-term strategic planning."

Another widely respected Democratic public opinion analyst, Stanley Greenberg, has conducted a series of focus-group studies on disaffected Democratic voters. Greenberg's work was underwritten by a variety of groups, including the United Autoworkers Union, the Pennsylvania Public Interest Coalition, the Michigan State Democratic Party, and the National Education Association; some of it was subsidized by his own company, the Analysis Group.

The fact that the party, as such, sponsors little strategic research on the electorate means that the party rarely makes effective use of the product. Many Democrats still think of polling as something to use in public relations, rather than in strategic planning. This makes sense in the heat of a campaign, when a poll can be useful in convincing reporters or donors that your candidate is gaining support. But often public-opinion findings are more useful for what they tell planners, and it is here that Republicans make more effective use of these techniques than Democrats. Often, Democrats get nervous lest polls reveal unpalatable findings. When one recent party poll revealed that a majority of voters thought labor unions had too much power, angry trade unionists demanded that the question be stricken from the poll. Leaders of women's groups looking at results of the same poll challenged the findings, on the ground that respondents did not seem sufficiently feminist.

Often, too, research results are used to produce support for a particular preconception rather than to inform strategy. One series of focus groups in 1985 produced a carefully qualified conclusion that Democrats should be careful about using the word "fairness" as a central party commitment, because to some voters, in some contexts, the word connoted welfare spending and special treatment for minorities. This led the then DNC executive director, Brian Lunde, who wanted the Democrats to move rightward in general, to counsel that the party should drop fairness as a theme entirely.

A further temptation for Democrats is to look at public-opinion analysis as a substitute for having core values. When the Democrats woke up last November 6 to find they had won an election, the feeling still lingered that Democratic beliefs were still somehow out of favor with the electorate. "Now," pronounced Democratic pollster Peter Hart, "the question is whether the party can find some good new tunes to sing." But the function of polling, surely, is to better understand the audience, not to divine the repertoire.

The Democrats in 1985 launched a program called Project 500, with a budget of $5 million, intended to target precincts in state legislative races and to prevent Republican state legislatures from dictating redistricting plans after the 1990 census. (After 1990, fifteen states are expected to have major redistrictings, because of significant population gains or losses.) Project 500 takes its name from the premise that Democrats must retain or pick up a total of 500 state legislative seats between now and the 1990 election in order to keep Republicans from making major gains in the House of Representatives through the redrawing of Congressional district boundaries. Since state legislatures draw district boundaries (within broad judicial guidelines), a state whose governor and legislature are controlled by the same party can strongly influence the balance of a state's congressional delegation.

In 1982, the Republican National Committee launched its own "1991 plan," aimed at electing enough Republicans to state legislative seats to elect a Republican House of Representatives in 1992. In the 1982 and 1984 elections, Republicans gained a total of 370 legislative seats. But in the 1986 elections, the Democrats made substantial gains, winning control of the Connecticut House and

Senate, the Minnesota House, the Nevada House, the North Dakota House, and tying the Republicans in Vermont. Democrats lost control of only one state chamber, the Montana House, where Republicans held a one-seat margin.

In all, Democrats gained 186 state legislative seats nationwide, the biggest gain since 1974. Democrats currently control sixty-eight state legislative chambers, compared to the Republicans' twenty-eight. Project 500, according to its director, Will Robinson, hopes to emulate and neutralize Republican efforts, by targeting close legislative districts and offering training seminars for candidates and campaign managers, aid in the form of polling and precinct targeting, get-out-the-vote drives, and media assistance.

On the Republican side, the RNC picks up the tab. Robinson has to go out and raise his $5 million budget. Recently, Robinson left Project 500 to work in the presidential campaign. On the Democratic side, the fast track is seldom the Party.

Another very significant form of campaign technology, where Democrats are competitive in technique but not in dollars, is electoral targeting. In any campaign, the most important piece of electoral intelligence is knowing where in the district to concentrate scarce time and resources. Once, this art of electoral targeting was the personal work of precinct captains. Lately, as urban machines have declined, it has depended on technology. Since 1980, the state-of-the-art targeting operation on the Democratic side has been a venerable group called the National Committee for an Effective Congress (NCEC).

NCEC began life as the first of the liberal PACs, having been founded by one of the leaders of the New York anti-Tammany reform movement of the 1950s, Russell Hemenway. For its first two decades, NCEC existed mainly to raise funds for liberal candidates. In the late 1970s, however, NCEC began to experiment with campaign technology. By 1982, NCEC was able to offer a package of services to liberal candidates for House seats, to help them formulate election strategies.

NCEC builds a computer voting history of each congressional district, sorted by precinct. The precincts are then ranked according to turnout (what fraction of voters actually voted) and performance (what fraction voted Democratic) in recent years. This analysis allows the campaign to focus on particular precincts—either for get-out-the-vote drives in the case of "core" Democratic areas, or for persuasion in the case of "swing" precincts, which have high numbers of independent voters—and thus helps to formulate a master plan that maximizes scarce resources. A second layer of targeting, which NCEC has begun to develop, overlays a demographic map on the precinct map, so that voters can be targeted block by block, or household by household, with appropriate thematic appeals. NCEC gives this service to progressive candidates as an in-kind contribution, and shares information with others in the Democratic Party coalition, including labor unions, and freestanding organizing drives like Project 500.

This incipient technical parity is a big step forward, but in contrast with the Republicans, two weaknesses are evident. First, NCEC's total resources of some $2.5 million a year are a fraction of what the GOP spends on precinct targeting. Second, NCEC is part of the progressive coalition but not of the institutional Democratic Party. Coalition politics, again, have both strengths and weaknesses: many heads are better than one, but many cooks can spoil the broth; NCEC produces first-rate targeting technology but also occasional infighting and rivalry over turf. A few candidates have told NCEC to keep its targeting, and send them cash.

In the same fashion, it remains a weakness that the labor movement in many parts of the country still functions as the *de facto* Democratic Party. Labor provides the big phone banks, the voter education, and the get-out-the-vote activity directed at its own membership. But broadly based as it is, it is only a minority in the old New Deal coalition. In some states, the AFL-CIO resists party-building that might dilute its own dominance of the state Democratic apparatus. Even at its best, labor's interests are narrower than those of the party as a whole. Even where labor still dominates the Democratic Party, the unions do not extend their voter-education and get-out-the-vote drives beyond union members and their immediate families, except where individual unionists help run party phone banks as volunteers. Compared to the Republicans, the Democrats are still more of a pick-up team than a national party.

As the Democratic Party rebuilds, sooner or later all of this work—the polling, targeting, focus-group work, technical assistance, get-out-the-vote drives, voter registration, and so on—will have to be brought in-house. Otherwise, the Democratic Party will remain an *ad hoc* coalition, with little year-in, year-out durability, and groups in the broader progressive family will continue squabbling for power, and reinventing wheels. Kirk's regime at the DNC has succeeded in eliminating some of the chronic fractiousness, but has not yet developed sufficient resources to insist on cooperation.

Campaign technology also needs to be kept in its place. Public-opinion sampling is surely helpful in targeting where sympathetic voters may be found, in developing issues, and in developing candidates' positions and rhetoric accordingly. But candidates and parties should not confuse political leadership with a search for current public-opinion preferences. The sudden hollowness of the Reagan presidency and its absence of an agenda reflected its heavy reliance on public-opinion technology. What is intriguing, when one compares the Republican process of issue development with its Democratic counterpart, is that few of the Reagan initiatives were driven by constituency demands. If the Republicans learn what the public wants via sophisticated polling techniques, Democrats learn because the phone starts ringing off the hook. This, again, is the Democrats' great strength and great weakness, but surely it is the more authentic and durable form of democracy.

The great hallmark—and ultimately the great weakness—of the Reagan era was its obsession with purely symbolic politics. In the 1980s, politics has been eerily disconnected. It is rarely something that affects people's material daily life, but rather has been a quest for themes that resonate emotionally. In this climate of disconnection and voter cynicism, a politics of symbolism dominated, and the Republican Party's institutional Teflon complemented Reagan's natural gifts.

I doubt that Democrats can ever beat Republicans at purely symbolic politics, nor should they try. Real problems have accumulated in America during the Republican period of supposedly benign neglect, and they demand public remediation. Politically, Democrats need to address these deferred problems, if they expect voters to support them in return. The Democrats do need to become competitive at polling, fund raising, party building, and the other paraphernalia of professional politicking. But the more difficult and more urgent task, both for the Democratic Party and the democratic polity, is to reconnect politics to people's lives. It was that connectedness which made Democrats the normal majority party between 1932 and 1968. How to restore it is the subject of the remainder of this book.

CHAPTER FOUR

VOTERS

I.

The political poignancy of the 1980s has been a sense on the part of most Americans that neither party offers them very much. Low voting turnouts, ticket splitting, polling and focus-group results, and interviews with voters all confirm this. For any voter under the age of forty, political memory winds back from Reagan to Carter to Ford and Nixon and the Watergate years, then to Johnson and Vietnam. Of all of these disappointing leaders, Reagan for a time seemed about to capture the allegiance of this emerging "baby-boom" cohort of voters, those born between 1946 and 1964, which has held such fascination for political analysts. As a genial, upbeat, "above-party" sort of figure, Reagan thrived personally as long as his program seemed to work. Ironically, however, even at the peak of his popularity, Reagan's strength as a nonpartisan kind of leader meant that little of his own popularity rubbed off on the Republican Party. By early 1987, when Reagan faltered personally, it was clear that the baby-boom generation was still distant from partisan politics, worried about its prospects, and very much up for grabs.

The great Republican disappointment of the Reagan era was the failure of the much-heralded partisan realignment to occur. At Reagan's zenith, in early 1984, partisan affiliation was briefly equal. By early 1987, Democrats had again opened up a gap of six to eleven points, depending on which poll you believed. The 1984 election, when Reagan carried forty-nine states, was less remarkable for its landslide than for its very low turnout and for the record percentage of ticket splitters. The two biggest partisan winners were Walter Dean Burnham's "party of nonvoters," and the party of disaffected, disaffiliated voters. The youngest voters, who seemed the most eager recruits to Reagan in 1984, fell away in the greatest numbers in 1986. No durable link was established between Reagan Republicanism and the electorate.

If there was no partisan realignment during the Reagan years, even less was there an ideological realignment. To a great extent, Reagan was popular *in spite of* his stands on many issues, not because of them. What fueled his popularity was his conviction, not his convictions. That is why Democrats miss the point utterly if they imagine they can recoup by imitating his policies. The only thing worth emulating is his resolve.

Ralph Whitehead, who has done extensive interviewing of "New Collar" voters, defined as nonrich voters of the baby-boom generation, says, "Voters tend to see the Republican Party as a force with a hard heart and a tough mind. They see the Democratic Party as a force with a soft heart and a tender mind. What voters would like, ideally, is a party with a soft heart and a tough mind. Unable to find one, they settled uneasily for the party with the tough heart and tough mind, in large part because they saw Reagan as an individual who could soften some of the hardness in that heart."

There is a great deal of evidence, in these final fading days of the Reagan administration, of accumulated populist frustrations. Reagan used a populist imagery without in fact enacting populist policies. The millions of "New Collar" voters who split their tickets to vote for Reagan *and* for progressive Democratic senatorial, congressional, and local candidates, have many economic grievances. They do not believe in the conservative doctrine that the free market will solve all ills. The 1986 election suggested that wage-earners of Middle America are prepared to vote for Democrats who are respectful of their cultural habits and willing to fight for their economic aspirations.

Among voters, the partisan loyalties of the New Deal coalition at the level of the mass electorate are not extinct, though they are faint. Most working-class voters are still not enthusiastic about voting Republican. They liked Reagan's patriotism, his optimism, his faith in them, and they forgave his more bizarre positions on social and foreign-policy issues. Only a minority shared his extreme conservatism or his ultra-*laissez-faire* economic ideology. (The Republicans had two opportunities to rally such voters to the Republican Party, under Nixon in 1972 and under Reagan in 1984, and they botched both.) The problem is that since 1968, the Democratic Party at the national level has given white middle-American wage-earning voters few affirmative reasons to vote *for* a Democratic president.

But in 1988 the field is wide open. The most hopeful development is that the Democratic Party has begun to recover its historic voice. Party documents, like the excellent 1986 Democratic Policy Commission report, "New Choices in a Changing America," point with pride to the accomplishments of Democratic state governors, even if they do not yet point out too loudly that the vehicle of these Democratic governors was . . . democratic *government.* Democratic politicians have stopped lacing their speeches with disclaimers that they don't like government, either. They have begun to return to the nation's unfinished business—like national health insurance, lifetime education, programs for the working family, affordable housing, and a more assertive trade policy. Much to their surprise (and that of the Republican right as well), it was the Reagan administration that began to say, "Me too."

The Democratic task is to alter the current climate of low voter participation and high voter cynicism. For, as I have suggested, such a climate is invariably both anti-democratic and anti-Democratic. When voters are disaffiliated, low- and moderate-income ones are the first to withdraw. Politicians get in the habit of playing to the interested and active voices, and they tend to be economically better off. "Liberal" and "conservative" come to be defined in cultural terms, or according to foreign-policy issues, neither of which is of much use in drawing nonparticipating Democratic voters back into politics. To the extent that liberal positions on social issues have any effect, they push white working-class voters to the Republican column. The challenge is to move economic issues to the forefront, and to restore the broad political participation of wage-earners. In all of this, the Democrats have a real opportunity, if only they will seize it. Most of the positions on public issues that seem to appeal to voters today are, basically, progressive ones, involving economic opportunity and security for working people.

II.

The Democratic prospect appears especially dismal at the level of presidential politics, where the "normal" arithmetic of the electoral college lately has become ever more heavily Republican. Although Democrats still outpoll Republicans slightly in congressional, gubernatorial, and state legislative elections, where turnout is lower, the presidential voters who emerge every four years seem increasingly Republican. In the five presidential elections that began with 1968, 23 states, with a total of 202 electoral votes, have been carried by the Republican *every time.* Thirty-six states, with 354 electoral votes (a clear majority of the electoral college), have gone Republican at least four out of the last five elections. In only ten states and the District of Columbia have the Democrats, with just 77 electoral votes, averaged a majority of the vote. Even most states that have voted for the Democratic candidate at least once have become less reliably Democratic. "Must" states for Democrats, like Texas, California, Michigan, New Jersey, though they have elected Democratic governors have become steadily more Republican in presidential politics. The South has remained more faithfully Democratic, but this is misleading because it reflects racial division. Blacks have voted in greater numbers, as faithful Democrats, while more southern whites have deserted Democrats for the Republicans. The more that national Democrats emphasize black issues, absent a common ideology of economic populism, the more they seem to alienate southern whites.

Conventional analysis has argued that this gradual erosion has occurred because the party is too left-wing. Because Democratic primaries are dominated by "activists" and party "interest groups," the argument goes, they tend to produce presidential nominees who are too liberal for the country—though this hardly describes Jimmy Carter or Walter Mondale. Because of the electoral college, campaign professionals analyze presidential politics in America geographically. They come, therefore, to believe that the electoral logic of presidential politics demands that the Democratic Party either explicitly move to the right or abandon tangible issues altogether in favor of amorphous "generational" or "thematic" or managerial politics; they think that the Democratic standard-bearer needs to do better in the white South, among males, among the young, in the suburbs, and in the West. This analysis is superficially accurate—the party does need to do better among all these groups; but it largely ignores the possibility of rallying real enthusiasm among nonvoters, or among grudging voters, by addressing their real needs. Instead, it concludes logically that since the white South is more nationalistic and fiscally conservative, that since male voters like *macho* leaders, that since the West resents domination from Washington, that since the suburbs are perhaps open-minded about gay rights and abortion but not about expensive social programs, and since the young crave optimism, the ideal Democratic standard-bearer must be a vaguely inspirational figure, younger and more charismatic than Mondale, tougher on defense than Carter, a trustworthy manager, and more conservative on fiscal, economic, and social questions than any Democrat in recent memory. The ideal Democratic candidate, seemingly, would be Jack Kemp.

This view of presidential politics ignores the fact that successful Democratic presidential candidates from Andrew Jackson to John Kennedy and Lyndon Johnson have increased both the participation and the enthusiasm of voters (and nonvoters) who previously saw little in the political system that spoke to their needs. It assumes a static electorate, which is more affluent, more conservative, and less partisan than a mobilized Democratic electorate must be or need be. In the absence of a party program that addresses the genuine economic needs of most Americans, the participating electorate is amenable to vague appeals to optimism, geniality, patriotism, and individualism, at which Republicans generally do better than Democrats. *But voters choose on this basis only when nothing better is available.* As a matter of ideological conviction, even the participating electorate is rather less conservative than is often supposed.

During the first three years of the Reagan administration, it was so taken for granted that public opinion had swung massively to the right that commentators and politicians alike were almost unwilling to believe what the polls showed. But people had voted for Reagan, it turned out, not primarily because they liked his positions on issues, but because they liked him personally and had lost confidence in Carter. In 1984, when Mondale lost to Reagan by an even bigger margin than Carter had, the election was even less a liberal-conservative referendum. Between November 1976 and November 1984, the percentage of voters identifying themselves as "conservative" increased only three points. In one of the most comprehensive analyses of the 1980 and 1984 elections to date, Warren Miller, using data from the University of Michigan National Election Surveys, calculated that the 1984 election was mainly an affirmative vote for the country's positive condition, and that Reagan's ideology substantially *detracted* from his electoral appeal. Satisfaction with the national status quo ("performance") added 25 percent to the vote for Reagan; ideological and partisan variables reduced it by 16 percent. This was precisely the opposite of the 1980 election, when voters disliked the centrist status quo and were prepared to try more conservative policies.

Since the 1984 election, public opinion has become steadily more liberal, though the Republican Party has retained an advantage as the party that voters consider better able to control inflation and government spending. The share of the electorate agreeing with the proposition that Reagan was "going too far in attempting to cut back or eliminate government social programs" steadily rose. By 1985, polls showed that people thought government was spending too little rather than too much on fighting crime by margins of

62–3, on fighting drugs (62–4), on health (58–5), education (56–5), the environment (54–6), energy (40–6), public transportation (33–6), and solving urban problems (39–9). They thought the government was spending too much on the military (37–14), space exploration (37–14), and welfare (37–14.) Sixty-nine percent thought middle-income families were paying too much in taxes and 80 percent thought upper-income families and corporations were paying too little. Large majorities wanted to see the government more closely regulate the storage of toxic chemicals, workers' health and safety, nuclear energy, and the ingredients used in foods. The percentage of people who agreed that the federal government in Washington was too powerful dropped from 48 in 1980 to just 32 in 1984, the lowest since 1964.

Most of the 53 percent of people who thought they would fare better financially under a Reagan government disagreed with Reagan's views on most issues. Among them, 63 percent disapproved of his handling of the economy; 66 percent disliked his foreign policy; 79 percent said they agreed with the Democrats on most issues; 81 percent thought Reagan sided with special interests, while 86 percent thought Mondale favored the average citizen. Only a tiny minority of 11 percent said they were voting for Reagan because he was a "real Republican," whereas 79 percent of the Democrats who voted for Reagan said they'd have been more likely to support Mondale if he had been "more of a strong Democrat."

Despite this evidence to the contrary, there was a strong sense during most of Reagan's presidency that Republicans and conservatism were on the march while Democrats, casting about for new ideas, hesitated to put forward their historic philosophy. Shouting "Tax and spend!" at a Democrat was like waving kryptonite at Superman.

By the 1986 election, both on the grounds of ideology and performance, Republicans were losing. While the White House put Reagan on the road to bless GOP senate candidates, the candidates struggled to distance themselves from their President. One GOP senate campaign commercial after another boasted that the senator had opposed the White House on social security cuts, on education funding, on jobs programs, on clean water. By January 1987, public satisfaction with Reagan's performance, as well as his ideology, had fallen sharply: 39 percent of poll respondents thought the next president should continue Reagan's policies, while 54 percent wanted a change of direction.

The weak and temporary gains of Republican Party identification among voters also began to fade during the second Reagan term. In March 1986, the Gallup Poll showed that people considered the Republicans the "party of prosperity" by a margin of 51–33; by late October this had narrowed to 41–30, while the number of respondents expressing little confidence in either party rose 13 points. In much of 1985 and early 1986, the Republicans had narrowly outscored the Democrats as the party "more likely to keep the United States out of World War III," but between March and October 1986, there was a swing of 12 points and Democrats outscored Republicans 34–29; at the same time, the fraction of voters who had confidence in neither party also rose 12 points. Often, a shift in public opinion from the dominant party to the "no difference/no opinion" category portends a shift to the opposition party.

These tendencies intensified after the 1986 elections. By February 1987, the percentage of people wanting the government to spend more on day care, for example, increased from 44 to 57; on college loans, from 34 to 46; on medicaid, from 49 to 61; on social security, from 51 to 63; and on medicare, from 33 to 74.

Of course, while these findings are congenial to traditional Democratic positions, they are of widely varying salience to voters. The voters' relatively liberal positions represent a vague state of mind, not an active state of political mobilization. Simply embracing a litany of activist proposals is no recipe for electoral success, because too much about the economy and the society has changed. Moreover, even if the voters are surprisingly supportive of public programs, they have been skeptical whether Jimmy Carter's party could be trusted to operate them. Yet these surprising voter attitudes offer a latent opportunity to reconnect with the Democratic rank and file, by meeting practical economic needs with traditional Democratic philosophy.

Many Democrats have been reluctant to seize this opportunity, however, partly because they have remained badly traumatized by the twin Carter and Mondale defeats, which convinced them that the party's primary task was to convince voters that Democrats had forsaken their evil tax-and-spend ways, their dependence on special interests, their unpatriotic pacifism, and their identification with the social lunatic fringe. Most Democrats were reluctant not only to champion "the failed programs of the past"; they were hesitant to advocate a strong public role for much of anything. Partly, too, these conclusions were reinforced by the people that the political elite sees day in and day out, people who do not share the pocketbook populism of the voters. In Washington, where Democrats like Senate Finance Committee Chair Lloyd Bentsen and Majority Leader Robert Byrd solicited $10,000 contributions from business lobbyists as the ticket of admission to private breakfast meetings, the average lobbyist that a Democratic senator sees is indeed an advocate for special interests—but not the special interests of wage-earners. Expanded public spending and tighter economic regulation are not on the minds of most legislative visitors.

III.

Despite the move of public opinion in the Democratic direction, it is well to remember that "issues," as conventionally understood, are misleading guides to the electorate's state of mind. Much of what is on the mind of ordinary voters today seems disconnected from politics altogether. As I have suggested, that means bad news for Democrats because Democrats stand for the proposition that the public weal has a coequal place in society with the private one. In a disconnected polity, conservatives reign.

The weakening of partisan allegiances generally and the particular dissolution of the bond between the Democratic Party and its wage-earning constituency seem to mirror centrifugal forces in our society, politics, and culture. The workaday world of ordinary people has changed in a way that our political system has failed to come to terms with. The normal world of wage-earning voters a generation ago—in which Father worked, Mother raised kids, people had stable jobs in mass-production factories or in well-structured corporate firms—has fragmented. Communities, career patterns,

tastes, lifestyles have all fragmented. Ralph Whitehead, bard of the
New Collar voter, says of his own family, "When I was a kid we all
had dinner at the same time, and we ate the same meal. In my house
today, we each eat something different and rarely at the same time.
Our parents embodied a particular era in American society. They
shared a common set of experiences—the Depression, the War,
and the postwar prosperity. That may have been exceptional, but
it seemed normal. It's over. We're in a new world, and we don't
quite know what it is yet. The political system doesn't know how to
address it."

For most moderate-income wage-earning voters, Democratic
Party fidelity was one of the constants in that stable world (except
when an occasional nonpartisan figure like Eisenhower happened
to run on the Republican line). Blue-collar parents of today's New
Collars belonged to a generation that expected a hand to fall off if
it pulled a Republican lever. "Liberal" and "conservative" had
practical meaning in that world, as did "Republican" and "Democrat." Today, a political candidate is one more product that television is hawking, for the voter to impulse-buy. "The baby boomers,"
says Richard Wirthlin, "are comparison shoppers. They will be
ticket splitters all their lives."

New Collar voters are the premier ticket splitters. In Whitehead's
calculations, they account for 15 to 20 percent of the total electorate. Most of them work in the service economy. They are neither
traditional blue-collar nor white-collar. If a yuppie is someone who
earns $40,000 a year or more, Whitehead calculates there are at
least six times as many New Collars as yuppies. They are the big
generational cohort to be captured by the majority party of the next
realignment. New Collar voters are often second- and third-
generation ethnics, sons and daughters of steadfast New Deal
Democrats. They are likely to be fairly liberal on social issues and
to be very concerned about their own economic opportunities.
Their views are complicated: they typically consider themselves
"better off" than their parents in some material ways, but with a less
secure sense of place or identity. Mom and Dad may not have had
computers and VCRs, but Dad had his job and Mom had her house,
and they seemed a lot less frazzled. One archetypal New Collar
campaign television spot commercial, on behalf of Joseph Kennedy

III, featured a young couple, baby in lap, wondering whether they would ever be able to afford to own their own home.

The practical issues that might secure the loyalties of these people are not firmly fixed on the political map. Many such voters voted for Gary Hart in the Democratic primaries in 1984, not, as many commentators concluded, because Hart was the yuppie candidate but because he seemed to represent idealism and hope. When Hart failed to get the nomination, most of them turned around and, despite some misgivings, voted for Reagan. Eighteen percent of them supported Democrats for other offices. Baby-boom voters are not, for the most part, hard-core rugged individualists. On the contrary, many have a nostalgia for communitarian values. But unlike their parents, who derived many tangible benefits from the New Deal social contract, they have been more or less cut loose to fend for themselves. If government seems unlikely to give them much, then the best they can hope for in a candidate are vague virtues like "leadership" and the advocacy of low taxes, which is to say, Reagan. Whitehead quotes a New Collar voter who cast ballots for Reagan and for the liberal Massachusetts Democrat, Senator John Kerry: "Give me a tax break and keep us out of World War III, and you've got a shot at my vote." A lot of Democratic elected officials have successfully competed for New Collar votes, Whitehead argues; if they hadn't, they wouldn't have been elected. "But as a party, we've been slow to give these people a face, a voice, and a connection to our philosophy."

When Whitehead and his wife, Barbara, a social historian, interview New Collar voters, they usually meet in people's homes after dinner. Barbara Whitehead often breaks the ice by asking to see family photos. From there the conversation progresses through family, work, opinions, values, and aspirations. At the end of one such interview, the hour well past eleven, the Whiteheads began to get up to leave. "But when are we going to talk about politics?" the wife wanted to know. "My husband went out and found out the name of our state senator." The most significant political fact about the New Collars is how few points of contact their lives ordinarily have with the political system or indeed with the government in the benign, New Deal sense. Politics is something "out there," and it doesn't seem to have anything to do with one's own needs, values, or aspirations. The Democratic Party, as the party of broadly diffused economic opportunity, logically ought to be the party of New Collar voters, but as yet it isn't.

The political scientist David Gopoian, in a series of focus-group interviews conducted in the working-class suburb of Parma, Ohio, identified several distinct types of weak New Collar and blue-collar Democrats who often vote Republican. Every voter invited to the focus group was a ticket splitter. Some were voting for the Democratic gubernatorial candidate, and for a Republican congressman; others were voting Democratic for Congress and Republican for local offices; many had voted for Reagan. Based on their responses, Gopoian divided them into four types, with these nicknames: "Harry the New Deal Hawk," "Mary Religion," "Janet the Loyal Democrat," and, inevitably, "Joe Six-Pack."

Each of these types is conservative in one or more respects. Harry admires Reagan's strong leadership and his willingness to use military force. He is your classic gun-toting, flag-waving blue-collar conservative, except that he is an active trade unionist. Mary thinks the Supreme Court shouldn't have banned school prayer, worries about sexual immorality, and opposes legalized abortion. Janet resents special treatment for blacks and other minorities. The one thing all these weak Democrats have in common is a gut-level economic populism. Harry thinks big business is too powerful, wants more government spending on toxic cleanup and on education. He doesn't like the New Right social agenda. Mary also distrusts big business, wants more spending on education and on toxic cleanup. Janet thinks the government spends too much on military weapons and not enough reducing poverty, even though she opposes racially oriented affirmative action. And even Joe, the most conservative of the lot, doesn't buy the idea that the free market would work well if government just got off business's back. The only Democratic issue which unites all these sometime Democratic voters is populist economics. Foreign-policy and social-policy issues intensify their divisions.

Stanley Greenberg, in a series of focus groups with similar voters in places like Manchester, New Hampshire, suburban Des Moines, Iowa, and Pontiac, Michigan, elicited comments of weak, hesitant affiliation with the Democratic Party, almost entirely on implicitly populist grounds: "Well, it's my understanding they're *supposed* to be for the worker." "They *seem to lean* toward the little man getting a start [and] taking care of his own self-interest." "They do *attempt to* help the working man." And "The Democratic Party, in my opinion, *seems* to look out more for the people."

Greenberg found resentment among white working-class voters that the Democrats favor giving blacks special breaks: ("They get more breaks than we do. It has gone too far.") The party's identity as the political home of the wage-earning class is evident but faint. "In the minds of potential Democrats, they make up a new middle class existing on the margins of society . . . living from paycheck to paycheck, and [their] children live with declining opportunities. Though it embodies the proper virtues, the new middle class sees itself as politically marginal, 'in the wrong category,' overlooked by parties, by politicians, and by government." Interviewees told Greenberg: "Low-income people pay next to nothing for taxes; the rich don't pay anything." "It's working-class people that are trying to take care of a family and survive. They are the ones who are getting a shaft."

By giving symbolic recognition to the economic frustrations of wage-earning voters, and combining that with a personal sense of optimism and leadership, Ronald Reagan could temporarily claim their affections. But Greenberg sees hopeful news for Democrats in a whole range of issues that more naturally belong to Democrats—issues concerning the ability of struggling middle-class people to survive the shifting economic and social tides. Greenberg identifies "the life cycle of the family" as a constellation of concerns where wage-earners both need and welcome help from government—to find adequate housing, to help make vocational transitions, to support daycare, to help finance education, and to help secure a safe retirement. "Democrats need to carve out a role for government that respects the family and that intervenes to help people during these difficult transitions."

One of the most astute pieces of political journalism in recent years was Jonathan Schell's two-part *New Yorker* article published in early 1987, interviewing two archetypal voters of this kind: the pseudonymous Bill and Gina Gapolinsky of Sherman Park, Milwaukee, and their extended family, about their reactions during the

1984 election campaign. Schell seemed surprised to discover that although Bill had very strong views, partisan politics was not a major part of his personal compass, nor politics generally. Bill explained that he actually agreed more with Mondale's views, but just didn't think Mondale was enough of a realist to make good on his promises. "Money runs the country," he said. "That's the part I hate about business and politics. . . . Reagan succeeds because he sees eye to eye with them. . . . I'm leaning to Reagan. I'm an optimistic American, I think America should be able to solve problems." Only when Reagan seemed to falter in the first televised debate with Mondale did Bill waiver: "If Mondale wipes out Reagan in the next debate, I'll vote for him." Ultimately, though, Bill stuck with Reagan. Although Bill embraced many populist values, the Democrats failed to reach him, because they offered little either in terms of expressing his values or programmatically. Instead, Bill's cynicism carried the day, and he voted for the tough guy.

Schell concluded that the settled world of Bill and Gina's parents was a kind of "Atlantis"—a submerged continent of social structures that appears to have vanished without a trace. As for the couple's own world, "There is a new life there, yet no picture of it has yet taken hold in the public imagination." In this new American life, personal concerns are still momentous and national problems pressing, but "politics" in the usual sense, mediating between the two, is less and less meaningful. Bill, Gina, and their friends did not discuss politics until prompted by the reporter, and often they guessed wrong about each other's leanings. "There is little indication that anyone who does not have a professional interest in politics takes it very seriously," Schell concluded.

The Schell interviews caused a minor sensation among operatives and pollsters who had been puzzling out New Collar voters and other "disaffected Democrats." They rang all too true. Gapolinsky was described as a regional salesman for a large snack-food company. His job required him to call on supermarkets and keep his product displays shipshape; he was constantly competing with other salesmen for shelf space. Whitehead observes that a New Collar worker like Bill Gapolinsky "internalizes the social Darwinism of Ronald Reagan's free marketplace." An assembly-line job of the sort Bill's father had requires cooperation and solidarity; a New

Collar job often implies competition. Bill's background and living standards may be blue collar, but his aspirations are entrepreneurial and his survival instincts are competitive rather than cooperative. He would like to believe in the softer, more humanitarian values that his wife (and Walter Mondale) profess. But as a breadwinner, the world he experiences is more like Ronald Reagan's. The Democrats might make headway with the Bill Gapolinskys of the world if they offered symbolic appreciation of their economic condition and some practical help. That doesn't mean trying to out-entrepreneur or out-macho Ronald Reagan. It does mean appraising the new condition of life for America's wage-earners with a clear head and addressing their needs.

IV.

In its heyday, the Democratic Party was an alliance of the working middle class with the needy lower class. Today, the disaffection of the New Collar class from active politics is compounded by the declining voting participation of the lower class. The polls show that poorer and less well-educated people vote at substantially lower rates; they do vote more heavily for the Democrat—*when they vote.* This class disparity in voting has widened as the electorate has become more disaffiliated. The percentage of well-to-do people who vote is still almost as high in the U.S. as it is in Europe. But while middle-class citizens register disaffection by splitting tickets, low-status citizens just stay home. Yet the modern institutional Democratic Party has not done enough to improve the turnout of its own natural voting base. These realities of contemporary electoral demography have become such a basic part of the landscape that they get surprisingly little attention.

In the 1986 election, the percentage of voting-age Americans that actually voted fell once again, continuing a twenty-year trend. An estimated 37.3 percent of eligible voters cast ballots in 1986, down from 41.1 percent in the off-year election of 1982, and the lowest turnout since the wartime election of 1942. Outside the South, the 1986 election had the lowest turnout of eligible voters since 1798. The same decline has been evident in presidential years. In 1960, 65.4 percent of the voting-age population cast ballots; by 1984, that had dropped to 55 percent. Though the overall poor turnout gets most of the publicity, it is the class skew that has the most powerful political implications and that should concern us here. In the 1980 presidential election, 73.8 percent of people with incomes of $25,000 and over actually voted, but only 48.8 percent of those with incomes between $5,000 and $9,999 cast votes. In 1984, 71.8 percent of people who owned their own homes, a pretty good measure of the middle class, voted; 43.7 percent of renters voted. What this all means is that more affluent people have about one and one half ballots for every ballot than poorer people have.

Educational attainment, like family income, is also highly correlated with the likelihood of voting. In their classic study *Who Votes?* the political scientists Raymond Wolfinger and Steven Rosenstone reported that only 38 percent of people with less than five years of schooling went to the polls, compared to 59 percent of those who finished eighth grade, 69 percent of those who graduated from high school, and 91 percent of those with more than five years of college. A 1985 census study showed that 79 percent of college graduates voted in the 1984 election, compared to 44 percent of people who had not finished high school.

These statistics, which are all ultimately derived from census data, probably understate the class disparities in voting, because people are often ashamed to tell the census taker that they failed to vote, and low-status people misreport more often than high-status ones. A study by the political scientists Michael Traugott and John Katosh indicates that 22 percent of low-income people falsely told the Census Bureau they were registered, compared to only 12 percent of middle-class ones. Overreporting by blacks occurred at twice the white rate. So the class gap in voting participation is even wider than usually reported.

These demographic realities are entirely consistent with long-standing findings about social class, perceived efficacy, and political participation. The working-class base tends to be more alienated, more cynical, less inclined to believe that voting is a civic duty, or that it will make a difference in their own lives. That attitude changes only when particular leaders, or parties, prove their efficacy and establish bonds with these people.

In an effort to see how this class divergence in participation influences politics, Walter Dean Burnham compared two Massachusetts towns, working-class Lowell and affluent, suburban Weston. The results are striking. In 1960, 10.6 percent of Weston's eligible voters failed to vote, 15.8 percent of Lowell's. By 1980, the nonvoters in Weston had increased to 19.9 percent, but in Lowell, nonvoting had skyrocketed to 50.4 percent. Meanwhile, the partisan balance in Weston had moderated, from 65–25 Republican to 50–30 Republican. This double shift, in Burnham's view, reinforces the "yuppification" of the Democratic Party. In Weston, most people vote and some voters can be persuaded to vote for a socially liberal, economically centrist Democrat. In Lowell, the Republican share of the vote stays low, but a lot of disaffected Democrats don't vote at all. Many suburban towns actually deliver more Democratic votes than blue-collar towns of the same size. Democratic politicians, therefore, pay a lot more attention to Weston than to Lowell and conclude that what Weston wants is just what will get them victory. Playing to the social liberalism of the suburbs does help some centrist Democratic governors, but it is lethal for the long-term fortunes of the Democratic coalition. Those same suburbs voted heavily for Reagan, while the Democratic base sat on its hands.

The United States is unique among industrial democracies in this class divergence in voting patterns. In Western Europe, not only are voting percentages much higher throughout society, but low-status voters vote at almost identical rates as high-status voters, partly because the state takes responsibility for maintaining voter lists, and partly because labor or social-democratic political parties explicitly identify with the working-class vote. Most observers attribute the class dropoff in American voting to the fact that the United States has far weaker institutions for mobilizing low-status voters. The Democratic Party, of course, has been such an institution during much of its history, and it could be again.

Race, as always, is a complicating factor in the special American experience. Until recently, the poor voting record of low-status voters was partly due to the fact that many blacks were barred from voting. But as black turnout in most states has increased to the point where it nearly equals white turnout, the overall voting participation of lower-status voters has *still* continued to decline. So the class chasm in voting is even worse than it appears, because an underlying trend has been partly camouflaged by the belated normalization of the black franchise.

Racial divisions are a special problem for Democrats as a coalition party. Many Democratic strategists in recent years have worried that as the party has become steadily more dependent on the loyalties of blacks, this tends to drive away working-class whites and creates electoral dependence on a group which, historically at least, votes less frequently. But this dilemma is all the more reason why Democrats must emphasize economic issues. Civil rights, unavoidably, is a "racial" issue. But social security, medicare, national health insurance, home-ownership opportunity, public education, job mobility, minimum wage, pension rights, daycare, and so on reflect economic issues—and offer economic benefits. They win black support to the extent that black voters are not independently wealthy; they win white support on the same grounds. They remind voters from different ethnic backgrounds of social commonalities, and they engender social and civic cohesion. Democrats, more often than not, tend to be liberal on a whole range of issues involving social tolerance. But only when the party delivers the economic goods to socially conservative working-class voters is it forgiven for its social cosmopolitanism. It takes a Harry Hopkins to buy the political space for an Eleanor Roosevelt.

Occasionally, an individual Democrat manages to combine these appeals superbly—like Robert Kennedy, whose affinity with working-class Democrats of all ethnic backgrounds overcame their mistrust that he might be "too liberal" on race. Jesse Jackson has done best when he recasts racial issues as class issues. Most successful Democratic politicians retain at least some ability to appeal to voters multiracially, on economic grounds.

That poorer, lower-status people still favor Democrats is heartening, in one respect, even though they vote less reliably. It suggests that the Democratic Party's historic identity as the party of the common citizen is still potent. Some of the correlation between low-income and Democratic voting has to do with the strong loyalty blacks have to the Democrat Party, but an analysis of the 1986 Senate elections shows that in nearly every state, less affluent whites tended to vote Democratic disproportionately, too. For example, in California, where the Democrat, Alan Cranston, won the election 51–49, he took 58 percent of white voters with incomes of $12,500 or less and 52 percent of those earning $12,500–$25,000. He lost in higher-income categories, where voters earning over $50,000 backed the Republican two to one. In Georgia, with a heavy black vote, the Democrat, Wyche Fowler, received only about 40 percent of the white vote overall, but he did better among poor and moderate-income whites, winning about 46 percent of whites with household incomes of $25,000 or less. His opponent, Mack Mattingly, swept the white upper-class vote, 72–28. But Fowler won the election. In Missouri, where the Democrat, Harriet Woods, lost narrowly, she won among voters with incomes of under $25,000 but not by a wide enough margin to offset her opponent's overwhelming win in the upper-bracket groups. The more an election was posed along populist lines, the greater the class skew. This pattern held strongly in every state except Colorado and Florida, where neo-liberal Democrats defeated extreme conservative Republicans fairly evenly across the income brackets, among white voters.

These income and educational voting correlations suggest just what the Democratic Party is at its best: an alliance of wage-earning people who vote Democratic out of class self-interest with very well-educated people who support Democrats out of a commitment to a just society. (And yes, the postgraduate crowd undoubtedly includes "special interest" professionals like schoolteachers and cancer researchers whose work depends on federal funding.) What the party cannot be is an awkward alliance between rich eccentrics and the dependent poor. In a society where most people are not rich, the party that speaks for the common citizen is the natural majority party. But the party's advocacy of the interests of the common people must be as authentic as it once was. The problem is not that citizens have suddenly become too affluent to vote Democratic; on the contrary, most households have less real income now than a decade ago. The problem is that Democrats have not yet adjusted their message to fit the practical economic needs of today's voters. If they can articulate such a message, Democrats could once again rouse their natural base of voters. Indeed, if people with household incomes of $25,000 or less voted at the same rate as wealthier people, Democrats again would overwhelmingly be the majority party.

V.

Looking at politics strategically, from the viewpoint of Democratic candidates hoping to win elections, one encounters a strange indifference to the chronic low turnout of low-status voters. It is almost universally argued by practical political strategists that elections are won or lost in ticket-splitter territory. In a typical district, 20–30 percent of voters have weak partisan loyalties, and it is presumably easier for a candidate to persuade an undecided voter than to animate a probable nonvoter. Almost any political professional will advise a candidate to concentrate on "persuadable" voters and will say that turnout in a given year is generally a function of contextual factors such as who else is on the ticket and whether it happens to be a presidential year. Even though many candidates do win insurgent races for local offices or Congress by mobilizing small armies of eager activists, it remains a virtual truism that a candidate in the "middle of the ticket"—say, for Congress or state legislature—cannot increase the turnout. Even the best Democratic campaign professionals advise candidates to "concentrate on the persuadables."

The National Committee for an Effective Congress, as part of its package of "targeting" services to liberal candidates, produces a computerized analysis of voting behavior, precinct by precinct, ranking precincts by voter "turnout" and by Democratic "performance." If turnout for a particular precinct is listed as 65 percent, it means that 65 percent of registered voters turned out to vote in some recent baseline election. If "performance" is listed at 55 percent, it means that 55 percent of the voters in that precinct voted for the Democrat. The NCEC data strikingly confirm, precinct by precinct, what the census shows in the aggregate: there is an almost perfectly inverse relationship in most parts of the country between Democratic turnout and Democratic performance, because upper-middle-class and wealthy people tend to participate at a substantially greater rate. The precincts that go Republican by more than 60 percent generally have turnouts up in the healthy range of 65–75 percent. The most faithful Democratic areas often have turnout rates of less than 50 percent and sometimes below 40 percent. The NCEC's usual advice to candidates is to take these realities as given and make the best of them.

Consider, for example, a typical NCEC precinct analysis, in this case a targeting and strategy memo to Congressman "John Doe" of a border state. Doe is a moderately liberal Democrat representing a district which is 10 percent black and only barely held by the Democrats. In the 1984 Reagan landslide, he ran sixteen points ahead of Mondale and survived with a bare 50.1 percent of the vote. Doe was a priority for 1986. The 1986 NCEC strategy memo for his campaign observed, "There are an estimated 34,000 registered voters who could be persuaded to vote for Doe if they voted at all," but, the memo went on, the estimated 31,000 ticket splitters were far more important. "A 30 percent Democratic performance precinct with a 25 percent persuasion percentage is more important to the Doe campaign than a 55 percent Democratic performance precinct with a 15 percent persuasion percentage." In other words, if the candidate could convert 25 percent of the voters in a largely Republican area, that would be time better spent than in a low-turnout, loyally Democratic area. In short, the candidate should spend his time going after swing voters and not trying to boost turnout among the alienated and nonvoting Democratic base areas. The memo added bluntly, "All early scheduling should avoid the black wards. There are simply no ticket splitters and therefore no votes to be won or lost in these wards." Very similar advice was given to other candidates.

Another interesting artifact, a campaign manual by two well-respected Democratic campaign strategists, Ann Beaudry and Bob Schaeffer, entitled *Winning Local and State Elections,* counsels progressive candidates: "The people most likely to vote in your election are those who regularly vote in similar elections. And their voting pattern will most likely resemble those of previous years.

Never get the idea that your campaign is going to magically transform the electorate."

The NCEC and Schaeffer and Beaudry have undoubtedly helped many good progressive Democrats win elections. Their advice is fine as far as it goes. But its cumulative long-term effect is to ignore the disaffiliated, potentially Democratic base of wage-earning voters, who then justifiably see little in politics that serves their interests.

An even more pernicious problem is that some Democratic office-holders have a distinct interest in holding *down* the turnout. In the remnants of big-city machines, local ward bosses still have a firsthand knowledge of neighborhood participants in politics. The last thing such leaders need is new, unfamiliar voters whom they don't control. In local elections, such voters are occasionally mobilized by reform candidates or by a candidate representing a previously silent ethnic group. Even though in the urban north there were no legal barriers to black voting participation, black turnout was chronically depressed until serious black mayoralty candidates began to run, because the white city machines had no use for high black turnout and ordinary black voters had little enthusiasm for the machines. The 1983 candidacy of Harold Washington, Chicago's first black mayor, boosted black voting turnout in Chicago from 55.4 percent in 1982 to 70.4 percent in 1983.

Once in office, however, many black officeholders in solidly black areas behave just like their white counterparts. They want to make sure their own supporters get to the polls, but they are far less interested in boosting turnout generally and may even actively oppose it. In some localities, like New York City, the political culture is so seriously decayed that in many minority districts, even those with black congressmen, less than 15 percent of voting-age citizens turn out to vote. Thus while the national Democratic Party wants, and desperately needs, increased political participation of its wage-earning base, practical local Democratic politics (and "all politics is local") often fails to encourage turnout and even actively discourages it.

"The Democratic Party wants the working class to vote, but not necessarily in this election in my district," says Linda Davidoff,

director of Human-Serve, a New York-based national group devoted to increasing voting participation. "A lot of elected officials
cannot stand the idea of people being allowed to register on election day, because that means a whole bunch of new voters, whom
they haven't contacted, would come out of the woodwork." Since
the usual campaign apparatus is based on contacting *registered* voters, determining their likely preference, and then getting them to
the polls, new, previously unidentified voters are wild cards.

Edward Schwartz, who organized a small army of volunteers to
win city-wide election as a "pro-neighborhood" candidate for the
Philadelphia City Council, made the point eloquently in his testimony before the Democratic Party's Leland Commission:

> Why has the Democratic Party been so reluctant to respond to its
> obvious strategic requirement for success? It has not been hesi-
> tant to support federal programs that will benefit low-income
> citizens, so much so that much of the population has come to
> resent them. Why hasn't the party accompanied this legislative
> program with an organizing drive designed to insure that poor
> people will vote their interests when the time comes, and support
> the party that has more consistently supported them?

The point here, despite Schwartz's emphasis on "poor people," is
that the Democratic party needs to increase the registration and
voting turnout of *all* wage-earning citizens. Schwartz continues:

> The answer, I think, is that while it has been in the interests of
> the national Democratic Party to mobilize the poor every two and
> four years, it has not been in the interest of the local party organi-
> zations to do so. To a presidential candidate, an aroused elec-
> torate means millions of additional votes. To a local party
> organization, or a local party elite that has chosen to suppress its
> low-income citizens, the same electorate may present a major
> threat to entrenched local political power.

In Philadelphia, as Schwartz notes, an attempt by then Mayor
Frank Rizzo in 1978 to win an unprecedented third term by ram-

ming through a change in the city charter finally galvanized the opposition to him. Between January and November 1978, opponents of a third Rizzo term registered 204,849 new voters in a city whose entire population was 1.7 million. Schwartz observes, "That the charter-change coalition could *find* over 200,000 nonvoters attests to the effectiveness of the Party's nonregistration program over the years." In that 1978 election, actual turnout in the newly animated poor and mostly black anti-Rizzo wards of Northwest Philadelphia—63 to 67 percent—actually exceeded the turnout rates of most of the more affluent areas of Philadelphia.

In Schwartz's own electoral district, he brought registration postcards to the door of every unregistered voter and raised the number of registered Democrats from 278 to 380 in the first year; follow-up work by his volunteers raised it further to 508. This local work produced an 86 percent turnout for Jimmy Carter in 1976 in a low-income, substantially black neighborhood. Schwartz declared, "Who says the quality of local party organizations makes no difference in voter participation today? . . . If I worked my division—meaning personal, door-to-door canvassing before the primary and general election, coupled with ongoing block-organizing and constituent service—I would raise the turnout at least 15 percent above the city-wide average every time." People were voting not out of a vague civic duty, but out of enthusiasm for a democratically elected representative who they believed was serving their interests. "I had managed to convince them that voting was not simply a test of a candidate's power, or of my own power, but of *their* power," Schwartz says.

VI.

The most fundamental, and still the most radical, instrument of political democracy is the universal franchise. When people of all economic classes have an equal say in governance, it transforms power relationships. Propertied elites, even when they support democratic mechanisms, have been fearful of masses of wage-earners casting ballots. In Western Europe, it took more than a century to extend the franchise from a narrow landholding class to all adult citizens. The German economist Adolf Wagner, writing just ninety years ago, predicted that universal franchise would lead inevitably to working-class demands for economic leveling, an enlarged state, and economic ruin. "Wagner's Law" is often cited by political conservatives as the prophetic explanation for the ruinous expansion of the welfare state.

In reviewing our own variation on this history of the expansion of the popular franchise, we Americans tend to view it in the same way we view so much else, as the natural forward march of progress. Once there were barriers; today, happily, the barriers have been dismantled. An alert ninth-grader can tick off the milestones: universal white manhood suffrage in the Jacksonian era; the black vote, at least in principle, in 1865; women's suffrage in 1920; the gradual abolition of the poll tax; the Voting Rights Act of 1965; and the eighteen-year-old vote in 1971.

Unfortunately, history is not always the linear forward march of progress that it seems, because these things don't always stay put. Universal suffrage remains a very radical idea, and it tends to be eroded by the natural power of economic elites, unless constantly reinforced by vigorous institutions of mass political participation. Just as the eighteenth-century American Founding Fathers, their twentieth-century segregationist descendants, the British Tories, and German Junkers all feared the potential radicalism of mass enfranchisement, economic and political elites today continue to resist easy universal voting. Before the 1965 Voting Rights Act, in many parts of the Deep South, harassment of prospective black voters was deliberate and flagrant. For example, a "literacy" test used in Alabama selectively asked such questions as "Would you name the county judges?" or "What is the name of the fourteenth state admitted to the Union?" or "How many people are there on the U.S. payroll?"—questions that, if asked of everyone who came to the polls, would have disqualified every voter in the country.

As recently as 1986, when a Republican "ballot integrity program" turned out to be a crude device for intimidating black voters, systematic attempts have been made to disqualify voters expected to vote for progressive candidates. No less than William Rehnquist, Chief Justice of the United States, as a young Republican Party militant in Arizona, once helped to organize a poll-watching operation in black precincts that threatened black voters with voting-fraud prosecutions. He was nearly denied Senate confirmation when this was revealed.

In general today, barriers to voting are more subtle. But a class bias persists, and the obstacles serve the same function—giving the political elite a stable, manageable electoral environment. The conventional wisdom is that lower-status people don't bother to vote because they have less civic consciousness, and since they are less likely to be well-informed on the issues, it's probably a good thing that they don't cast ballots.

For example, voting registration forms are often difficult to read and understand. And if people have ever had a brush with the law or are in debt, they may be reluctant to fill out an official form, mistakenly fearing that a minor arrest record bars them from voting or that the form will somehow be used against them.

Often, low-income people who do register face further subtle obstacles to casting their ballots. Linda Davidoff, director of Human-Serve, says, "Very few people are highly motivated to vote. People are generally cynical, but they will cast a ballot if they are allowed to. In a polling place in a black or Puerto Rican neighborhood, the lines are often three times as long as elsewhere. If people are just getting off work, it's dark by six o'clock in November. In rough neighborhoods, people often don't like to go out after dark. An impermeable system reinforces low motivation, and that's just the way the political establishment wants it. I have tried to get candidates to walk the streets of East Harlem. You can watch their faces tighten. If these people don't vote, then you don't have to campaign at them. We want to start by removing the barriers to registration and voting. If we can remove the barriers, then we can concentrate on improving the motivation."

The government spends millions of dollars encouraging people to register with the armed services, but spends almost nothing encouraging them to register to vote. Ironically, there is something called a Federal Voting Assistance Administration, and it is located in the Pentagon. Its principal function is to help Americans based overseas—mostly military personnel and corporate employees—to cast absentee ballots. Federal law requires some agencies, such as

employment service offices, to distribute military recruiting literature but officially prohibits certain other agencies, like antipoverty
offices, from registering people to vote. States that have adopted
voter-outreach programs generally have to put them in agencies
like motor-vehicle registries that do not receive federal funds.

Low voting participation in the United States is relatively recent.
When European democrats were still fighting to expand the franchise, the United States already had something close to universal
participation of what was then the electorate. Professor Burnham's
classic work, *Critical Elections and the Mainsprings of American Politics,*
recounts that voting participation in the United States began rising
dramatically during the Jacksonian era, and by the 1830s was already generally higher than it is in most states today. Between 1848
and 1896, roughly 75 percent of eligible voters turned out to vote.
At that time, in most states, there was no such thing as voter
registration. People simply showed up at the polling place, gave
some evidence of their identity, and requested a ballot. No sooner
did large numbers of wage-earners begin to vote than various devices were invented to restrict participation, invariably described in
high-minded terms as restricting "voter fraud." This continues to
be the favorite Republican argument today whenever such reforms
are proposed as postcard registration or election-day registration.
Images are concocted of big-city bosses slipping a couple of dollars
and palm cards to the town drunks and "voting them" for the
straight Democratic ticket.

When Pennsylvania enacted an early voter registration statute in
1837, according to the historian Joseph Harris, it was widely argued
"that the law was passed as a party measure, designed to cut down
the vote of Philadelphia, that it fostered rather than prevented
fraud, and that it took away the right of suffrage from the poor and
secured it for the rich." Harris quotes a Democrat named Porter,
from Philadelphia, who complained to a party convention:

> When the assessors went around, the laboring men were neces-
> sarily and of course absent from their homes, engaged in provid-
> ing subsistence for themselves and their families; and not finding
> the men at home, did not go again. When the election came on

these men appeared to vote, and were spurned from the ballot boxes. They were told that their names were not on the registry, and that, therefore, they had no right to vote. . . . But how was it with the rich man? The gold and silver doorplate with name was enough, and there was no danger that the assessor would overlook that.

By the 1880s, most states had enacted some form of voter registration law. In the 1890s, many began to shift the burden of establishing eligibility from the state or county to the prospective voter. Politically, the desire of usually Republican economic elites to restrict voting participation was affected by a number of factors—the influx of immigrants, who were often allied with urban Democratic machines; the populist revolt of 1882–96, which briefly put radicals in positions of real political power; and the existence of some voting fraud. As so often in the American experience, procedural civic reform was allied with the interests of the economic elite. When registration requirements were tightened, they came to include requirements that the citizen appear before a registration board prior to each election, periodic "purges" of the rolls, and long waiting periods between registration and voting.

Some states actually applied more stringent requirements for large cities than in the countryside. For more than a decade, for example, Republicans from upstate New York pressed for differential treatment for New York City. In 1880, the New York legislature mandated registration for cities with populations of over 16,000. These discriminatory statutes were eventually overturned, with the result that registration barriers were extended statewide. In the South, statutes devised primarily to reduce black voting participation had the effect of reducing participation generally. Voting participation dropped dramatically during the first two decades of the twentieth century, from 78 percent in 1898 to 74.3 percent in 1906, 71.6 percent in 1910, 64.8 percent in 1918, and 56 percent in 1928. It began rising again during the New Deal, and falling dramatically after 1968. Today, only the state of North Dakota, which still preserves its legacy of prairie populism, has no voter registration at all. It shocks out-of-state observers to learn that in North Dakota, you simply present yourself on election day, show an ID, declare your-

self a citizen under penalty of perjury, and vote. This system seems
to have done North Dakota no visible harm.

No other nation erects such barriers to voting participation. In
most of Western Europe, where there is not the same cultural
resistance to state recordkeeping on citizens, the state simply main-
tains a registry of important demographic events for each individual—births, deaths, marriages, divorces, and changes of address.
This census is the source for an electoral register of qualified voters, which is printed out prior to every election. Nobody has to
register to vote, since the government already has the information.

In some nations, such as England and Canada, where the state
does not keep systematic track of changes of address, the government does a special canvass to produce a current list of qualified
voters. In England, it is established in each parliamentary constituency for each election: town clerks send forms to every household,
by mail; if the form is not returned, canvassers known as electoral
registration officers follow up with house calls. Canada has a Chief
Electoral Officer, who is responsible for drawing up and posting
the list of voters prior to elections. Official enumerators nominated
by the major parties conduct a house-to-house canvass to list
names, and the lists are closed two and a half weeks before election
day. The Canadian government estimates that at least 98 percent
of potential voters are listed. France's system is like ours in the
sense that the citizen is supposed to take the initiative and register.
But the state has the responsibility for keeping a permanent voters'
list and periodically updating it. Every December, a special municipal commission meets to strike the names of voters who have
moved or died and to add newly qualified ones. Since the French
central statistical office keeps vital statistics on every citizen, the
local commissions have no difficulty in obtaining this information.
In Sweden, complete voter lists are maintained by the national tax
board.

Throughout Europe, there is only minor class variation in voter
turnout, partly because the state takes responsibility for maintaining voter lists, and partly because most of Europe has labor or
social-democratic political parties explicitly identified with the
working-class vote.

The claim is oft heard that voter registration is necessary to

prevent fraud. But oddly enough, once an American citizen has run
the gauntlet of voter-registration procedures, enforcement against
his casting a fraudulent vote is virtually nonexistent. No state has
even a systematic program of spot checks, and the system is operated as if its purpose were to erect barriers to voting, not to catch
cheaters. In fact, individual voter fraud is rare and mass fraud even
rarer. If any party makes a coordinated effort at ballot-box stuffing,
it is usually spotted by the opposition party. If conservatives were
truly concerned about voter fraud, they would support a European-
style system of universal registration, which of course they don't.
It is not necessary to believe that these barriers are deliberately
contrived to see that they are functional: Looked at casually, our
system seems irrational, but understood in class terms it is functional indeed.

Though the concept of voter registration is peculiar to the
United States, and not even part of our original electoral system,
most citizens and politicians can't imagine the system operating any
other way. Linda Davidoff says, "The idea of a universal franchise
is something we think we believe in, but it turns out to be more
radical than we think it is. The notion creeps in that people should
deserve the right to vote; when you talk about removing obstacles
to voting, people say, 'it ought to be a little difficult.' "

Human-Serve—the name stands for Human Service Employees
Registration and Voter Education Fund—began in 1983 as the
brainchild of political scientist Frances Fox Piven and sociologist
Richard Cloward, activist-scholars long associated with poor people's movements. After spending nearly two decades working on
welfare rights and similar issues concerning the political participation of poor people, Piven and Cloward arrived at the most radically egalitarian act of all—voting. Their idea was that the voting
participation of poor people could be increased dramatically if the
officials who operate human service programs registered their clients, at welfare and food stamp offices, for example. The proposal
was endorsed by the National League of Cities, the National Black
Caucus of State Legislators, and by some thirty national human-
service professional associations.

A few venturesome mayors and governors, including those of

Texas, Ohio, New York, Montana, New Mexico, and West Virginia, issued executive orders allowing registration at welfare agencies, but they did so reluctantly. For the plan seemed to confirm the most lurid conservative notions about a symbiosis between the welfare state and its dependent clients. Welfare recipients, according to this view, were in voting terms the modern counterparts of the town drunk; welfare workers, with a selfish interest in electing tax-and-spend liberals, were acting like modern ward heelers. Even worse, it reinforced the awkward image of the Democratic Party as an alliance of professional do-gooders and the undeserving poor.

In reality, Human-Serve never quite conformed to the caricature—it favored voter registration at *all* public agencies, not just welfare offices—and it soon evolved into something rather more sophisticated and irreproachable. Human-Serve today doesn't try to go out and register people, though other organizations do. Instead, it functions as a national clearinghouse, research organization, and lobby for the dismantling of obstacles to voting. In a sober postmortem on their 1984 experience, Piven and Cloward wrote, "The unprecedented voter registration campaign of 1982–84 ended in a class stalemate. . . . The solution is to reform the voter registration system so that low-income citizens can participate more easily. But a realistic reform strategy must confront the entrenched opposition of the national political parties, neither of which wants the electorate expanded from the bottom."

Linda Davidoff says, "There are never going to be enough volunteers. We think registration should be a function of *citizenship*. From the beginning, we've been urging that government take over the task of active registration. Get-out-the-vote is entirely separate. Having to do both jobs with volunteers thins out resources."

VII.

It seems evident that the Democratic Party needs both to lower barriers to registration, and to encourage other avenues of political participation. For the first, the simplest solutions would be Election Day registration, universal postcard registration, and an Election

Day holiday, so that wage-earning voters wouldn't have to decide whether to brave long lines in the evening. Human-Serve, which supports all three approaches, has also been advocating something called "Motor Voter," which would have state motor vehicle bureaus register people at the time they obtain or renew drivers' licenses. Admittedly, this would slightly skew the effort toward the middle class, but less so than the present pattern of voting. Davidoff says, "If you get a motor vehicle agency to accept responsibility for registering voters, you're creating for the first time an obligation on the part of a public agency to see to it that citizens have an opportunity to register."

Seven states now allow personnel to register voters at motor vehicle bureaus and/or at social service agencies. Seven others distribute voter registration literature at their government agencies, but leave it up to the citizen to mail in the materials. Michigan, which set up the first motor-voter program in 1975, has seen a steady increase in its registration rates, and in 1984 had about 90 percent of its voting-age population registered. In Colorado, where a motor-voter program took effect on July 1, 1985, 140,000 people were newly registered to vote, increasing Colorado's pool of registered voters by 11 percent.

In the last presidential election year, various liberal partisan and nonpartisan organizations worked to register voters. About $7 million was spent on organizing volunteers, and more than three million new voters were registered. The Republican National Committee, with a $10 million budget for voter registration and get-out-the-vote, and its allies in the conservative movement registered at least that many. The Democratic Party, which had talked of putting $2.5 million into voter registration, actually spent only a small fraction of that, at most a few hundred thousand dollars. The proposed campaign was another casualty of party infighting, since Tony Harrison, in charge of the project, was a protégé of the mayor of Gary, Indiana, Richard Hatcher, and never enjoyed the full confidence of top officials of the DNC and the Mondale campaign. The biggest magnet for black voter registration was Rev. Jesse Jackson, and leaders of the party establishment were reluctant to boost either his grass-roots strength or his financial resources.

Thus while both the national Democratic Party and a lot of local Democratic parties remained committed to broadened voting participation, this was only in theory, not in practice.

The efforts to increase the voting turnout of poor people and minorities included many foundations and groups privately sympathetic to the Democratic Party. But as nonprofit, tax-exempt organizations, they could not explicitly give money to specific campaigns, and they were gun-shy because of previous brushes with the IRS. After the Ford Foundation underwrote major voter-registration drives quite openly aimed to help elect black mayors in the late 1960s, Congress sharply limited foundation electoral activity, and required that any voter-registration group work in several states and be scrupulously nonpartisan. Some well-known Democratic fund raisers, such as former Commerce Undersecretary Frank Weil, built conduits to ostensibly nonpartisan voter registration, encouraging big Democratic donors who had "maxed out" in campaign donations to give additional tax-deductible money to voter-registration drives.

Voter-registration politics on the liberal side was further hobbled by characteristic battles over turf. The traditional recipients of foundation money for voter registration had been black groups like the Atlanta-based Voter Education Project. VEP, founded in the 1960s, had once been run by the civil rights leader (now Congressman) John Lewis. Another group with a good reputation for actually getting voters was the A. Philip Randolph Institute. A group called the National Coalition on Black Voter Participation, directed by Gracia Hillman, served as a clearinghouse for minority voter-registration efforts and operated Operation Big Vote, a registration campaign working mostly through black churches. Newer groups included Project Vote, run by an aggressive white liberal activist named Sanford Newman; it funneled foundation money to local groups, which it also supplied with training materials, including videotapes and "block captain kits." Another predominantly white group, the Citizen Leadership Foundation, ran programs in affiliated statewide citizen-action organizations, primarily in white working-class areas. Among groups aimed at Hispanic voters, the Southwest Voter Registration/Education Project has had excellent success in raising turnout among Mexican-American voters, and a counterpart group, the Midwest Voter Registration/Education Project, began in 1983–84. However, a certain amount of ethnic and territorial rivalry complicated these efforts. In particular, black groups, many of which had been working on voter registration since the late 1950s, resented the diversion of funds to Hispanic and white-led groups.

The pioneer Voter Education Project, meanwhile, was a casualty of poor administration and haphazard leadership. In 1984 the foundations, long critical of its deteriorating management, reluctantly ceased to fund it. This, along with the new competition from white-led, liberal voter-registration groups, raised suspicions in the black community that the white foundations and wealthy Democratic partisans were not sincerely committed to increasing black turnout, or at best did not want the money going to build black political strength, least of all Jesse Jackson's. "In 1984, voter registration politics mirrored coalition politics at its worst," says Ann Lewis, former political director of the DNC.

By 1986, some of these tensions had subsided. Foundation money was flowing once again to local groups, both directly and through umbrella groups like Project Vote and Operation Big Vote. However, the tension persisted between wanting to be partisan and needing to appear nonpartisan. An evaluation of the 1984 efforts candidly observed that foundation-funded voter-registration drives, by their very nature, "must observe strict standards of nonpartisanship. This inhibits their ability to engage in carefully planned cooperative ventures with electoral campaigns."

In some states, progressive organizations stayed within the letter of the law by having a political arm that could overtly help a specific candidate and a nonprofit arm that took foundation money to register voters. Some postelection literature in 1986 noted joyfully the (narrow) victories of Senators-elect Wyche Fowler, Terry Sanford, and Brock Adams—all in states that had had voter-registration activity, and of course all Democrats. The Republicans, with more partisan money than they could usefully spend, had no such tightropes to walk.

Many political scientists and some of the nonpartisan voter-registration groups have misconstrued the relationships among political participation, social class, and progressive politics. One can demonstrate statistically that nonvoters are not so different from voters except in their perceptions of political efficacy, and conclude from this that an increase in turnout would have little partisan or ideological effect. It is also true that first-time voters tend to be influenced by whoever is temporarily in ascendance; in 1984, new voters backed Reagan by about the same percentage as voters generally. The League of Women Voters always insists that an enlarged franchise would not benefit either party disproportionately. The Committee for the Study of the American Electorate insists that "Contrary to theory, most nonvoters are not more Democratic than voters," though "they do come from families whose voting history is slightly more Democratic than the rest of the electorate." But of course the assertion that nonvoters are no more Democratic than voters is in a sense meaningless, because nonvoters by definition do not cast votes, until they decide to become voters. Their sense of political connectedness is lowest of all groups. The historical evidence is that nonvoters come from demographic sectors that, when they decide to switch from nonvoting to voting, favor Democrats.

The standard political-science view confuses a civic understanding of what voter participation means with a dynamic, political understanding of voter mobilization, and it ends up with a misleading, static picture. It is certainly true that increased voting turnout has no particular implications for social class or political party, *other things being equal.* But obviously, most of the great historic surges in political participation have occurred along with partisan realignments, not with neutral bursts of civic consciousness. Voting participation among low-status groups does not increase because people suddenly decide to do their duty but because they perceive that political activity might serve their interests. In 1936, voting participation rose dramatically because working-class people turned out to vote for Roosevelt. In the 1960s, newly enfranchised black voters were heavily Democratic, because the national Democratic Party had fought for civil rights. Increased participation per se would do little for progressivism or for the Democratic Party, but coupled with a strong, economically progressive program, increased voter mobilization would have significant partisan consequences.

VIII.

I have suggested in this book that several factors have eroded the bonds between Democratic Party and common citizen: a breakdown in social and cultural patterns that once included Democratic Party allegiance; a decay in the party machinery; a weakened linkage between people's private needs and the effect of government programs sponsored by Democrats; and a perception by many white working-class voters that more divides them from racial minorities and the very poor than unites them. The so-called New Collar voter expresses all these factors.

What prospect exists for restoring the bonds between party and people? What new forms of political participation are stirring? One interesting development is the growth of statewide "citizen action" organizations, whose members are precisely drawn from those groups that survey researchers would call weak Democratic voters, based on an agenda that is in essence economically populist. These groups have names like the Ohio Public Interest Campaign, the Illinois Public Action Council, the Pennsylvania Public Interest Coalition, and the Massachusetts Fair Share. Some of them operate under the national Citizen Action umbrella, and share a national lobbying office and facilities for training organizers; others, like the Association of Community Organizations for Reform Now (ACORN), often operate in *de facto* coalition. Two characteristics stand out: all of them are economically populist rather than liberal in the classic sense of the term; and many are rapidly becoming part of the *de facto* Democratic Party machinery, filling an institutional vacuum with a popular ideology, practical links to working-class voters, and seasoned and eager ground troops.

In a political culture in which reformers are often the "morning glories" that Plunkitt of Tammany Hall claimed they were, these citizen-action groups are also noteworthy for their longevity. Some of them have been in existence for well over a decade, and they are just now attaining full political maturity. In their infancy, they avoided electoral politics and concentrated on organizing citizens to take action on working-class economic issues such as mortgage red-lining, utility rates, toxic hazards, discriminatory tax assessments, and so on. While they lobbied vigorously, they did not support political candidates. But then, in 1980 and 1981, they made a concerted decision to enter electoral politics on the side of progressive/populist candidates, though they are nominally and legally nonpartisan. In this respect, they walk the same tightrope as the AFL-CIO, which is effectively an adjunct of the Democratic machinery. And in our disaffiliated political culture with a decayed party infrastructure, the citizen-action groups that entered electoral politics instantly became the second-most important organizations in the Democratic base.

In at least ten states, a candidate who has the endorsement of such state citizen-action groups acquires a formidable volunteer organization. In Ohio, Illinois, Pennsylvania, Iowa, and Washington, among others, citizen-action groups have begun to supply both rank-and-file volunteers and campaign professionals. They received substantial credit for helping to elect Ohio Governor Richard Celeste, Illinois Senator Paul Simon, Iowa Senator Tom Harkin, as well as several congressmen, many of whom went on to found the Congressional Populist Caucus.

In Pennsylvania, PennPIC, which has been active in electoral politics since 1982, has 250,000 dues-paying members and a budget approaching $2 million. In a congressional campaign, it can field several dozen volunteers, and several hundred statewide. It has staffed offices in seven cities, with ten full-time organizers, and a total field staff of sixty. PennPIC not only brings to bear the resources of its own members, but helps to rouse the dormant other pieces of the Democratic coalition, such as labor, environmentalist, neighborhood, and senior-citizen groups. For example, PennPIC often asks unions to let it run phone banks out of a union hall: It organizes the canvass, finds the rank-and-file unionists, and helps mobilize them to be activists.

Trade unionists credit PennPIC and groups like it with breathing life back into coalition politics. Because the citizen-action groups are close to, but not part of, the labor movement, they are often able to broker alliances around particular issues. Because they are more committed to bottom-up politics than many entrenched local labor leaders, and because they have resources, they can often shame the less venturesome labor people into paying more attention to their own rank and file.

The Ohio Public Interest Campaign, the oldest and probably most influential of the citizen-action groups, pioneered in a canvass of voters, which now raises about $2 million a year from nearly 300,000 Ohio households, through a sophisticated phone and door-to-door canvass. In some Zip Code areas, OPIC membership approaches 15 percent of all households. OPIC uses its canvass both to raise money and to see what is on voters' minds. It lobbies, campaigns, organizes, and educates on such "fair share" subjects as local tax and education policy, utility and insurance rates, development politics, jobs, and the environment. OPIC has among its staff people several dozen people well-equipped to run the field organization of a political campaign. Its new computerized list of donors is the most formidable roster of progressive voters in Ohio.

OPIC began as a Nader-style public-interest lobby, all head and no body, but gradually metamorphosed into a mass-membership organization. Its founder and still its director, Ira Arlook, has become one of the most respected political professionals in Ohio. In a state where the institutional Democratic Party machinery is weak, OPIC sometimes functions like a surrogate party. Its well-respected office in Columbus is the most effective progressive lobby in town, substantially more visible than the official state Democratic Party. OPIC has backed candidates for dozens of state and local offices, most prominently Governor Richard Celeste, and had a good deal of influence in formulating his program. Jay Westbrook, the most visible progressive in the Cleveland City Council, is a former OPIC organizer. The governor's issues director came out of OPIC, as did several other key aides.

These groups suggest a new political type—the reformer as regular. Political scientists such as James Q. Wilson have long argued, as Plunkitt once did, that liberal reformers are usually hopelessly elitist. This was certainly the pattern of the first wave of reform in the late nineteenth century, which was a kind of uptown, Civic League conspiracy against the raucous populism of Tammany. Wilson thought he detected the same antipopulism in the movements of well-educated, ideologically liberal postwar "reform" groups that he studied in his famous book *The Amateur Democrat*—the California Democratic clubs, the anti-Tammany New York reform-club movement, and the Independent Voters of Illinois. What distinguished these groups from traditional Democrats, he contended, was less their penchant for clean politics than their disdain for working-class needs. That disdain was reciprocated. The AFL-CIO's Committee on Political Education, Wilson wrote, "regards the CDC and its clubs as both a rival for political influence and as a source of irrelevant and possibly dangerous ideology." In general, Wilson argued, traditional mass Democratic politics, corrupt or not, was a rough-and-tumble politics that served working-class material needs. "The amateur Democrat is not part of this tradition and indeed rejects many of its essential features. He seeks to mobilize intellectual, not material discontent; to obtain recognition for the cosmopolitan middle class; not for the disadvantaged lower class."

Since these words were written in the early 1960s, Wilson has blossomed from a defender of working-class Democratic Party regularity into a full-blown neo-conservative. And citizen-action groups have invented a marvelous fusion of civic reformism and working-class politics. They have created many skilled political activists whose agenda is precisely one of "working-class material needs" just when party regulars were turning away from the working class. Far from competing with the labor movement, they work in close alliance with it on such issues as plant closings, worker health and safety, and jobs programs. In this respect, they have far more in common with the populist working-class reform movements that Wilson overlooked, like the Democrat-Farmer-Labor party of Minnesota or the Non-Partisan League of North Dakota, both of which seized power from entrenched machines and enjoyed long tenure in office.

These new citizen-action groups bring to American politics the first new ideology of practical populism since the Democratic Party's great schism during the late 1960s and early 1970s over the Vietnam War. Many of them provide congenial settings for hard-hat conservatives and onetime antiwar activists to come together around such practical issues as whether there should be laws giving a worker the "right to know" what toxic substances he may be handling. Although some of the citizen-action leaders were once long-haired protesters in the shaggy 1960s, they have learned to be culturally respectful of mainstream working-class America. Spiro Agnew's fatal trilogy that supposedly described protest-era Democrats—"Acid, Amnesty, and Abortion"—are nowhere on the citizen-action agenda, but more authentically radical economic ideas are. Interestingly, the Democratic neo-conservative school has no more use for citizen action than they had for McGovernism.

The very existence of citizen-action groups pushes the Democratic Party in the direction of economic populism, restores the cultural and issue-related bonds among its disparate elements, and makes labor more a coalition partner and less an interest-group pariah. The citizen-action movement also helps to educate politically a new generation of activists too young to remember the Vietnam schism, and and it has helped to convert once elitist liberal positions on environmentalism and women's rights into populist causes that can restore alliances between wage-earning voters and liberal intellectuals.

In several cities where these groups are allied with neighborhood organizations, they are part of the same general phenomenon that has seen a rebirth of Democratic organizations around populist mayors—like the longtime Schaefer organization in Baltimore, George Latimer's regime in St. Paul, and Charles Royer's in Seattle, where a loose network of working-class neighborhood groups serves as the mayor's *de facto* machine. These mayors and their supporters have something of the same ideology, and often include the same activists.

Citizen-action movements are sometimes criticized from the left as being composed of white lower-middle-class homeowners rather than very poor people. But these are precisely the portions of the electorate that have been most seriously disaffected from the Democratic Party and from democratic, participatory politics. Moreover, the agendas put forward by these groups include the sort of class issues that can transcend racial ones; in practice the citizen-action groups are where one finds the least racist of white working-class voters.

These groups, to be sure, have their limitations. The fund-raising canvass, in some states, is accomplished with sleight of hand: an eager-sounding activist, apparently a volunteer, makes a pitch about his group's good work to keep cancer out of your drinking water, and comes away with a ten-dollar pledge and a "membership" from you. More often than not, this turns out to be a paid solicitor, and six or seven of your ten dollars goes for his commission. Often, you are nothing more than someone talked out of ten dollars. But still, the canvasses often do yield authentic supporters for a cause, and start the process of political mobilization. Many voters who first make contact with the citizen-action groups via the telephone or door-to-door canvass become genuine activists. And a wage-earning voter rallied to this set of issues eventually finds it harder and harder to accept the Republican view of the world, or to accept patriotism and the mythic free market as useful substitutes for practical economic benefits.

These groups do not yet have a full-blown populist agenda. The one subject that seems to work most powerfully is concern about toxic chemicals. It is in working-class neighborhoods where toxic chemicals are often found in the drinking water. In Pennsylvania, where several gritty cities now boil their water and deer hunters trip over mine tailings, environmentalism is anything but an elite issue. The evidence of dirty drinking water supports the populist argument that private corporate interests are not always the same as the general social interest and that regulation is often a good thing. But worries about industrial pollution, utility rates, and mortgage red-lining do not quite add up to a comprehensive program. Nor do they address the closer-to-home worries over jobs, housing, health, schooling, and adequate family income.

Nor have these groups yet mobilized anything like a majority of working-class voters, as the labor movement once did. Still, their sense of the world is congruent with the aim of restoring links between wage-earning voters and a progressive, majority Democratic Party. They are an encouraging start, as well as a fine laboratory. As the Democratic Party begins to put back together its historic coalition of the working middle class and the poor, citizen-action groups suggest the kind of ideology and programs that offer credibility as well as practical benefits. Bill Gapolinsky, let us recall, was sympathetic to Mondale; he just doubted that Mondale could deliver. As it happens, the Sherman Park section of Milwaukee is honeycombed with community organizations. To reconnect the Bill Gapolinskys of America to Democratic politics, the network of participatory institutions will have to become more effective, and national and local Democratic candidates must learn to find such voters on their map, both symbolically and practically.

While imagery and symbolism are useful in getting the voters' attention and suggesting uplifting themes, thematic politics has little staying power, especially for Democrats as the party of have-nots. Only a broad economic program that speaks to black and white, middle class, "new collar," blue collar, and poor alike can restore its weakened links with the electorate. And this is a task not primarily for electioneering, but for governing. Sooner or later, events will thrust a Democrat into the White House. And it is in office, not on the campaign trail, that Democrats will succeed in restoring the alliance between party and voter—or fail. The Democrats need to return to the inclusive vision that uses government to serve American people *as citizens* and not as members of special groups. Although America today is more affluent than it was during the New Deal, the vast majority of voters today are not independently wealthy; they live from paycheck to paycheck. Whatever their needs may be—job retraining, daycare, or home-ownership opportunity, rather than the work-relief and retirement benefits that loomed so large fifty years ago, it is still true that the government should help to provide them with economic opportunity and security—and could, if only it *would*. Without this governmental commitment, both the Democratic Party and our political system itself will continue to seem remote, if not irrelevant, to most citizens. And "symbolic" or "generational" politics alone are unlikely to reverse the decline.

CHAPTER FIVE

IDEOLOGY

I.

As I have suggested, the implicit Democratic Party ideology has been one of opportunity, inclusion, and the affirmative use of the government to temper the extremes of the market. But for almost a generation Democrats have largely failed to act on this ideology and to connect it to voters too young to remember the New Deal. Lately, the Democratic posture has been primarily reactive. The party has been influenced by intellectual currents that commend to the Democrats a philosophy of modified Republicanism. These currents—neo-conservatism, neo-liberalism, and *laissez-faire* economics—each in its own way severs the Democratic Party both from its principles and from the political logic that connects it to voters. In recent years, progressive populism has existed mainly as a party memory and a set of icons—a sentimental faith that once rallied voters to the Democratic side but that is now somehow ill-suited to the times.

In a climate of self-confident conservatism and Democratic confusion about goals and means, occasional Democratic invocations of old ideals and unmet social needs invited editorial derision and conservative cat calls about the same old failed stuff. The instinct to use public spending aggressively was short-circuited by both the federal budget deficit and by the bad memories of the 1970s. The populist impulse was undercut by the party's felt need to stand for economic growth, which in the 1980s seemed to mean being pro-business. And the impulse to alter Reagan's foreign-policy priorities was undermined by the presumption that Democrats had to be as tough-minded on national security as Republicans. In this climate, the "neo" movements attracted many Democrats.

These impulses are both defeatist and self-defeating. Though the specific needs have changed, the political logic of a mixed economy remains intact and persuasive, if often ignored. There *are* politically effective alternatives to neo-Republicanism that can rally disaffiliated voters, especially of the New Collar generation, to the Democratic side. But before turning to them, it is worth pausing to take a closer look at the siren call of the neo's.

Neo-conservatism began as primarily the reaction of several centrist Democratic intellectuals to what they viewed as the excesses of the 1960s. Often, it expressed disagreement with the prevailing Democratic foreign policy toward the Soviet Union and toward national liberation movements. Neo-liberalism mainly concerned domestic policies; it was a reaction by a small group of intellectuals to what they viewed as the excesses of big government and interest-group politics. Neo-conservatism was explicitly ideological; it kept its guns trained on the left. Neo-liberals were self-consciously iconoclastic and sprayed rounds on everyone. On some issues—the alleged "overload" of large entitlement programs like social security and their corrosive effect on the polity—the two agreed, and most economists cheered them on. Both movements were purely cerebral, elite movements of literary and public-policy intellectuals. When *The New Republic,* whose stance sometimes reveals elements of both philosophies, published a taxonomy of different types of "-con," the magazine received a hilarious letter from a French teacher, chortling at the unintended (and unprintable) added layer of meaning. Meanwhile, the average voter doesn't know (or care about) the difference between a "-con" and a hole in the ground.

It is ironic that leftist intellectuals should thus live to see a time in America when ideas truly mattered—and to have the ideas reflect mainly right-wing fervor. But the *neo-* movements have exercised substantial influence on both the reigning Republican Party and the opposition Democrats. As Peter Steinfels wrote in his 1979 study *The Neoconservatives,* "As experts in particular fields relevant to public policy, [intellectuals] work out the details of particular measures. But as traffickers in society's symbols and values, as keepers of its memories, as orchestrators of its spectacles and images, and . . . as shapers of general ideas, intellectuals are *legitimators."*

Intellectuals and professional economists newly infatuated with Adam Smith have been splendid legitimators of *laissez-faire* politics. For Republicans, neo-liberalism and neo-conservatism have created a muscular public philosophy, rather more coherent and marketable than the older forms of purely negative and self-serving business Republicanism. For Democrats, the *neo-* movements, each in its own way, created ideological static, making it harder for the party to remember its progressive, populist roots.

Like many of the Democrats' big campaign contributors, the *neo-* movements are philosophically coherent but politically androgynous, flying party banners as flags of convenience. While most neo-cons by the early 1980s had become partisan Republicans, they continued memberships in several purportedly Democratic organizations and continued to lecture Democrats on the dangers of "McGovernism" as a force that weakened the Democratic Party. They liked to contend that they hadn't deserted the Democratic Party, the party had deserted them. On the other hand, neo-liberals insisted, for the most part, that they were true modern Democrats, trying to save the party from its habit of pandering to interest groups.

While these two movements were ascendant, Democratic progressivism was all but ideologically silent. In the past decade there has been no vigorous institution, no prominent journal, no clear party *tendance* expounding a clear, modern form of Democratic progressivism, little vigorous advocacy of a mixed economy, and few loci of progressive scholarship. The party's own economic advisors have been coaxing it to move rightward. A handful of individuals did good and serious work, but unlike the neo's, they had only the most rudimentary networks and little bench strength. The debates of the period were, for the most part, between a resurgent, intellectually alert right, and a confused, hesitant center. To a Hoover Institution conference on the constitutional limitation of taxes, in 1981, for example, a few token liberals were invited, the Hoover Institution having graciously scanned the available field for candidates. But the liberal delegation was hesitant, eager to please, and a good fifteen years older, on average, than their conservative hosts.

Many fairly liberal Democrats agreed with just enough of the neo-con and neo-lib arguments to blunt the essential progressivism of the party's message and suffuse the party itself with self-doubts. Some government programs *were* a mess, weren't they? Democrats worried about proving that they were good managers, and as fiscally prudent as Republicans. Just as Republicans were discovering the political exhilaration of big deficits, and populist imagery, Democrats embraced the economics of Herbert Hoover—with Hoover-like political results. And on the foreign-policy front, the Democrats kept suffering the aftershocks of Vietnam. Détente with the Soviet Union was apparently something only Republicans could get away with. When the Soviet Union invaded Afghanistan in 1979, President Carter made the incredible statement that he hadn't realized how untrustworthy the Russians were. The party that had bungled the Vietnam war in the 1960s and had "lost China" in the 1940s had a new version of an old problem. Once again, it had to digress from its own economic high ground, to seem reliably and fiercely anti-Communist.

The Carter administration, the one Democratic administration of the past twenty years, was a battleground between Democratic hard-liners and soft-liners on this national security front, and between New Deal/Great Society progressives and neo-liberals and fiscal conservatives on the domestic front. Relative progressives dominated some areas of domestic policymaking, such as labor, housing, and welfare. Like other minimalist liberals, Carter could agree to spend money on social problems, but not to fundamentally challenge the free market. His chief economist, Charles Schultze, was among his most conservative appointees, and throughout the administration Schultze championed economic deregulation and waged a successful battle against any form of economic planning.

For the most part, the soft-liners had the upper hand in foreign policy, though a fierce tug-of-war persisted between national security advisor Zbigniew Brzezinski, the hawk, and Secretary of State Cyrus Vance. Despite the infighting, the Strategic Arms Limitation Treaty, Carter's effective pressures on dictatorships to restore human rights, and the Camp David initiative that led to a peace treaty between Israel and Egypt remained among Carter's most notable accomplishments. Carter's final two years, however, brought a shift. In the first two Carter budgets, military spending had been trimmed. The last period of the Carter administration saw a military buildup, a harder line against the Russians, drastic cuts in domestic spending, and more enthusiastic economic deregulation. Carter, who had begun as something of a hawk and something of a neo-liberal, skeptical of government programs, returned to his roots. He also returned to Georgia, repudiated by the voters.

II.

Neo-conservatism, as a movement, began two decades ago. It was initially a reaction on the part of once liberal intellectuals, many of them Jews, against the turbulent events of two decades—the 1930s of their youth and the 1960s of their middle age. In the 1930s, several of the neo-cons had been marxists—not just any sort of marxists but intricately accomplished theorists and members of purist Trotskyist splinter factions. It was a training ground in Talmudic disputation and sectarian infighting that would serve them well.

The end of ideology that seemed a permanent condition in the 1950s was very congenial to this group of intellectuals. Almost to a man, they came to find political passion of any variety dangerous. The fierce ideological battles between European left and right had, they reminded us, ended with Hitler. The German left had predicted, "After Hitler, us," but instead Hitler wiped out the humanistic left, along with six million Jews. The only leftists to succeed Hitler did so in Eastern Europe, and they were brutal Stalinists.

The younger radicals of the 1960s New Left seemed to have no appreciation of this history. As the Vietnam war worsened, and liberal protest turned radical, the New Left quickly evolved from being an idealistic, democratic-socialist resurgence into a hate-America carnival of nihilism—or so these intellectuals thought. The people who became neo-conservatives found the radicalism of the 1960s culturally repugnant. They found it appalling that good "liberal parents," as the title of Midge Decter's 1975 book had it, would spawn "radical children." As intellectuals and as Jews, the neo-conservatives had a profound respect for the values of tolerance and moderation, and for the American Constitution. The Federalist Papers and the Constitution itself, with their deep skepticism regarding human nature and their ingenious restraints on majoritarian whims, were perhaps the best gift Protestants ever gave Jews. The Founding Fathers' dour conception of human passions conformed all too well with the Jewish historical experience. The New Left (also substantially Jewish) had no respect for this, it seemed, no understanding that passion could become pogrom.

As they looked at domestic public policy, the neo-conservatives were disturbed at the tendency of interest-group liberalism to invite popular demands that the polity was incapable of fulfilling. As the civil rights movement mutated into a Black Power movement, they faulted establishment liberalism for helping to create the mutation. They were disturbed by the social engineering that created separatist, federally financed poverty-program machines, undercutting settled democratic and Democratic municipal politics, and seeding only "maximum feasible misunderstanding." They did not like federal affirmative action requirements for minorities, which seemed both an affront to true liberalism and uncomfortably close to the admission quotas that had once held back Jews. The Black Power rhetoric quickly connected to a Third World rhetoric of revolutionary nationalism, which in turn encouraged Palestinian nationalism. Two decades later, when the New Left was long defunct, the neo-conservatives could trace a direct line from the internationalist radicalism of the early SDS to the crude anti-Semitism of Louis Farrakhan.

In the 1960s, most of these intellectuals still considered themselves Democrats, and indeed, it was as Democrats that they
mounted much of their critique of the New Left. The romantic and
elitist marxism and, later, the cultural Dada of the New Left, they
contended, alienated the white working class and turned blacks into
cultural nationalists. Youthful white radicals were nothing but a
"new class" of pampered middle-class kids gone slumming, in cos-
tumes that the real working class would never accept. The New Left
kids, trained in the best universities to be society's governing class,
were class traitors. Even worse than the avowed marxists were the
antiwar activists who stayed in the Democratic Party—the "McGovernites." When the labor leader George Meany declined to endorse
McGovern's presidential candidacy, it seemed to confirm the neo-
conservative view that the New Left was wrecking the party's
chances to govern the country.

The neo-conservatives honed their rhetoric, their ideas, and
their ideology in journals, most notably *The Public Interest* and *Commentary. The Public Interest* was founded, in 1965, by Irving Kristol,
once a member of Max Shachtman's breakaway Trotskyist group,
later an anticommunist editor of *Encounter,* and by the sociologist
Daniel Bell. Others in the core group included the social scientists
Daniel Patrick Moynihan, Nathan Glazer, Seymour Martin Lipset,
Martin Diamond, Robert Nisbet, and Samuel Huntington. *The Public Interest* at first published mostly the work of moderate liberals
and former socialists, all of them first-class thinkers, including
James Q. Wilson, Edward C. Banfield, Ben Wattenberg, Paul Sea-
bury, and Walter Laqueur. Later it published more conservative
writers, like the supply-side economist Arthur Laffer, his best-
known publicist Jude Wanniski, Michael Malbin, and Martin Feldstein. By the mid-1980s, Bell had quit the masthead, Moynihan was
again sounding like a good partisan Democrat, but Kristol was a
Reagan Republican and the magazine was at the epicenter of a
network of conservative Republican ideology building.

The early *Public Interest* was born in ideological passage. In the
sixties, the original *Public Interest* group mostly still viewed themselves as liberals. What troubled the *Public Interest* fraternity was
that the well-intentioned antipoverty efforts of the Great Society
had so often gone astray. The magazine was a true symposium; it

ran articles by socialists as well as by incipient neo-conservatives. Its first issue featured articles on automation by the economists Robert Heilbroner and Robert Solow, both men to the left of center, as well as careful, moderate essays on why the poor are still with us by Nathan Glazer and Evelyn M. Burns. Glazer, foreshadowing the more full-blown neo-conservatism that would come later, observed, "In many of our great cities, the majority of those who seek public assistance are Negroes," and concluded his essay with the thought, "It is axiomatic to me that Negro organizations—whether they educate, train, advise, employ, organize, or what not, can potentially do far more with Negro clients than can governmental organizations."

Kristol had a keen eye for the implicit, real philosophical issue underlying an ostensibly technical policy debate, and for the social question that was not quite yet explicitly formulated but deserved to be. He had an editor's gift for helping academics to write cogent prose and, later on, polemic. Over the years, he published many seminal essays of social criticism, including more than a few by liberals. This was every intellectual's dream of a journal; only slowly did it mature into a coherent ideological organ, and by the time it did so a grateful Republican administration was there to use the product. It offered intellectuals real power. While most quarterlies dwelt in the wilderness of adversary culture, *The Public Interest* discovered the intellectual joys and financial security of celebrating what Irving Kristol called, with no fear of oxymoron, "business civilization."

As the *Public Interest* matured, its neo-conservatism became more explicit and more strident. By the late 1970s, it became possible to identify a generic *Public Interest* article, a sort of template that would shape any presenting social dilemma. The argument went like this: Well-intentioned reformers had tried to ameliorate a given situation, but the government intervention backfired. It served mainly the interests of the providers, those of the new class. It actually made the lot of its intended beneficiaries worse off. In the process, it overloaded the public sector, and undermined the authority of the polity itself. Moral: leave things alone. If you must meddle, make sure the means are privatized. Distrust the motives of new class intellectuals, except those who write for *The Public Interest*.

One such *Public Interest* article, which nicely displays the entire formula, is entitled "Educating the Handicapped: Reforming a Radical Law" (Winter 1982), by John C. Pittenger and Peter Kuriloff. The law in question is a 1972 Massachusetts statute known as Chapter 766, which became the model for a 1975 federal law that in effect gives handicapped children the right to "appropriate" public schooling. Though the federal entitlement is less sweeping, in Massachusetts this turns out to mean that local public schools have to "mainstream" moderately handicapped children if at all possible, and give them additional supports to enable them to stay in the public school. As a last resort, they can be sent to special schools with state, school district, and parent sharing the additional cost. As part of the compliance system, a school district or parent can request a special evaluation to be done to determine the child's special needs.

Pittenger and Kuriloff found this law to be a radical new entitlement whose costs far exceeded its projections. They argued that the law increased litigation, "exacerbated relations between the state and local schools," and that "professionals often coped with [paperwork] requirements in ways that had perverse effects"—for example, they "discouraged parents from seeking evaluations." Because wealthier parents were more sophisticated at using the law, the authors speculated that the effect was perhaps to "increase the disparity between the special education services available to children at opposite ends of the social ladder." They conceded that the law is an "enormous advance in civic sensitivity" to the handicapped, but ultimately they came down on the side of warning of fiscal ruin, lawsuits, disappointed handicapped teenagers finding a hostile job market, and loss of political support for the public schools.

In fact, in Massachusetts, the act has been widely conceded to have done immense good. It is admittedly one more complication for public-school principals, but hundreds of thousands of children who might have been shunted and stigmatized have stayed in public schools. Because of the required evaluation process, schools have become alert to the special needs of borderline children earlier in their schooling. Millions of other children have been, as the authors admitted they would be, sensitized. (Our five-year-old came home from kindergarten to announce that "David," badly crippled from cerebral palsy, is "just like anybody else, except he's handicapped." Today, David is still in public school, a much-loved fourth-grader.) All this has to represent a net gain for society. The alternative would have been elite special schools for a few well-to-do families and warehousing for the rest. To be sure, middle-class parents are more astute at taking advantage of Chapter 766 than poor ones, but there is less class bias in the system than there would be if parents of handicapped kids had to rely exclusively on private resources. Yes, the act has added one more claim upon state resources. But *The Public Interest,* in shedding crocodile tears for different educational constituencies competing with each other, never thinks to sacrifice a battleship instead.

Though the pose of the generic *Public Interest* article is one of neutral scholarship, it has an unmistakable bias against the public remedy. It goes to heroic lengths to find flaws, and it short-shrifts advantages. Benefits are conceded, mainly in polemical service of the credibility of the article's punch line, which invariably is that the program is a bad idea. (One archetypal, antiregulation polemic, "Richer Is Safer" by Aaron Wildavsky, made the ingenious claim that since in richer societies people generally have longer life expectancies, health, safety, and environmental regulation is actually bad for public health, because it retards growth and, hence, life.)

Another representative article, by the Harvard economist (and later Reagan's chief economic advisor) Martin Feldstein concerned the high costs of health care. This appeared in the summer of 1977, early in the Carter administration, at a time when national health insurance was back on Congress's agenda. In the decade since medicare had been enacted, hospital costs had soared, and now Congress was considering not only broadened coverage but tighter controls. Most analysts, especially those familiar with the institutional details of health policy in other nations, concluded that the medical inflation reflected the fact that the U.S. government had assumed responsibility for underwriting the service without having obtained the authority to regulate the costs. Feldstein, however, had a different explanation. Health costs had inflated in America, he calculated, because Americans were overinsured. They were overinsured, he wrote, because insurance premiums are tax-favored, which leads rational, profit-maximizing households to buy more insurance than they really "need." Rather than more regulation, he advocated that the solution was to get rid of the tax favoritism for insurance premiums.

This analysis largely ignored not only the structural imperfections of medicaid and medicare and their political genesis, but also their unequal class impact. While some families conceivably overinsure themselves because of tax angles, tens of millions of people had no insurance at all. But articles like this posited atomized individuals functioning like Adam Smith monads and deflected attention from structural analyses and regulatory solutions.

The other major neo-conservative organ, *Commentary,* was altogether different in tone. Whereas *The Public Interest* strove to sound reasonable, *Commentary* delighted in polemic and invective. It had begun in 1946 as a moderately liberal journal published by the American Jewish Committee. When its editor, Norman Podhoretz, was reborn in the 1960s as a neo-conservative, so was the magazine. Whereas *The Public Interest* specialized in genteel debunking of the logic of social entitlement, *Commentary* went after misguided individuals. *Washington Post* writer Sidney Blumenthal, writing about Ronald Reagan's counterestablishment, was struck by how much its sectarian style resembled that of the Old Left. "Shadow leftists," he called the neo-conservatives: "In many important respects, neo-conservatism is the political culture of the Old Left preserved in aspic." Where once as marxists they fiercely attacked liberals, now they attacked them from the conservative side.

By the 1980s, there were a dozen more such journals—four published by the American Enterprise Institute alone, plus the Heritage Foundation's *Policy Review,* a journal on foreign policy (*The National Interest*) financed by the Olin Foundation, a religious journal (*This World*), and one on the arts (*The New Criterion*). It was a heady time for aspiring neo-conservative social critics. Ideologically conservative foundations were raising tens of millions of dollars from business groups. There were plenty of grants, plenty of mentors, plenty of publication outlets. A graduate student could submit a manuscript to Irving Kristol, be certified as the latest neo-conservative find, have the article distilled on *The Wall Street Journal*'s editorial page, be quoted in the Mobil Corporation's op-ed ads, appear before sympathetic congressmen, do a stint in a think-tank, and later go to work in the Reagan administration.

For conservatives, *The Public Interest, Commentary,* and the later imitations represented a stunning advance over the *National Review* of the 1950s and 1960s. The older conservatism of William F. Buckley and James Burnham was in the musty tradition of grand theory, highly principled and several feet off the ground. "Policy" was something mundane, and suspiciously liberal. The *National Review* could offer a conservative good sound philosophical grounds for opposing, say, medicare, but it had little to contribute to the nuances of a medicare legislative battle. The newer conservative journals did not debate first principles; they knew what their principles were and spent their energy linking policy expertise, political maneuver, and ideological marketing.

And despite the conservatives' sincere insistence that they were the beleaguered cultural minority, no such energy, resources, or conviction appeared on the liberal left. In a funny way, despite its marxian lineage, the neo-con pose was the converse of Lenin's. Lenin represented a tiny minority within a minority, but he called his faction the Bolsheviks, meaning "majority." Long after they were being toasted at the White House and their ideas were influencing Abe Rosenthal's *New York Times* as well as Sun Myung Moon's *Washington Times,* Podhoretz and Kristol kept modestly insisting that they were a tiny group surrounded by a large, potent, hostile liberal establishment. Lenin would have applauded the stratagem.

If the neo-conservatives were the 1930s preserved in aspic, the aspic was the adversary culture of the 1960s. Everywhere they kept seeing ghosts of George McGovern. Joshua Muravchik, writing in *Commentary,* claimed that the real failure of Mondale's campaign in 1984 had been that it was dominated by McGovernites. This analysis must have been amusing to the party's centrist technicians and their financial backers, who had made sure that Mondale took a hard line on defense, on budget balancing, and that he eschewed any domestic economic initiatives requiring substantial public expenditure. The most emphatic interest-group heresy that Mondale indulged in was the same one commended by Muravchik's brand of neo-conservatism—an intimate alliance with the old guard of the

AFL-CIO. Elliott Abrams, a former aide to Democratic Senators Henry Jackson and Pat Moynihan, the son-in-law of Norman Podhoretz, and an armchair general in the Contra war, epitomizes the neo-conservative tendency to see the world in terms of the cultural battleground of the 1960s. His former Harvard roommate, Harvard Professor Steven Kelman, another veteran of the 1960s sectarian wars, said of Abrams's generation of neo-conservatives, "They're still acting as if SDS was about to take over the United States."

Had the neo-conservatives simply cashed in their former party identify—"liquidated their Democratic assets when the bidding price was high," as Blumenthal wrote—that would have been windfall enough for the right. But a great many kept a foot in the Democratic Party. The Coalition for a Democratic Majority, for example, was founded as a reaction against the short-lived McCarthy-McGovern dominance over the institutional Democratic Party. The CDM people were, characteristically, Democrats who ended up as "Democrats for Nixon" or "Democrats for Reagan." Most of the founding group had been associated with Senator Henry M. (Scoop) Jackson; after Jackson's brief 1976 run for the Democratic nomination failed, many went on to support Reagan. The closest thing to the original CDM manifesto was a 1970 book by Richard Scammon and Ben Wattenberg, *The Real Majority.* Scammon and Wattenberg's basic point, in this wide-ranging sweep of the electoral scene, was that "Americans have begun casting their ballots along the lines of issues relatively new to the American scene. For several decades Americans have voted basically along the lines of bread-and-butter economic issues. Now, in addition to the older, still potent economic concerns, Americans are apparently beginning to array themselves along the axes of certain social situations as well. These situations have been described variously as law and order, backlash, antiyouth, malaise, change, or alienation. These situations, we believe, constitute a new and potent political issue. We call it the Social Issue."

For Wattenberg, a "Scoop Jackson Democrat," the social issue was worrisome because it drove wage-earning Democrats into the arms of right-wing populists like George Wallace and eventually into the arms of Republicans. As a Democrat, Wattenberg lamented the same phenomenon that had led Republican strategist Kevin Phillips to celebrate an "emerging Republican majority" in his 1969 book of that title. It was the same set of electoral dynamics that had troubled James Q. Wilson when he noticed the distance that separated reform Democratic clubs from the base voters. Elite views on social reform, "limousine liberalism," and foreign-policy pacifism left out the white working class. The Roosevelt coalition, Scammon and Wattenberg wrote, was made up of "tens of millions of ordinary Americans who felt commonly about certain issues— mostly economic issues—and voted for the man who acted in their interest." They counseled Democrats, *"Capitalize on economic issues* and even expand on them: Be for a higher minimum wage, higher social security benefits, expanded Medicare for children ('Kid-dicare') and eventually for the entire population; be anti-inflation, antirecession (standard out-party economic themes); be for the little guy, black and white. Say, 'It's time to get America moving again.'" [italics in the original]

This insight was exactly right. But Wattenberg went on to make the contradictory argument that Democrats had to find the "center ground in the attitudinal battlefield." And in his later lobbying work as head of the tiny and misnamed Coalition for a Democratic Majority (CDM), he positioned himself on the weak side of his own insight. Instead of rebuilding a Democratic majority by emphasizing the economic populism that had built the Roosevelt coalition, Wattenberg promoted cultural and foreign-policy conservatism and largely ignored working-class economic issues. This was generally true of the entire crowd. The anti-McGovern Democrats became so obsessed with foreign policy and social issues that they abandoned the economics of the little guy entirely. Muravchik's broadside, for example, had nothing at all to say about working-class economic issues, except to ritually support the labor movement in a tactical marriage of convenience with the AFL-CIO's generally hawkish foreign policy. CDM literature and advocacy have almost exclusively concerned themselves with foreign and military policy. Its impressive letterhead group of Democrats signed pamphlets and lobbied for a hard-line foreign policy, and had nothing to say on domestic economic and social questions.

By the eve of Reagan's election, the original neo-conservative movement had split along partisan lines. A few people who genuinely worried that social and foreign-policy divisions were bad for the Democratic Party went back to emphasizing economic populism and remained, essentially, progressive Democrats. Among these were the social scientists William Schneider, Seymour Martin Lipset, and Daniel Bell, and Senator Daniel Patrick Moynihan. Schneider, who had once served on Moynihan's Senate staff, described the competition for Moynihan's ear as one between "the left-wing Catholics against the right-wing Jews." The liberal Catholics advising Moynihan, led by Timothy Russert, later an aide to Mario Cuomo, encouraged him to go left on domestic economic issues. The neo-conservative Jews, led by Elliott Abrams, pressed Moynihan to be a foreign-policy conservative. With the Republican right controlling the Senate, Moynihan re-emerged as a Great Society Democrat, much to the disappointment of the neo-conservatives. A few neo-conservatives, like Penn Kemble and Ben Wattenberg, continued to fight a rearguard action within the Democratic Party, though exclusively on foreign-policy issues. But most of the small band became *de facto* or *de jure* Republicans: Jeane Kirkpatrick became Reagan's UN Ambassador; Max Kampleman became his chief arms negotiator; Elliott Abrams became Assistant Secretary of State. The insight that Democrats had better downplay cultural radicalism the better to spotlight economic populism got lost altogether.

Closely allied with CDM, with heavily overlapping leadership and membership, is a group called Social Democrats, USA—or SDUSA. An officer of both groups is Penn Kemble, vice-chair of SDUSA and chair of the executive committee of CDM. SDUSA (pronounced like the word "seducer" in a Woody Allen accent) epitomizes Blumenthal's observation that the neo-conservative right behaves just like the Old Left: It is best described as a cell, having begun as a splinter of a splinter—a minority faction of Max Shachtman's breakaway Trotskyists—which careened rightward while most of the rest of the Shachtman group reaffiliated with Michael Harrington as democratic socialists in the Norman Thomas tradition. For all intents and purposes, CDM and SDUSA are the same people, a few dozen Washington and New York activists, most of whom have come to recognize that their true home is in the Republican Party. But SDUSA and CDM continue to maintain the pose that they are good partisan Democrats. As such, they do real damage.

Social Democrats, USA, took a very hard line on Vietnam and on other foreign-policy questions. Several of their leaders subsequently took jobs in the Reagan administration. Carl Gershman, a leader of the group, became head of the Reagan administration's Endowment for Democracy. Gershman, in turn, funded others from the SDUSA group, including Penn Kemble, who organized a lobby for the Nicaraguan Contras called ProDemCa, and his sister Eugenia Kemble, who runs a right-wing labor/foreign-policy institute. Chris Gersten, also part of the SDUSA group, now heads the National Jewish Coalition, the Jewish affiliate of the Republican National Committee. Linda Chavez, who is married to Gersten, is another SDUSA product who became a full-fledged Reagan Republican, holding a U.S. Civil Rights Commission appointment, a White House public liaison post, and finally running for the U.S. Senate from Maryland in 1986. When the Endowment for Democracy paid for three "social democrats" to attend the meeting of the Socialist International (which is made up of genuinely social democratic parties like the British Labor Party, the French Socialist Party, and the West German SPD), the American group turned out to be Sidney Hook, a genuine albeit conservative social democrat, Midge Decter, and former Republican Treasury Secretary William Simon!

SDUSA retains influence in some segments of the AFL-CIO, notably via foreign policy, since many labor leaders continue to pursue a hard line on the Cold War. CDM has invested great energy in cultivating House Armed Services Committee Chairman Congressman Les Aspin, applauding his gradual transformation into a national security hawk. Jay Winik, on Aspin's staff, is CDM's former executive director. And when the Democratic Policy Commission created a foreign-policy task force chaired by Congressman Stephen Solarz of New York, pressure by CDM president Peter Rosenblatt, a panel member, had the effect of forcing "compromise" language representing views of a minority on the task force, toning down criticism of the Administration and muting an attack on U.S. aid to the Nicaraguan Contras. This happened in July 1986, on the eve of the Iran-Contra scandal, at a time when Democratic National

Committee polls were showing that only 15 percent of Democrats favored aid to the Nicaraguan Contras.

Apart from the substantive issue of whether Democrats ought to espouse a hard line or a soft one on the Nicaragua question, people who are basically partisan Republicans have no business advising the Democratic Party. The Republican National Committee is far too astute to permit this sort of Trojan Horse within its walls. But as a broad, open, coalition party, the Democrats have no credentials committee, nobody to remind the Coalition for a Democratic Majority that several of their members are across the street working for Reagan and are therefore unwelcome. CDM and SDUSA epitomize the neo-conservative conception of "new class" intellectuals. They have no mass membership, no large following among Democratic legislators, and consistently find themselves on the losing side of issues among the Democratic electorate.

III.

Peter Steinfels concluded his 1979 study *The Neoconservatives* with the observation: "The great danger posed by and to neoconservatism is that it will become nothing more than the legitimating and lubricating ideology of an oligarchic America where essential decisions are made by corporate elites, where great inequalities are rationalized by straitened circumstances and a system of meritocratic hierarchy, and where democracy becomes an occasional, ritualistic gesture. Whether neoconservatism will end up by playing this sinister and unhappy role, or whether it will end as a permanent, creative and constructive element in American politics, is only partially in the hands of the neoconservatives themselves. It will also be determined by the vigor, intelligence, and dedication of their critics and opponents."

One might have expected the neo-conservative challenge to engender an equally vigorous response from progressive intellectuals. But the most visible countermovement that arose to meet the challenge was neo-liberalism. The core premise of neo-liberalism is that the alliance between populist goals, public-sector means, and animated voters is fatally flawed. Where neo-conservatism is politically strategic to the point of being Machiavellian, neo-liberalism is often antipolitical. Whereas neo-conservatism is explicitly ideological, neo-liberalism is wishfully post-ideological. Its conception of the political process is Rousseauist. All politicians should somehow look to a higher common good and not dirty their hands in the stuff of politics, namely delivering benefits to the electorate. Like neo-conservatism, neo-liberalism has at its epicenter a journal, the *Washington Monthly*. The editor of that journal is Charles Peters, a rumpled, cranky, and endearing West Virginian, once an official of John Kennedy's Peace Corps, and a man who insists he is still a liberal. Like *The Public Interest,* the *Washington Monthly*, now in its twentieth year, is a superbly edited product. Its style is dry irreverence, which it usually earns by careful, often lethal reporting. It has a real flair for making public-policy issues entertaining without trivializing them in the process; it is the kind of magazine you pick up and read cover to cover. Peters, almost singlehandedly, has trained many of the most thoughtful political journalists of this generation, talented magazine writers now in their thirties and early forties who share with him a skepticism about the public sector, an idealistic disdain for interest groups, and a studied denial of the relationship between class and political power.

James Fallows and Nicholas Lemann (now at *The Atlantic*); Michael Kinsley (at the *New Republic*); Joseph Nocera (at the *New England Monthly*); Walter Shapiro (at *Time*); Jonathan Alter, Gregg Easterbrook, Mickey Kaus, and Timothy Noah (at *Newsweek*); and Arthur Levine and David Ignatius of *The Washington Post* all learned their craft from Peters. Peters also has a soft spot for Ralph Nader and occasionally publishes populist alumni of the Nader network such as Jonathan Rowe, Mark Green, and Robert McIntyre.

In the *Washington Monthly* view of the world, public and private bureaucracies reign. Interest groups are seen as perils, whether those representing Head Start children or the Fortune 500. The *Washington Monthly* can be equally harsh on domestic social programs, trade unions, big businesses, and the armed forces. It can be dewy-eyed about entrepreneurship. Its view of interest-group politics is Pogo's—we have met the enemy and he is us. Overall, neo-liberals tend to be deeply idealistic about the Republic and deeply cynical about actual political institutions. In the first paragraph of his "Neoliberal's Manifesto," published in 1983, Peters declared, "We still believe in liberty and justice and a fair chance for all, in mercy for the afflicted and help for the down and out. But we no longer automatically favor big unions or oppose the military and big business. Indeed, in our search for solutions that work, we have come to distrust all automatic responses, liberal or conservative."

During and after the Carter administration, a period of liberal malaise, this view had immense appeal, for it seemed to offer liberals a certified way of remaining true to their liberalism while jettisoning unfashionable baggage—big government, big unions—thereby preempting some conservative appeal. It seemed to appropriate the nonideological high ground of the New Deal and the New Frontier—Roosevelt's famous pragmatism and Kennedy's idealism. Implicitly it suggested that solutions to social and political problems had to be technical. If only politicians were as disinterested and virtuous as the *Washington Monthly,* good policies would prevail and grateful voters would keep the selfless politicians who advocated them in office.

Though the *Monthly* had only the most high-minded and genuinely liberal motives, its effect was often to reinforce the impulse to apologize for the Democratic Party's populist roots. A very good illustration of the neo-liberal disdain for politics can be seen in its view of social security. As Peters put it, "What we did with social security was we bribed the middle and upper classes to support a system that was needed for the poor . . . we're wasting tremendous amounts of money on people who don't need it. It has never been made clear to the public that vast numbers of the affluent are getting these programs: social security, veterans' pensions, unemployment compensation." James Fallows made a similar argument in an *Atlantic* article, "Entitlements," concluding, "The people who really *need* help need more than they are now getting. If they are to have it, other people must have less."

Peters, whose fondness for anecdotal evidence rivals even Reagan's, loves to point to his Aunt Alice, "who is rich and who uses her social security to go to Europe in the summer. Or the fellow who uses his unemployment compensation to go to Florida . . ."

In general, the view is that social programs generally should be means-tested, that is, restricted to the certifiably needy, so as to get the resources more efficiently to the people who genuinely deserve them.

There are both empirical and political fallacies in this view of social security and of social programs generally. First of all, citizen-entitlement programs like social security, medicare, unemployment compensation, and veterans' pensions were never conceived as programs "for the poor." They were intended as benefits for the broad, wage-earning class. Although an argument can be made, and often is, that the first generation to collect social security benefits got a windfall, all wage-earning Americans generally view social security as an earned right, not as welfare. The genius of social security is that it manages to redistribute a great deal of money to the poor and near poor precisely by putting them in the same program with the middle class. A low-wage worker gets a far higher return on his social security payroll taxes than a high-wage worker; as a result, the pensioner class exists in a kind of welfare-state afterlife, where income is more substantially equalized than during the working years.

Although there are undoubtedly a number of "Aunt Alices" going to Europe on their social security pensions, the vast bulk of social security money goes to people who depend on it for a minimally decent standard of living. Only one elderly household in ten makes enough income ($25,000 for a single, $32,000 for a couple) to pay tax on benefits. Statistically, social security redistributes four times as much income as all other explicitly redistributive programs combined. As a report by the Villers Foundation recently pointed out, there are still more elderly poor, proportionally (15.2 percent), than any other age group, and for elderly households with incomes between $10,000 and $20,000, social security contributes fully 46 percent of what comes in. Without it, 47.6 percent of the elderly would be poor.

In a democratic polity that also happens to be a highly unequal market economy, there is immense civic value to treating middle-class and poor people alike. A common social security program, or medical care program, or public school program, helps to create the kind of cohesion that Europe's social democrats like to call "social solidarity"—a sense that basic humanity and citizenship in the political community require equal treatment in at least some areas of economic life. And by doing so it also creates a reliable constituency for the Democratic Party. America's older voters who support Democrats and social spending do not do so because they have suddenly gone soft in the head as they approach retirement age, or because it is normal for people to become more liberal as they grow older. They do so because the Democratic Party upholds a functioning social contract that meets real human needs. To view this social solidarity and political compact as merely "bribing the middle and upper classes" is to read one's own cynicism into an admirable policy, and to miss the point utterly.

In theory, targeting social spending to the certified poor would make for a more efficient as well as a more equitable welfare state. This is a perennial conservative argument for means-testing. But liberals, neo- or otherwise, should know better than to advocate means-tested social programs. The practical problem when programs are only for the poor is that the broad constituent support for them evaporates, and then the task of certifying need leads to invasive procedures and other indignities, and the quality of the programs erodes. The most tested axiom of social policy is that "programs limited to the poor are poor programs." Compare medicare, which is for the middle class, with medicaid, which is for the needy. Medicaid has less of a political constituency, its reimbursement schedules are lower, and many doctors refuse to participate in it. There is a further "notch" problem, in that a family whose income is slightly too high for the medicaid limits can suddenly find itself with no health insurance at all. This notch problem is entirely manmade, an artificial consequence of having no comprehensive health insurance program for everyone.

The fallacy of the means-testing solution emerges even more clearly when one considers America's most venerable, expensive, and universalistic social program—public education. It would save a lot of money to limit public schools to the poor, or to charge middle-class parents tuition based on their income. But the broad constituency for public schools would vanish overnight. It is certainly fair to debate the limits of social entitlement: in how many areas, such as health, education, and retirement benefits, do we as a society want to offer citizenship entitlements on the basis of need, and at what level? But to means-test the benefits is to defeat the programmatic logic, the social logic, and the political logic.

Many neo-liberals use the term "means-test" imprecisely. The term normally means to determine eligibility for a program that has been limited to people of a certain income. A means-tested program like Aid to Families with Dependent Children is the opposite of a universal citizen entitlement like public education or medicare. Some neo-liberals, like former Arizona Governor Bruce Babbitt, say they favor a "universal means test" for all social spending. When pressed, however, he explains that he wants that only as an ideal and in practice would settle for *taxing* benefits. Taxing social benefits, in general, is a good idea, because it injects an element of payment according to need without creating two classes of program and two classes of beneficiary. We sensibly adopted part of this approach when we began to require retired people to pay taxes on half of their social security benefits if their total earnings exceeded $25,000 annually. But this should not be confused with means testing, which is something else entirely.

Another neo-liberal variation on the social security critique is the general claim that the old are living too well at the expense of the young, largely because of the government's tax and income-transfer policies. As Philip Longman wrote in a *Washington Monthly* article entitled "Taking America to the Cleaners," "If ever there were a generation that had reason to take to the streets, it was this one." Longman subsequently became research director of a group called AGE—Americans for Generational Equity, dedicated to the proposition that the welfare state which serves the old (through social security and medicare) must be pruned back to reduce the tax burdens on the young. While it is indisputable that the real living standards of young families have declined since 1973, and that the income distribution among working-age people has become significantly more unequal, it seems odd to choose as the target the one demographic group where income equality has improved (thanks to social spending). The primary engine of inequality among the young—and old—is market-determined income and wealth, not the welfare state. Young people are hurting because wages have not kept pace with living costs. The tax system is admittedly not nearly so redistributive as it should be, but this is hardly an issue of age equity. Yet AGE and the neo-liberal critics of "generational inequality" seem oddly oblivious to the inequalities engendered by the market, and are largely silent on the issue of redistribution *within* the working-age population, which has much more extreme chasms of wealth and poverty. Seemingly, an egalitarian would want to redistribute from rich to poor, whether working age *or* elderly. A cynic might conclude that the "generational equity" lobby were using the issue as a stalking horse for a more general attack on the welfare state itself.

Neo-liberals disdain the available instruments of twentieth-century liberal politics—namely, government programs that benefit a broad range of citizens—yet they can wax sentimental about the politics of a bygone era. A favorite neo-liberal nostrum is to propose abolishing the civil service and bring back raw patronage. It is hard to imagine how firing most of the 3 million federal employees every time the White House changed hands would create a more efficient and responsible public sector, but Peters is convinced that it would.

By the same token, the neo-liberal movement can be oddly misty-eyed about the values of mandated social cohesion. The *Monthly* cherishes milieus that mix social classes. The Kennedy Peace Corps is Peters's alma mater. Better public education is a *Washington Monthly* favorite, as is compulsory national service. (I second both objectives.) Yet national service, in practice, would surely present the same sort of bureaucratic target that the *Monthly* is so quick to lambaste when the government program is actual rather than hypothetical. Of course, it is proper for defenders of the public sector to demand the highest standards and the greatest democratic accountability in public programs, and to criticize the corruption of such programs; but the *Monthly* often crosses over the line into ritual ridicule of the public sector itself, its interest groups, careerists, and inevitable profiteers. One wonders how such a public sector could be entrusted to operate compulsory national service?

A second favorite neo-liberal target is the labor movement. In 1983, two broadsides against trade unions appeared back to back, in the May *Atlantic Monthly* and the June *Harpers*. Gregg Easterbrook's "Voting for Unemployment" (in the *Atlantic*) pointed out that employed union workers with seniority, who usually make up a majority in the bargaining units, have a vested interest in demanding raises even when the result is fewer jobs for others. During the long period when American industry was insulated from global bargaining, unions were the junior partners in the oligopoly, and industry-wide "pattern bargaining," with regular raises, became the rule. Eventually, many union workers priced themselves and their junior coworkers out of jobs. "Unions have come full circle," he wrote. "Conceived and developed as a voice for the average worker—and winning many important social victories on the average worker's behalf—they now represent an elite of workers who are highly paid and elaborately protected." Easterbrook made the usual criticism of "adversarial" labor-management relations and concluded that worker flexibility, cooperation with management, wage restraint, and profit sharing would be far better for workers, unions, and American industry.

The analysis is flawless as far as it goes, but it doesn't go nearly far enough. For nearly a decade now, many unions have attempted precisely the sort of social bargain Easterbrook commends, yet the power balance between management and labor is currently so lopsided that the innovative unions are being swept aside right along with the adversarial ones. If industry would offer labor a bargain whereby the workers traded wage restraint and flexibility for real job security and recognition of the union's right to exist, labor would break out the champagne. But nobody is proposing such a bargain. And Easterbrook neglects to consider the useful function unions fulfill in an industrial economy: as a democratic counterweight to organized business and as organizations that help form the constituency for a progressive political party. It is precisely in nations where organized labor's very existence is not challenged that unions can be the restrained and responsible industrial citizens that Easterbrook wants them to be.

Mickey Kaus's piece, "The Trouble with Unions," in *Harpers,* is cruder. Kaus goes through some of the same arguments, throwing in some good featherbedding horror stories, and contends, with Milton Friedman, that gains by unions must necessarily come out of the pockets of even worse-off, unorganized workers. "For every Norma Rae breathing cotton dust fumes, there is . . . a union like the UAW, whose workers make far above the national median, standing in the way of the more efficient production methods that might revitalize its industry." Seniority systems, according to Kaus, create "an incentive to work only well enough not to get fired." He blames rigid work rules on unions, although labor historians have suggested that work rules were more often a management response to labor power.

Kaus, like Easterbrook, has a *deus ex machina* solution to the problems he describes—worker ownership. He has no idea, politically, how we might get from a situation like the present day, where corporations ruthlessly break the most moderate of unions, to one where workers come to own the means of production; but he suspects that such a reform will require breaking the AFL-CIO's stranglehold on the Democratic Party. As in so many other neoliberal essays, the assumption is that the power of argument is the only power that matters, and technical insights will set the world to right. There is no appreciation whatever for the truth that unions, with all their blemishes, have been the principal engine of most progressive legislation enacted since World War II and that the unions' recent parochialism is a symptom of labor's weakness, not its strength.

In a similar vein, Professor Martin Weitzman of MIT, much esteemed in neo-liberal circles, thinks he has a solution to the perennial "trade-off" between inflation and unemployment. Weitzman contends that the habit in market economies of paying some workers "too much" while other workers are left unemployed is not an inevitable capitalist flaw, but the result of the particular system we have for compensating workers, namely fixed wages. In his book, *The Share Economy,* Weitzman makes a technically ingenious argument that if industry shifted to a system of flexible compensation, where a substantial portion of the workers' pay packet depended on the profitability of the firm, not only would there appear the oft-remarked productivity benefits of profit sharing, but the economy as a whole would tend to stay closer to full employment without inflationary pressures. *The New York Times* hailed this proposal as the best new economic idea since Keynes. But in this proposal for a whole new system of labor compensation that has workers assuming more of the risks of entrepreneurship, Weitzman has nothing to say about how or even whether the control of corporate governance should be altered. In this respect, the proposal is pure neo-liberalism; its emphasis is on technicalities and it fails to consider the political aspects.

Not just labor unions but interest groups in general are a neo-liberal *bête noire.* Interest-group politics, Peters has written, "has divided the nation and produced a politics of selfishness that has governed the country for more than a decade. . . . I think the only possible salvation for this republic is a citizenry that is determined to inform itself on a broad range of important issues—and that will vote for an elected official on the basis of his or her stand on *all* the issues. We now have a Congress that is petrified of offending any single passionate group—be they private boat owners or banks—and that won't change until the members know we're not going to throw them out of office on any basis other than overall performance."

This view has an attractive idealism about it. The election of 1984 seemed to confirm Peters's darkest fears, both for the democracy and for the Democratic Party. Walter Mondale, who appealed little to the party's voting base, nonetheless captured the nomination by creating a "politics of inevitability" among Washington insiders— the interest groups. The premier interest group, big labor, failed even to deliver its own voters in the important New Hampshire primary, where the labor rank and file voted for Gary Hart. Mondale was widely faulted for seeing voters only as members of organized groups, and labor for being the supreme case of a Democratic special-interest group. When the AFL-CIO made the tactical blunder of treating Mondale as a wholly owned subsidiary, Hart, who has an exemplary pro-labor voting record, began talking about Mondale as the candidate of the special interests. And after the 1984 election many Democrats took pains to distance themselves from the labor movement.

The phrase "interest-group liberalism" comes from an influential 1969 book by the political scientist Theodore Lowi, *The End of Liberalism.* Lowi's book attacked both interest-group politics and the prevailing political-science view that "pluralism" was something to be celebrated as essential to democracy. Lowi believed, with Key, Schattschneider, and Burnham, that parties were better means of achieving democratic ends than pressure groups. He warned that just as Adam Smith's invisible hand did not always produce the best outcome in the economy, the sum total of interest-group maneuvering did not necessarily lead to the fairest political outcome, since some interest groups were more powerful than others. He observed that the liberal political formula of doling out benefits to organized constituency groups was already coming a cropper, which it was. Although Lowi, like Peters, articulated an idealistic-sounding Rousseauist form of democracy, one read his book in vain looking for another form of liberalism. Neither man has offered an alternative practical politics that excludes non-elite interest groups altogether.

What we have here, on closer examination, is an old demon, the False Dichotomy. The most effective Democratic presidents have managed both to deliver tangible benefits to interest groups of the non-elite, *and* to appeal to all voters as American citizens. FDR was president of all the people, except for a few Republican royalists, but that didn't prevent him from providing extensive benefits via his alphabet soup of New Deal agencies. Indeed, it was the concrete benefits that gave the larger symbolic affiliation meaning. The most potent programs, like social security, were not for interest groups, but for everyone. Likewise, John Kennedy could appeal to all voters as Americans, but he recommended specific programs for the party base. Democrats, surely, ought to be able to appeal to working-class voters in general without savaging the labor movement!

The other unpardonable fallacy in the neo-liberal logic is its failure to recognize, with Lowi, that all interest groups are not created equal. How can one morally or politically equate lobbies representing the Business Roundtable and the black right to vote? Irving Howe, editor of *Dissent,* has written:

There is a long tradition in this country to which the rhetoric of "special interests" is related. It is the tradition of an elite gentry, a self-ordained patrician class, which supposes itself to be above "mere" material needs. This political tradition claims to care only about higher-minded, moral concerns; it presents itself as the advocate of "higher" values. I think such claims are delusional. . . .

Isn't there, however, a discernible general or national interest, transcending the interests of discrete social groups? On some matters (clean air, safety rules at work, national security, and so on) there no doubt is. But the neoliberals have been a bit too enchanted with the notion of a general interest transcending the limited interests of various social groups. Neoliberals tend to speak of special interests as if there were no crucial moral and social distinctions to be made among them; as if it weren't clearly in the common good to further some and oppose others.

Among the intellectually subtlest of the neo-liberal journalists is James Fallows. Fallows writes with great precision and refinement, invariably basing his findings on careful research. With no special background in military affairs, he nonetheless boned up on defense procurement and produced one of the best books on the logic of Pentagon wastefulness. When he gets to domestic social questions, however, Fallows's message is ambiguous. In an article entitled "America's Changing Economic Landscape," Fallows reminds us of the inevitability of industrial change. Once, three-quarters of American workers were farmers. Whole industries, like cooperage and buggy-whip manufacturing, have disappeared; yet after a period of disruption many of the workers displaced from them ended up better off. Fallows sets his scene in a gritty Chicago neighborhood where industrial workers are struggling to save their jobs. His message is that history has probably doomed these people. He mentions a much-reviled Carter administration document, *Urban America in the Eighties,* which concluded that some older cities were probably beyond revitalization, and that instead of fighting natural economic forces public policy should go with the flow. Fallows also quotes, approvingly, studies that "nearly unanimously conclude that people who pull up stakes fare better than people who stay behind." A few paragraphs sympathize in a faintly patronizing manner with people who have a sentimental attachment to place ("How can you go to Texas when Aunt Maria's seventieth birthday is coming up?"), but he concludes by quoting the author of the Carter study, who finds it ironic that people whose own forebears were recent immigrants have an irrational attachment to old neighborhoods and dying industries. As policy recommendation, Fallows in passing commends a "people not places" approach of subsidizing transitions to facilitate mobility.

The trouble with this kind of argument, like Easterbrook's, is that it stops just where it should begin. Of course industrial change is inevitable. The real political issue is who benefits, who suffers, and how should society lubricate the change? What would a policy of "people, not places" really mean? To what extent should we let the market do the job, and to what extent should society intervene? To what extent must we fight to assert the principle that the market by itself can't do the job humanely? Who are the constituents for such policies? What do they cost? The societies that have paid the most attention to facilitating industrial change are social democratic ones, with strong unions, vigorous working-class voters, and an ideological approbation for such intervention. But alas, the article has no sequel. Fallows is more intent on showing how misguided are those whose industrial jobs cause them to resist change than he is on thinking through what to do about it.

This essay suggests what is lacking in neo-liberalism as a public philosophy. Neo-liberals make provocative social critics, but they are unreliable as ideological stewards of the Democratic Party. Fallows, despite his humane disclaimers, comes perilously close to saying that if the industrial workers in Chicago's old neighborhoods choose to go down with the ship, it's their own fault. As Plunkitt of Tammany Hall, or for that matter Harry Hopkins, might have reminded Fallows, these are good Democratic voters you're talking about, son. It's one thing for a new-class intellectual to write such people off; it's quite another to commend this view as a philosophy for the Democratic Party. The carefully qualified tone notwithstanding, there is almost nothing in Fallows's essay, ideologically or politically, that wouldn't have warmed the heart of Milton Friedman.

In their eagerness to demystify and debunk, neo-liberals tend to cast a cold eye on human suffering, and occasionally they almost sound like social Darwinists. They are reminiscent of the nineteenth-century upper-class reformers who wanted purist solutions uncomplicated by messy complexities of place and politics. They recall the tale Lincoln Steffens tells on himself about an encounter with the ward boss Martin Lomasny, who counseled him that what the people needed was "none of your law and your justice, but help." The unconscious presumption seems to be that all people have, or ought to have, the same boundless opportunities as the Ivy League grads who become successful journalists. As a group, the neo-liberals lack imaginative empathy; it is hard for them to grasp that for many ordinary Americans, drastic economic change is an ordeal rather than an exhilarating challenge. "Place"—which is to say, community—is at the very center of local, neighborhood-based politics, the revival of which is beginning to breathe life back into democratic polity and the Democratic Party.

In another recent essay, Mickey Kaus argued that the definitive solution to the conundrum of how to get people off welfare is mandatory jobs. The work ethic, Kaus wrote presciently, is "an idea that seems more Democratic than Republican. . . . The current workfare boom gives liberals a chance to achieve, through the back door, the ancient Democratic dream of a guaranteed job." But Kaus's proposal is simply to force anyone on welfare to take a minimum-wage job or lose his or her benefits. In making this proposal, he tries to debunk the more humane versions of "workfare," such as the Massachusetts Employment Training program, and, as a good union baiter, he blames the Democratic Party's failure to embrace such a program on the public-employee unions that oppose it, since they resist the low-wage competition. Though his proposal is ostensibly represented as an alternative to those of the neo-conservative Charles Murray, in effect Kaus's subtext is quite the same as Murray's: the government welfare program is substantially responsible for creating and sustaining the black underclass, and the only solution is to take away the checks and make the bastards work for a living like everyone else.

What is sad is that Kaus takes what could be a bridge issue and turns it back into a wedge issue. The broadest, most embracing theme Democrats have is that they are committed to the idea of equal economic opportunity. When Michael Dukakis, running for re-election, ran a spot advertisement touting his widely praised Employment Training program, it featured a black nurse's aide saying, "I used to be on welfare. Now I have a job. And I owe it all to one man, Michael Dukakis." Stripped of the campaign hyperbole, the ad suggested different but complementary messages to black and white viewers. To black viewers, it shows what Martin Lomasny meant by "help." To white viewers, it shows that Dukakis is making these people take jobs, albeit gently. Every white viewer would surely rather see the woman helping a patient than collecting a welfare check. But Kaus's version of the idea stresses not opportunity, but society collecting a pound of flesh. His "jobs" would not be any sort of opportunity ladder, like ET. They would simply require welfare recipients to sing for their supper and, as such, would be resisted by every self-respecting black politician.

When I suggested this to Kaus, his response was that he is only a journalist, not a Democratic Party tactician. Fair enough. The neo-liberals are a little like Wernher von Braun in the Tom Lehrer ditty: he just sends the rockets up; he doesn't worry about where they come down. (" 'That's not my department,' says Wernher von Braun.")

IV.

The term "neo-liberal" is also used in Europe, but somewhat differently. Since in Europe, where democratic-left parties are typically labor or social-democratic ones, "liberal" retains its older meaning of denoting a party or person who supports *laissez-faire,* Europeans use "*neo-*liberal" to describe people newly enamoured of free markets; the phrase implies a turning away from mixed economies toward deregulation and privatization. That also applies in the United States in one respect: the free-market orientation of most economists and the neo-liberal rejection of public-sector solutions to economic problems tend to reinforce each other. In this sense, the fiercest neo-liberals are professional economists.

Classical economics is both a discipline and an ideology. In debating government policy, economists are potent ideological allies of both neo-liberalism and neo-conservatism. Since Adam Smith, classical economics has used a model of human behavior that presumes a self-regulating economy and posits a rational, utility-maximizing individual exercising free choices in a social vacuum. Since Smith, economists have held that the sum of individual free choices adds up to the optimal social outcome. By definition, no political intervention can improve on market-determined prices, quantities, products, or income distributions. In a famous epistemological sleight of hand, economists offer this model both as a description of the way the world actually is, and as an ideal of the way the world should be. Which is to say that classical economists function as a secular capitalist priesthood, both certifying the scientific accuracy of *laissez-faire* and commending its use. In this respect, they are useful handmaidens of economic elites and natural adversaries of progressive politics.

John Maynard Keynes and the Great Depression persuaded most mainstream economists that in some circumstances the Invisible Hand does not always produce the best of all possible worlds. But Keynes's revisions of the classical model were broadly accepted only to the extent that he taught that *laissez-faire* fails to optimize the outcome at the level of the whole economy. This is the famous Keynesian concept of "aggregate demand." As Keynes's ideas were incorporated into what came to be called the "neo-classical synthesis," orthodox economics accepted his insight that total purchasing power—aggregate demand—could sometimes slip into self-intensifying cycles of boom and bust, which required the government to use fiscal and monetary mechanisms to manipulate demand. But orthodox economics continued to insist that markets should set prices and patterns of capital allocation; it never really accepted Keynes's idea that government should also sometimes second-guess private investors; it saw trade unions as monopolists interfering with the natural pricing mechanism, and it only reluctantly accepted the creation of government-funded social programs and modest income redistribution as necessary concessions in an imperfect political world. In general, classical economists still believe that the most "marketlike" solution is likely to be the best one. They tend to look disdainfully on the political arena as one in which the state, which is clumsy and vulnerable to improper pressures, illegitimately distorts the market, which is efficient and by definition likely to produce the "correct" outcomes.

Most progressive policy innovations made by the U.S. government in recent decades, except in macroeconomics, have been made over the objections of the Democratic Party's own professional economic advisors. Social security, national health insurance, all kinds of subsidy and regulation tend to make neo-classical economists uneasy because they override market pricing mechanisms. Any form of economic planning and any revision of the free-trade dogma are particularly repugnant to them. In the past twenty years, as more overtly conservative economics gained currency, such as monetarism and supply-side economics, even "neo-Keynesian" economists have become less Keynesian and more *neo-* (that prefix again!). As a result, Democrats often find that their best political instincts are pronounced scientifically unsound by their own economic advisors. Europe, at least, has influential social-democratic economists. The United States does not.

As the economy has become the dominant problem of public policy, most policy questions have come to be defined as falling within the province of professional economists. The Democratic Party's habit of depending on expert advisors who are congenitally opposed, by professional training, to much of the party philosophy, is perhaps best illustrated by the Brookings Institution. Strictly speaking, Brookings is nonpartisan, but it is widely considered as the Democrats' unofficial economic think-tank, and it strives to be just that. In fact, Brookings began life, in the 1920s, as a fairly conservative outfit, and it opposed much of the New Deal. It briefly took on a more progressive coloration in the 1960s, during the zenith of neo-Keynesian manipulation of deficits and surpluses, when the prestige of economic technicians was at its peak. But more recently, Brookings has been a powerful conservatizing force on the party.

For a couple of decades, Brookings has had something close to a permanent seat on any Democratic President's Council of Economic Advisors. The late Arthur Okun, Lyndon Johnson's chief economic advisor, was a Brookings man. One of Okun's most notable works was a book arguing that equality and efficiency must, unfortunately, be traded off. To increase equality, Okun deduced, is necessarily to retard economic growth. That syllogism has done untold damage in paralyzing the progressive impulse. Charles Schultze, Carter's chief economist and a vigorous opponent of any form of industrial planning, was also a Brookings man. Alice Rivlin, whom the Democratic majority named as first director of the influential Congressional Budget Office, in 1974, came back to Brookings as director of economic studies in 1982, frazzled after a decade of budget skirmishing and fed up with Congress's inability to follow the fiscal routine. Under Rivlin, the fiscal view expressed in Brookings annual studies took a marked turn to the right. And George Perry, a leading Brookings macroeconomist, was a top advisor to Walter Mondale; he was widely expected to head Mondale's council had Mondale been elected. When Senator Joseph Biden tossed a tentative hat in the presidential ring in late 1986, he called on two economists to set up some seminars for him, Robert Litan and Robert Lawrence—of Brookings. (The last real liberal to chair the council was JFK's economic advisor, Walter Heller, who was appointed as an alternative to the more left-wing John Kenneth Galbraith. The greatest exception to this dismal lineage was that crusty populist, Harry Truman. When he appointed the chairman of the very first Council of Economic Advisers, Truman picked a vigorous advocate of economic planning and full employment, Leon Keyserling, who was not an economist at all.)

Brookings is not exclusively conservative; on a set of older issues, where the liberal position is fairly settled, it can be fairly progressive. For example, Martha Derthick, former director of its Governmental Studies program, and senior fellow Henry Aaron, former assistant secretary of HEW, are among the nation's leading scholarly defenders of social security. And Joseph Pechman, a longtime Brookings stalwart, is Mr. Progressive Tax Reform. But these voices have been drowned out by younger, more conservative ones preaching *laissez-faire* and budgetary austerity.

In 1984, Brookings's annual volume, *Economic Choices*, outdid even the Republican view about budget balance, advocating a virtually balanced budget by 1989. This, it said, would require freezing the spending levels for 1985, and "additional cuts in domestic spending must be considered." Though a deficit in the range of 5–6 percent of the GNP, which was Reagan's deficit at its peak, cannot be sustained, a moderate deficit of 2 percent of the GNP is probably tonic for the economy, and the difference between a 2 percent and a zero percent deficit is about $80 billion that could be devoted to needed social spending. Brookings's austere fiscal view crowds out any venturesome view of the public sector and even contradicts another chapter in the same book, where it is conceded that economic transition has costs, and recommends job retaining and relocation subsidies. The same volume further reversed Brookings's long-standing advocacy of progressive tax reform, much to Pechman's chagrin, and advocated a convoluted brand of consumption tax. This prompted an essentially accurate headline on *The Wall Street Journal* editorial page, "Brookings Joins the Supply Side."

Unlike the avowedly conservative foundations, Brookings disclaims any ideological stance or agenda and instead fancies itself as a kind of dispassionate graduate school mercifully free of graduate students. Yet now and then it does take off its gloves to argue a point of view vigorously, and it is invariably a conservative one. Brookings has been at the forefront of the fight against any form of industrial policy; it has vigorously advocated a purist view of free trade; and one of its most influential young economists, Robert Lawrence, has challenged the evidence that low-wage jobs are proliferating and the United States is becoming a two-tier economy. Brookings, of course, has a right to its views. But the Democratic Party needs other views.

The coup de grace for this brand of economics was Mondale's 1984 campaign. Brookings economists and fiscally conservative veterans of the Carter administration came together to convince Mondale that the single most important task the Democrats had was to show the public that the party could be fiscally responsible. Carter's chief domestic-policy advisor, Stuart Eizenstat, had become converted to the view that "constituency demands have outstripped government capacity." Bowman Cutter, who had been Carter's budget chief, argued that Carter had lost the 1980 election because the liberal wing of the party had blocked his efforts to cut the budget more deeply. Thus fiscal responsibility became Mondale's centerpiece—both as a matter of personal vindication and as conservative fiscal policy. Arguably, this was defensible economics, but without any support for offsetting affirmative government programs, it was terrible politics. The Democrats' economists, like their money men and their neo-conservative tutors, were perfectly androgynous. Virtually all of their advice might have been given to traditional Republicans—and was.

A good example of how this school of economics inflicted ideological paralysis on the Democratic Party was something called the

Bipartisan Budget Coalition, which was the creation of former Republican Commerce Secretary and investment banker Peter G. Peterson. In late 1982, at the peak of the worst economic slump since World War II, Peterson and other business leaders became convinced that the greater peril was not recession but the "structural deficit" and the risk of rising interest rates. The deficit, of course, was in fact the fruit of Reaganomics—a huge increase in military spending coupled with an excessive tax cut, which failed to produce the added revenues that its supply-side sponsors forecast. Peterson circulated for signature full-page ads to run in newspapers calling for drastic cuts in federal spending and a tax increase. The idea of reducing demand in the midst of a deep recession is economically perverse, not to say antiprogressive, because it only deepens the slump. Yet the Democrats were so hung up on the need to seem fiscally responsible that Peterson was able to recruit dozens of prominent Democrats to his cause, including several economists. This occurred during the the 1982 off-year elections, when the party surprised itself by sounding more populist than it thought it really dared and made a significant electoral comeback.

Economic orthodoxy also dominated Democratic thinking about the closely related issues of trade, economic planning, and management of the dollar. Most economists—left, right, and center—would agree that our problems with a large trade deficit and an overvalued dollar are partly connected to the enormous budget deficits. The logic works like this: when Congress authorizes a big deficit, the Federal Reserve Board must attract foreign capital in order to finance the deficit; to attract it, the Fed keeps domestic interest rates higher than those in other countries, which works in the short run, but in the long run has the effect of overvaluing the U.S. dollar; this makes American products uncompetitive in world markets and causes the trade deficit to worsen. Eventually, the United States ends up as a major debtor and its national balance sheet grows ever shakier.

This analysis is accurate as far as it goes, but orthodox Democratic economic advisors took it to an extreme. They insisted that the *only* problem afflicting American industry was the overvaluation of the dollar. This means there is no need for an industrial policy or a more aggressive trade policy, only a need to cut the federal budget deficit so the dollar's value will fall. Some of them even rejected the idea of central banks making a coordinated intervention in currency markets as an unwarranted interference with the free market. The market, they claimed, was reading the dollar's value all too accurately and would continue to do so until the deficit was cut.

In September 1985, the Republican Treasury Secretary, James Baker, outflanked both the Reagan administration's economists and the Democratic Party's: he negotiated an agreement with other major nations to depress the value of the dollar independent of what Congress did about the budget deficit. Baker was convinced that markets were simply reading the value of the dollar wrong. Once the other nations went along with his plan to give the dollar a shove, it started to fall . . . and fall . . . and fall, losing more than half of its value against the Japanese Yen and the West German Mark. Yet the big trade deficit moderated only slightly.

This stubborn persistence of the trade deficit had to do with several factors, including other nations' mercantilist habits, the depression of Third World purchasing power, the fact that many U.S. producers buy components overseas and must pay more for them when dollars are cheap, and the fact that many of our trading partners, like Korea, Taiwan, and Brazil, keep their currencies pegged to the dollar. But the Democrats' best-known economists kept insisting that the only problem was that the dollar hadn't yet fallen far enough against the Yen and the Mark. As the economic priesthood, they ruled out alternative policies—fixed exchange rates, industrial strategies for ailing industries, or a different sort of trade regime. Democrats who nonetheless began to explore such alternatives—correctly, in my view—felt they were doing so without benefit of clergy. Economists who did subscribe to such economically heretical (but politically mainstream) views were often on the margins of their profession.

Almost everything its economists were proposing was totally at odds with the party's most important institutional base, the labor movement. The economists, despite their "neo-Keynesian" label, were all too willing to tolerate 6 percent unemployment as a redefined rate of "full employment." The contrast with what was going on on the conservative side is dismally instructive. On the

Republican right, well-subsidized intellectuals were making a coherent case for low taxes, privatization, deregulation, and the high
public purpose of the business establishment, just as the party
needed them to. On the Democratic left, such as it was,
neo-conservatives were courting organized labor, mainly because
it was a handy Cold War ally; neo-liberals were attacking labor as
a selfish special interest; and economists were pronouncing the
party's persistent populist instincts as scientifically unsound. No
wonder Democrats seemed to be groping for "new ideas"! One
might say to the conservative economists urging fiscal austerity and
laissez-faire economics on the Democratic Party what Speaker Sam
Rayburn said of the Cambridge intellectuals planning the escala-
tion of the war in Vietnam for Lyndon Johnson: "I'd feel a whole
lot better about them if just one of them had run for sheriff once."

V.

In the aftermath of Jimmy Carter's defeat in 1980, party thinking
floundered badly, and the *neo-* movements impeded the subsequent quest for Democratic principles. Though Carter wasn't much
of a liberal, much less an economic populist, his loss was taken as
a repudiation of Democratic progressivism. Democrats spent the
early 1980s in search of a philosophy and a program.

Although conservatives found the word "ideology" useful—it
forced you to define what you believed in and relate it to the lives
of ordinary citizens—in Democratic circles the word was not mentioned in polite company. Instead, Democrats backed into a bloodless search for "new ideas," implicitly conceding that there had
been something fatally wrong with their old ideas. Therefore, their
search was disabled from the start by several presumptions: the
new ideas could not require the expenditure of much money; they
could not be too populist, since Democrats were supposed to be
reassuring the commercial elite that they cared about the business
climate just as much as Republicans did; they could not frontally
challenge the ideal of the free market, which was assumed to be
intellectually ascendant, scientifically correct, and politically popular; and they could not be divisive. In short, the Democrats' new

ideas had to be *ad hoc,* technical adjustments, and these were unlikely to excite anyone but other technicians.

A related problem is that "new ideas" per se do little to attract
voters. Democrats used to build their constituency by delivering
material benefits once in office—by taxing and spending. But the
new attitude was that taxing and spending was a habit to be shaken.
So what was there to be instead? Undoubtedly a number of "new
class" yuppie intellectuals thrill to new policy ideas out of sheer
intellectual joy, but they don't add up to a majority of the electorate.

Democrats began creating think-tanks. Unlike the dozens of conservative research institutions that were founded during the 1970s
with lavish support from business groups, the Democratic think-
tanks were for the most part operated on the cheap, with scant
ideological conviction. More often than not, they served to dissemi-
nate available material on the usual subjects written by centrist,
well-established policy intellectuals. Unity was the order of the day,
and they were neither insurgent nor ideologically forceful. Idea
factories founded since 1980 include the Center for National Policy
(annual budget: $650,000), the Roosevelt Center ($2.8 million),
the Policy Exchange ($150,000), and the Center for Budget and
Policy Priorities ($600,000), all in Washington; the Democracy
Project ($150,000), in New York; the Institute for National Strategy
($250,000), on the West Coast, plus several others that were mainly
fronts for individual candidates. The most attractive new face in the
1984 election, Gary Hart, built his entire primary campaign around
"new ideas." He became the first Democratic candidate to prepare
for 1988 by founding not a Political Action Committee but an
institute: Hart's Center for a New Democracy was established in
early 1985, budgeted at $500,000, with an initial staff of seven and
a plain mission to establish Hart as the premier idea man among
the Democrats. Other potential candidates grasped this new idea
fast. Senator Bill Bradley set up a tax-policy foundation; Senator Al
Gore created an institute; Governor Bruce Babbitt set up a leadership foundation; Representative Richard Gephardt was a prime
mover behind the Democratic Leadership Council; and the official
Democratic Party, not to be outdone, established its own policy
council.

Out of office, the Democrats sought to play fox to Ronald Reagan's hedgehog. In his famous 1951 essay, the political philosopher Isaiah Berlin quoted the Greek poet Archilochus that "The fox knows many things, the hedgehog knows one big thing." Sir Isaiah observed, "There exists a great chasm between those, on the one hand, who relate everything to a single central vision . . . a single universal organizing principle . . . and, on the other side, those who pursue many ends, often unconnected and even contradictory, connected if at all only in some *de facto* way . . . related by no moral or aesthetic principle." Sir Isaiah, as it happened, was writing about Tolstoi and Dostoevski. But his well-known distinction aptly describes the great chasm between Reagan and the squabbling Democrats. Reagan was the consummate hedgehog. He asserted one big thing: government is bad; *laissez-faire* is good. His administration employed a lot of idea mechanics to produce small ideas in the service of that one big idea. And he managed to articulate his big idea in a manner that the broad public could support, even though lots of little publics had trouble with many of his little ideas.

The Democrats, on the other hand, *used to* have a few big ideas: the free market can't do everything; the state is a very useful counterweight to the market; the little guy deserves more breaks than the marketplace delivers. And the Democrats had a lot of particular policy approaches informed by their convictions. Most Democrats still considered that their party was the party of the little guy, but they were no longer quite sure what to think about state and market.

In this ideological vacuum, "new ideas" simply for the sake of new ideas was hardly a substitute for the coherent world view the Democrats lost. It was only the political equivalent of the newsmagazine notation "TK," which means "copy to come later." But that doesn't work very well in politics. Before 1980, the American Enterprise Institute, the Heritage Foundation, the Hoover Institute, *The Public Interest* quarterly, and the *Wall Street Journal* editorial page had actually done for the conservative movement and the Republican Party all the things the Democratic think-tanks hoped to do: they redefined the public agenda, built networks of young conservative scholars, took over the op-ed pages, gave substance and weight to conservatism, and laid the groundwork for Reagan. The conservative new ideas were powerful precisely because they were driven by one big idea. And the Democratic counterpart was

weak because it was not. All the little foxes chewing at ideas didn't create a convincing hedgehog, only a lot of hedging. The cartoonist Dan Wasserman lampooned Gary Hart in dialogue with a citizen:

> HART: America needs new ideas.
> CITIZEN: Could you name one?
> HART: I just did.

The premier new Democratic think-tank was the Center for National Policy, which began in 1981, at first calling itself the Center for *Democratic* Policy, but it dropped the partisan word lest it invite trouble from the IRS. The goal of the center, according to Theodore Van Dyk, its first president, was "consensus building—to take the difficult policy questions and bring about a consensus that would not be possible without us." Van Dyk, who had once worked for Hubert Humphrey, did not consider himself a liberal counterpart of, say, Irving Kristol. "We have no litmus issues, we don't have a lobbying agenda, we do not attract ideological money, the way a Heritage Foundation does. Instead, we're a kind of clearinghouse, putting ideas out into the intellectual marketplace," Van Dyk explained.

At its best, the "clearinghouse model" might indeed sort out contending visions of a liberal resurgence. But in practice, the center seemed more like the cerebral counterpart of the Mondale campaign—a guarded attempt to build consensus via coalition. In six years, the center published some two dozen monographs and "occasional papers," and sponsored several conferences. Its work is, on the whole, decent enough. For example, monograph number 18, entitled "Tax Policy: New Directions and Alternatives," published in late 1984, began with a short essay by the economist Walter Heller persuasively arguing the case for a tax increase, and the rest offered several possible approaches: closing loopholes, enacting new energy taxes, a "progressive expenditure tax," a VAT, and so on. The authors were the usual suspects; their arguments were already available in Brookings papers, congressional testimony, and journal articles. The pamphlet offered nothing new, but at least it was well packaged and had the virtue of offering a consistent (if unpopular) prescription.

Several other center publications, however, failed even this test. "Budget and Policy Choices" (1983) contained one paper (by Carter's budget chief W. Bowman Cutter) making the now-familiar case for limiting "entitlements," and in the very next paper, Peter Edelman argued eloquently for new government entitlement for employment and retraining. "The cost of this 'entitlement,' " he concluded, "is clearly substantial. I believe the return is potentially even more substantial." The pamphlet lacked any ideologically consistent discussion of citizen entitlements, or a defense of them, a political analysis of where they go awry, or criteria to suggest when they are indicated. Rather than a clearing house, it was a grab bag and a fairly centrist one at that.

A third publication, perhaps the center's best known, prepared by a task force chaired by Felix Rohatyn, Irving Shapiro, and Lane Kirkland, called for a minimalist tripartite industrial policy with an "industrial development board," new research-and-development subsidies, and a bank. The proposal managed to be just controversial enough to seem outside the mainstream antiplanning consensus, without being bold enough to seem worth the trouble or to fire political enthusiasm. It was a technician's document.

If there was any over-all theme in the center's *oeuvre,* Van Dyk explained, it was "Growth *über Alles.* Stress growth even over equity, at least temporarily." But that, as an ideological theme, seems exactly wrong. You can get growth *without* sacrificing equity. If you think equity must be subordinated to growth, then you have accepted the assumptions of conservatism before the debate starts, and you might as well be a Republican.

The center's initial gravitational center might be described as representative of the late years of the Carter administration. The ideological assumption was the one that led Carter to distance himself from the New Deal and Great Society, and to try to convince voters that Democrats could be humane but parsimonious. It was the same impulse that fatally afflicted Mondale, who managed to be simultaneously pilloried as an old style, big-spending interest-group Democrat *and* as Mr. Austerity.

The center as a technocratic operation did not try to identify or to incubate a cohort of younger, ideologically driven intellectuals of the sort that magically blossomed in the conservative think-tanks

and journals in the late 1970s. In part, the operation failed to spawn new thinkers because it offered them neither philosophical affinity nor money. The ostensible message was New Ideas, but the medium broadcasted predictability and sameness. In 1986, the center recruited a new president, Kirk O'Donnell, former Speaker Tip O'Neill's chief political aide. O'Donnell resolved to make the place more partisan.

Another characteristic new think-tank was the Roosevelt Center for Public Policy Studies, bipartisanly named for Franklin, Eleanor, and Theodore, whose portraits grace its lobby. It is not altogether fair to categorize the Roosevelt Center as a liberal think-tank, for as its publicist Jill Leonhardt explained to me, "We are nonpartisan, nonpolitical, and nonideological. Everybody thinks we are a liberal think-tank. We have had that cross to bear ever since we were founded." But it is principally underwritten by Richard Dennis, a Chicago-based commodities trader whose wealth is said to exceed $100 million, and who is one of the Democratic Party's biggest fund raisers. Dennis was a backer of Adlai Stevenson III, and it was considered a significant coup for Bruce Babbitt when Dennis decided to support Babbitt's presidential effort. But Dennis has two somewhat divergent political hobbies: substantive support for the Democratic Party—and an interest in his own brand of "process populism." Dennis believes passionately that policymaking has become isolated from ordinary citizens. So rather than creating a think-tank that might help liberals and Democrats to reinvent their progressive ideology, Dennis underwrote an explicitly nonpartisan institute devoted to the goal of greater citizen involvement in the policy process. "There's a sleeping giant out there called the American people, that can throw its weight around and break through ideological and partisan deadlocks," its president, Roger Molander, says. Molander himself is a sort of born-again Jeffersonian. He spent eighteen years at the Pentagon as a nuclear engineer, worked on arms control at the White House under Presidents Ford and Carter, and in 1979 dropped out to found Ground Zero, a citizens-education project about nuclear proliferation.

The Roosevelt Center's specialty is devices that involve citizens in policy disputation. In a simulation game called DebtBusters, the center invites citizens to try to solve the deficit problem. To date, nearly all of the thirty thousand citizens who have grappled with the numbers and played DebtBusters have decided to cut defense and raise taxes as well as to reduce social programs. Roosevelt Center staffers see games like DebtBusters as a vast improvement on conventional public-opinion polling, which elicits misleading or simplistic pictures of what the public thinks. "We have the only real data on how the citizenry would break the budget deadlock," says Molander.

For 1988 the center hopes to sponsor a series of citizens forums for presidential candidates, as a way of getting away from negative campaigning and back to issues. As procedural, civic populism, this is nice enough; but as substantive populism, or as *politics*, it doesn't promise very much. The League of Women Voters has been doing this more proficiently and less pretentiously for decades.

Too few of the traditional think-tanks, new or old, seem interested in breathing life back into Democratic progressivism. Unlike their conservative counterparts, they are hung up on being nonpartisan, apolitical, and technically virtuous. To them, "policy" is something splendidly disconnected from politics, or connected only via a high-minded civic exercise.

The few institutions that have tried more explicitly to rebuild the intellectual foundations of progressivism are smaller, far clearer about their goals, and not in the business of "new ideas." Significantly, the core idea that all three have in common is economic populism. The Center on Budget and Policy Priorities, under the imaginative leadership of Robert Greenstein, has functioned as a combination truth squad and quarterback in the effort to keep Reagan from repealing the entire New Deal. Another admirable group, the Villers Foundation, was created as an advocate for the nonrich elderly. While many economists and neo-liberals were almost ritualistically repeating the statistical half-truth that the elderly are oversubsidized, Villers demonstrated the reality of a two-class world of senior citizens. And Citizens for Tax Justice exposed the perversity of Reagan's 1981 tax program. With a professional staff of just six, it won a remarkable victory when Congress in 1986 enacted something very close to its long-standing design for tax reform—broadening the tax base, eliminating loopholes, and cutting rates. CTJ also was crucially effective in preventing knee-jerk liberals from acting on their instinct that anything that reduces the top nominal tax rates on the rich (which were never paid in practice) must be bad policy. As CTJ kept pointing out, it was rising rates on working people that caused the tax revolt in the first place. The loopholes that Congress finally decided to close in 1986 had benefited mostly the upper class. Once the principle is established that loopholes should be closed, one can always go back and add a higher top rate later. CTJ, largely funded by trade unions, was also crucial in preventing labor from acting on its own parochial instincts and lobbying to kill the whole bill because it tightened the tax treatment of pension funds, and, in an early draft, killed the deductibility of state and local taxes, which was not good for state governments and hence public-employee unions. But unions this time were able to keep their eye on the big picture.

It might be said that these three groups are more lobbies than idea shops. But of course so are AEI, Heritage, Cato, and the other rightwing groups. Practical influence is what politics is all about. For the most part, the right has been far more strategic than the left about underwriting intellectual work as long-term lobbying. These smaller, more insurgent progressive groups had influence because they were clear about what they believed.

VI.

In the mid-1980s, two other new kids appeared on the progressive block. The economic populists in Congress decided to give themselves a clear philosophical identity, creating their own caucus, and the labor movement resolved to get serious about investing in ideological renewal. Labor had been largely in a defensive mode, concerned about keeping its losses to a minimum on the industrial front, while taking what it considered a bold political risk by investing heavily in a presidential primary in 1984. But after Reagan's re-election, several of the best progressive economic thinkers and union leaders realized they had a common problem. For its part, organized labor had a desperate shortage of scholarly allies. When it needed someone to attest that David Ricardo's theory of comparative advantage had not been handed down from God to Moses, or that economic regulation was sometimes actually useful, it kept turning to the same two or three renegades. The academy has not been licensing many liberal economists lately. For their part, the few progressive economic thinkers felt professionally isolated—former Labor Secretary Ray Marshall, MIT's Lester Thurow, Harvard's Robert Reich, Barry Bluestone of the University of Massachusetts, and one-time antipoverty activist Geoffrey Faux, who operated his own small institute. These men were a lot closer to the Democratic Party's New Deal–Great Society tradition than, say, Brookings is, but they did not belong to an established "school" of economics and were largely frozen out of the research networks that make it possible to foster graduate students of like mind.

Though labor was uneasy about underwriting anybody outside the labor family, and its leaders were a bit wary of Reich and Thurow, who could sometimes give short shrift to labor's institutional concerns, nine unions agreed to give this group of economists seed money totalling about $1.5 million to found an Economic Policy Institute (EPI) with Faux as director. EPI was also able to raise foundation support and money from industries harmed by the reigning free-market ideology. It has given small grants for work on trade policy, labor market policy, income distribution, and industrial strategy.

At about the same time, several members of the House and Senate founded first a caucus, then a New Populist Forum, to put economic populism back on the map as a real alternative to neo-liberalism and neo-conservatism. In the 1984 election they could boast that all twenty-two members of the House populist caucus, many of them in what were considered marginal seats, survived Reagan's landslide and won re-election. In 1986, Democrats won several improbable Senate victories by preaching economic populism. It made far more sense in the 1980s for progressive Democrats to run as populists than as liberals.

What is populism? Historically it was a home-grown, peculiarly conservative form of American economic radicalism, reflecting the demands of otherwise powerless groups, such as small farmers, for their fair share of the national economic product. It has usually fused demands for political empowerment with demands for economic justice. Populists have seen their constituents as victimized by distant economic organizations which they don't control—banks and absentee landlords and grain wholesalers—and fight to create local, democratically accountable economic institutions. In the heyday of nineteenth-century populism, the Farmers Alliance and the People's Party of the 1880s and 1890s mobilized millions of small farmers, elected senators and governors in several Western and Southern states, and in some places displaced Democrats as the second major party. In North Dakota, populists were for two decades the governing party; they devised a state-owned commercial bank, a state grain elevator, and other genuinely radical mechanisms of democratic ownership.

As an ideology, populism is problematic, because it has an ugly side. Though the original populist revolt of the 1880s was remarkably multiracial, as economic frustrations intensified, much of the movement became racist. Community is both an inclusionary and an exclusionary concept. In William Schneider's phrase, American populism is "ideologically ambivalent"—economically radical, but parochial and socially conservative. Schneider observes, "Elites tend to be rich and well educated, economically conservative and culturally sophisticated. Populism is anti-elitist and therefore just the reverse—left-wing on economic issues and right-wing on social and cultural issues." Economic populists like Tom Watson and William Jennings Bryan ended their careers as demogogic social reactionaries. Huey Long was a blend of economic radical and conservative near-dictator, but his populist values won him a fanatical following among Louisiana's little people.

In its more moderate form, small-p populism is simply a broad plea for economic justice. The New Deal fused elements of populism with aspects of the Progressive reform movement of the Theodore Roosevelt–Woodrow Wilson era, adding some *ad hoc* and social-democratic inventions of its own. But it definitely tapped the populist demand of economic justice for the ordinary laborer and farmer.

In recent years, the Democratic Party's caution on issues concerning the economy, combined with its cultural cosmopolitanism, enabled the Republicans to tap the populist impulse by appealing to working-class patriotism and social conservatism. If the Democrats seemed to project effete cultural values while failing to deliver much economically, the Republicans briefly seemed the more "populist" party.

Kevin Phillips, a prominent advocate of right-wing Republican populism, observed, "I started outlining *The Emerging Republican Majority* in the early 1960s at Harvard because it was clear that the Harvard Young Democratic Club at that time consisted of all these guys with IIIs and IVs after their names who spent their political lives escorting Muffies and Buffies to liberal parties. I said, well, hell, if this is happening at Harvard, then I know what is happening in Tennessee and Idaho and South Boston, because the two will always go in different directions."

However, Republican pose as the more populist party is anomalous and unnatural, given its core class support. After the Reagan presidency, there is bound to be a fierce battle for the Republican Party, between the economic populists such as Phillips, Jack Kemp of New York, and other congressmen of the Conservative Opportunity Society on one side, and country-club Republicans like George Bush on the other. Reagan was uniquely able to combine populist imagery and a few populist policies such as middle-class tax relief, with a program that essentially represented the interests of the business elite. It is hard to think of any other Republican now on the political scene who can duplicate that feat. Consequently, the opportunity exists for the Democrats to reclaim their mantle as the populist party.

In the rural South, the industrial Midwest, the nonsuburban West, and the ethnic working-class neighborhoods of the Northeast, there is simply more electoral pay dirt for Democrats in economic populism than in social and foreign-policy liberalism. That is why neo-liberals who keep counseling Democrats to ignore "place," and economists who advise austerity, and neo-conservatives who offer only the cultural conservativism and a "tough" foreign policy are offering such bad advice.

Frank Reissman, an editor of *Social Policy* magazine, observes that the new wave of populism is still "a mood in search of an ideology," and its several components are not always consistent with each other. There is first "an emphasis on traditional values like family, neighborhood, religion, and patriotism." Here, Reissman might be describing Jonathan Schell's quintessential disaffected Democrat, Bill Gapolinsky. Reissman cautions, "While recognizing the significance of these roots, we must distinguish between traditions that have a progressive potential and those that are narrow, provincial, parochial, chauvinistic, racist, and sexist. . . . Right-wing populists have an easier task as they can more uncritically accept traditions." Secondly, according to Reissman, populism emphasizes: "communitarian, cooperative, self-initiated activities emanating at the grass roots level. This bottom-up participatory approach is powerfully rooted in American traditions and has been powerfully reactivated." Finally, he writes, populism doesn't like concentrated power. "Large numbers of people feeling submerged and overpowered by big institutions and big government are attempting to get some controls over their lives. They are struggling for empowerment."

This dislike of big government and defense of often parochial and exclusive local cultures is what makes populism so "ideologically ambivalent." The populist heritage can be almost as resentful of big government as of private economic concentration. Some latter-day populists, including Reissman's own co-author, Harry Boyte, fault modern progressives for placing too much emphasis on statist solutions and not enough on local voluntarism and community institutions that "mediate" between the state and the market, rather in the spirit of Alexis de Tocqueville. "Progressives' failing is that they see mediating institutions as barriers to progress," Boyte writes, expressing the valid concern that government bureaucracies, at their worst, can indeed supplant rather than invigorate local democratic institutions, and alienate voters.

However, as Boyte concedes, populist movements have often relied on government programs to serve their own goals. The choice of government program versus local self-help can be another case of positing a misleading false dichotomy. For example, as I suggested in my 1984 book, *The Economic Illusion,* the Scandinavian system of home health care is a well-funded public program that employs tens of thousands of skilled professionals—in service of local self-reliance. These home health-care programs are typically run by local governments or nonprofit agencies and are anything but distant and bureaucratic.

Closer to home, one can think of government-assisted local housing or farmers' co-ops, as well as something as familiar as the local PTA—a voluntary self-help organization that exists in symbiosis with a government institution. As the "welfare state" has grown, its most effective agents have often been local nonprofit providers of services. One can also think of what I have termed "regulation as an organizing tool." The combination of Right-to-Know legislation giving workers information about toxic hazards at the workplace, coupled with federally subsidized "COSH groups"—COSH stands for Committee on Safety and Health—has breathed life into many union locals. In the same manner, federal regulation requiring banks to disclose the geographical pattern of their mortgage lending and requiring them not to discriminate against poor neighborhoods proved to be a powerful tool in the hands of neighborhood groups that mobilized to monitor their local banks. Government programs can be an ally or an adversary of popular economics and populist politics. A housing policy can subsidize developers or tenant co-ops. A farm policy can reward agribusiness or family farms. A health program can favor corporate hospital chains or consumer-controlled HMOs. The trick is to get the right constituency linked to the right policy. Liberals often ignore this aspect of social-program design, because they think the only important goal is to deliver the service. The 1960s antipoverty program can be viewed as a flawed experiment in populism—populist because it was participatory; flawed because it bypassed local government. It is always possible for government interventions to nurture rather than supplant the local democratic impulse. And for the Democratic Party that approach is a political necessity.

Several recently elected Democratic members of Congress and Senate are very much in this populist tradition. Senator Paul Simon of Illinois epitomizes the seeming contradiction: he combines a populist suspicion of big government with a belief that government should work for ordinary people. Simon is one of the few progressive Democrats who favors a constitutional amendment requiring the federal budget to be balanced. He is also the sponsor of an $11 billion WPA-style bill to put unemployed people back to work rebuilding America's roads, bridges, parks, and other public facilities. Presumably he would find the money for the jobs bill by reducing Pentagon spending and by taxing the rich. This is not contradictory; it is pure Harry Hopkins populism.

Possibly the shrewdest populist ideologue among Democratic elected officials is Jim Hightower, the elected state agricultural commissioner of Texas and the leader of the Texas Democratic Party's progressive wing. Hightower epitomizes the combination of an economic radical with a culturally mainstream politician. He won hundreds of thousands of votes from socially conservative working-class Texans, who split their tickets to vote for a Republican governor and for him.

The basic Hightower speech is worth quoting at length: This particular rendition happened to be at the National Press Club, in Washington, D.C., a good year before the Democrats' November 1986 electoral comeback. Hightower summarized his message with four points:

Number one, the great masses of middle America have not become nearly as yuppized, as Republicanized, as happy-faced as many of the pundits and other trend-spotters would have us believe. Number two, the political party that seeks refuge in the great yawning middle ground of American politics is destined to lose. Number three, Democratic leadership, contrary to popular opinion, is experiencing vigorous growth at the grassroots level among people who are running for and winning state and local offices. And number four, the Democratic Party can indeed be the majority party again if it will seize the populist moment that is presented to us today.

If you were to go and knock on the door of 1331 West Hall Street in Denison, Texas, you would be greeted by my old daddy. Now, you've got to beware of Texans bringing you "old daddy" stories, you know that, but I'm about to give you one here. If you were to ask him, Is he a liberal or a conservative, he's going to say, "I'm a conservative." But if you ask him what he thinks about the utility companies raising his rates on a regular basis and squeezing the little tiny profit margin that he's got; if you ask him about the multistate holding companies removing the source of capital from his hometown to the corporate centers in Dallas and, in fact, all the way up to New York City; if you were to ask him about the lobby clout of big business to write tax policies, to write regulatory authority, to write legislation that squeezes little people like him out of business, you would have tapped as progressive a human being as you would ever want to be face to face with.

In office, Hightower practiced what he preached by organizing farm-to-market co-ops, and creating outlets for homegrown Texas produce in local supermarkets. He became part of a coalition arguing that what farmers needed was not more federal subsidies, but more predictable and stable prices. Though Hightower locates his politics in a native populist tradition, it is thoroughly compatible with the implicit premise of mainstream Democratic progressivism that *laissez-faire* markets cannot be trusted to give little people a fair shake. Hightower has a far shrewder feel for popular thinking and for electoral demographics than a great many campaign professionals. He declares:

My point here is that the great center of American politics is not square dab in the middle of the spectrum, equal distance from conservatism and liberalism. Rather, the true center is populism, which is rooted in that realization that too few people control all the money and power, leaving very little for the rest of us. And they use that money and power to gain more for themselves. Populism is propelled by the simmering desire of the great mass of people to upend that arrangement. Now, this is hardly a centrist position, if by centrist you mean moderate. But it is at the center of most people's political being, and it is a very hot center, indeed.

If you will just go down and greet and meet the morning bunch at the Chat-and-Chew Cafe, you will quickly tap a deep strain of populist resentment of the powers that be—the bankers and the bosses, the politicians and the press, the big boys, and what is generally referred to as "the bastards." Middle Americans are not meek centrists, which we are being told is the majority constituency the political parties are supposed to be pursuing . . . they are antiestablishment malcontents . . . they are mad about what is happening in their own lives.

Even as we sit here partaking of this good meal, people are out there at the clubs right now enjoying a midday repast of cool melon melange and asparagus and goat cheese and a delightfully fruity and frisky California wine. But most of America doesn't live there. The majority of Americans are down at the 7-11 picking up a Budweiser and a Slim Jim and wondering if there's anybody in America who's going to stand up on their side. That is the populist constituency. . . . And those are the people that the Democrats must begin to speak to.

This man was elected, statewide, in Texas, midway through Ronald Reagan's first presidential term. At first, Hightower was taken as a regional oddity. After the 1986 election, he began getting more invitations than he could handle to speak at Democratic gatherings in other states.

Populism is not an easy catchword in American politics. It may have a Huey Long/Father Coughlin connotation. Yet populism as an ideal is probably the oldest and soundest of the Democrats' "new ideas." But any word that requires footnotes on its bumper sticker is probably not a good word to describe a majority movement. "Progressive" is probably a better word than populist.

Lately, even the Democratic Party's centrists have tried to make off with the word "progressive." At the Democratic Leadership Council's summit conference in Williamsburg, Virginia, after the 1986 elections, one speaker after another spoke of the importance of dropping party "interest groups" and speaking to the electoral center. But DLC Executive Director Alvin From explained that the DLC's preferred label was not "centrist" but "progressive." The current DLC chairman, former Virginia Governor Charles Robb, a leader of the party's center-right faction, spoke of the DLC's role "as a sounding board for progressive ideas."

To help the DLC appropriate the progressive label, the group invited William Leuchtenberg, the biographer of FDR and Truman, to give an address on "The Progressive Tradition of the Democratic Party." Either the DLC hadn't read his book or Leuchtenberg took the assignment more literally than intended. As most of the prominent centrist Democrats in the hall stared at their plates, Leuchtenberg gave a barn-burning speech in the best progressive/populist tradition: "History simply does not show that moving to the center is a guaranteed route to success," Leuchten-berg said.

> Certainly, Democrats must adapt to new circumstances, but if Democrats become preoccupied with graphing precisely where the center is and positioning there, Democrats run the risk of losing identity, of no longer being, in Emerson's phrase, not only the party of memory but the party of hope. For perhaps the single characteristic that Democrats have had most in common has been the capacity to inspire the country with the conviction that we are not helpless creatures of destiny, but can affect our own fate, a conviction that united FDR's "We have nothing to fear but fear itself" with Jack Kennedy's call to get the country moving again. . . .
>
> If Democrats are soon to enjoy the kind of election night cele-brated in 1936, 1948, and 1964, it will be, I believe, because the next Democratic presidential candidate has that kind of spirit, because he takes pride in the magnificent legacy that is ours, and because he affirms that government is not part of the problem, it is part of the answer.

The room echoed with polite applause, except for a few ringers at the press table who were clapping wildly. It was well worth the trip.

CHAPTER SIX

DEMOCRATIC OPPORTUNITY

I.

It is often said of American politics that our presidential elections are seldom contests over competing visions of the future but rather backward-looking referenda on the incumbent administration. In this respect, the abrupt collapse of Reaganism offers Democrats an unexpected opportunity to win the White House in 1988 simply based on the swing of the pendulum. If much of Reagan's personal popularity was built on "performance" rather than ideological appeal, little of that performance remains. The shake-up of the administration in the aftermath of the Iran scandal also limited the influence of the hard-core right. By the spring of 1987, the once highly doctrinaire Reagan presidency had become a regency, operated by competent and moderate men of the Republican center.

But the economic and political forces that have made Republicans the stronger party and split Democrats from their own roots are likely to persist. Though Reagan's personal fall and the circum-

stantial reversal of Republican fortunes lifted the Democrats' spir-
its, it will be of only temporary benefit to Democrats unless they
seize the moment, to govern effectively and to use their next period
of incumbency to rebuild not just their party, but the political logic
of a mixed economy where people are citizens as well as buyers and
sellers and community has an equal place with market. They now
have a real opportunity to recapture the allegiance of voters and to
re-establish that nexus between party, state, program, and electorate which is their most attractive and necessary quality. They must
restore civic consciousness among ordinary wage-earning citizens.
They must reinvent a functioning social contract. In Robert Reich's
phrase, the "myth of the benevolent community" has been a powerful animating theme in the American experience, just as potent
as the opposite myth of the heroic individual. But in recent years,
as the old linkages of community have weakened, we have been at
a loss to know what we want the social contract to provide, or how
we expect it to work.

As they develop their policy ideas and rhetorical themes Democrats need to be politically strategic. That means not just finding
the votes to kick Republicans out of office and to enact Democratic
programs, but thinking through how each policy rebuilds the base
and restores the links. The next party program that Democrats
propose must pass two separate tests: it must be feasible and make
good policy sense in its own terms; and it must give something
tangible to the electoral base. The policies should strive to
strengthen the link between party, government, and voter and
thereby reclaim the civic ethic as a counterweight to the market
ethic. Progressives ought to be as explicit and canny about that goal
as conservatives are about radical individualism and privatization.

II.

Early in the Reagan administration, *Conservative Digest* published a
now famous special issue on "Defunding the Left." Howard Phillips, director of the National Conservative Caucus, argued that
many federal agencies, including Vista, the National Legal Services
Corporation, the Community Services Administration, subsidize

"advocacy groups." If these programs were eliminated, the caucus contended, it would put a lot of left-wingers out of business. Phillips was correct, though not quite in the way that he thought. For progressives, the value of public programs is not literally that they keep a lot of activists on the payroll (though that occasionally happens), but that they create space where an ethos of public-mindedness can flourish, in which competent people can work together toward goals other than private profit-maximizing ones.

For example, the U.S. Public Health Service does an immense amount of tangible good in bringing medical services to forgotten corners of the country. Even more importantly, for health professionals who work in it, however briefly, it is a consciousness-raiser. That some doctors survive their medical education with social conscience intact often has a lot to do with having spent a couple of years with the Public Health Service. Arguably, replacing this public program with vouchers for indigent people to use at private clinics might be equally cost-effective, but it would represent an incalculable loss for social solidarity.

Or consider the National Legal Services Corporation. It has indeed, as the right claims, been a hothouse of socially conscious lawyering. In a litigious society, giving poor people the legal resources to press economic claims against landlords, elite-influenced bureaucrats, law-breaking employers, and so on is a radically egalitarian act. It also creates a subculture where socially conscious professionals can make a modest living, and thus offers an alternative role model for lawyers. When the Harvard Law School in early 1987 announced a policy of partially forgiving tuition loans for lawyers who took lower-paying jobs in social agencies, it was acknowledging how hard it is for that alternative legal culture to survive in a purely market system, where aspiring lawyers who are tens of thousands of dollars in tuition debt answer the siren call of elite corporate firms all too easily. Again, replacing Legal Services with vouchers for the poor to use with regular lawyers, as conservatives propose, would eliminate all this. The ostensible conservative target is budgetary, but the bigger target is the alternative legal milieu. Many of those Democrats with postgraduate degrees who keep anomalously turning up in the survey research are lawyers and doctors who did time in public agencies. A Demo-

crat who overlooks these linkages in the name of some Rousseauist
Higher Good is committing political suicide.

A good public school is perhaps the most powerful example of
a public sociopolitical space. While the ethic of the pure marketplace is social Darwinist, a public school is essentially egalitarian,
because it has the goal not only of helping the brightest to excel,
but also of teaching everyone to read, write, do sums, and reach a
basic level of civic participation. For most of us, nothing, with the
possible exception of military service, is so egalitarian as our years
in public school. The school treats the rich kids in the class pretty
much the same as the poor ones. The hindmost are not left to the
devil, but are kept after school. The problem is, schools in poor
districts have fewer resources than rich ones, and over the years
children from affluent professional families tend to have their education more consistently reinforced at home than the poor ones.
Conservatives try to hoist the welfare state on its own petard by
demonstrating that publicly funded programs are often somewhat
skewed to the better-off parts of a society, and that is sometimes
true. But at least the public school seeks to counterbalance that
class tendency and creates a space with public and civic values.

The health care delivery system, as we now call the business of
doctors and hospitals, is a dramatic illustration of how haphazardly
and imperfectly public policy has created such spaces. I vividly
recall sitting beside a recent immigrant from Greece, waiting in the
emergency room of a prestigious Boston hospital. My son had a
baseball injury. His daughter was having delicate emergency surgery. The man, from a rural village, could not get over the fact that
in America it did not matter at all how much influence he had; his
daughter was getting the same advanced care, with the same dig-
nity, as the richest banker's daughter. Nobody was making him feel
like a charity case. As the man described these wonders of his
adopted country, I felt a burst of patriotic pride in splendidly
egalitarian America. The problem is that this ethic of equal treatment for the sick or injured leaves out about one-quarter of the
population. The man and his daughter were part of the great
American middle-class health system because he happened to have
a job with an employer who provided comprehensive health insurance. Most of us would agree in the abstract that one's purse should

not determine one's access to health care, yet we have devised a system where 37 million people have no health insurance at all and another 23 million are in the vastly inferior medicaid system, and both groups are indeed made to feel like charity cases.

Even within the insurance sector of the system, the rich can purchase better treatment than the nonrich. For example, medicare stipulates cost-control rules—cataract surgery, say, can only be reimbursed as an outpatient procedure—but rich people can choose to buy the more comfortable way out. (What do you mean Grandma can't go into the hospital for her cataract operation? Send me the bill.) Similarly, Blue Cross can decide that a heroic procedure is not warranted and refuse to pay for it, but a well-to-do patient can pay himself. In our mixed system of health-care delivery, where insurance companies provide reimbursements, public hospitals who must treat all comers are forced to compete with profit-making hospital chains that offer gold-plated treatment to the must lucrative and highly "reimbursable" customers. Big-city hospitals once relied on the profits from their paying patients to subsidize their nonpaying ones. But this makeshift form of social-ism-on-one-ward doesn't work when resources keep draining out of the public, need-driven sector of the system and into the private, purse-driven sector. A single, universal health-insurance system would be a net gain for efficiency and for equity. And as a frank political matter, placing all people in the same system—retired, working age, rich, middle class, and poor—would be an immense gain for our sense of public space, and for the Democratic Party as the guardian of that space.

When the Reagan administration cut the funding for America's public spaces—the places in our mixed economy where civic values flourish—and when Reagan persuaded too many Democrats that the voters expected them to do likewise, he indeed "defunded the left," not the left in the sense of an extreme ideological splinter but in the sense of a broad, popular political center that values commu-nity alongside individualism. He deprived us of programmatic re-sources, of social solidarity, and of ideological capital. Even if most neo-liberals did not appreciate the important linkage between pub-lic programs and progressive politics, the strategic right did.

A society must be something more than a giant marketplace of disconnected individuals. Even in libertarian America, most citizens intuitively grasp that imperative. Social tissues include purely private relationships, obviously, but civic ones as well. This is the historic public philosophy of the Democratic Party, and it is a philosophy Democrats would do well to reclaim.

III.

In this century, Democrats have used such slogans as New Freedom, New Deal, Fair Deal, New Frontier, and Great Society to convey what they were about. The New Deal was probably the best of these, capturing both the idea that the people deserved a better hand than the one they had been dealt, as well as a better social bargain. The party needs to convey something of that again, whoever the Democratic nominee is in 1988. It needs to reinvent a social contract and a new sense of community.

The new community must repair and celebrate the concept of reciprocity and mutual obligation. In the heyday of the Democrats' majority, reciprocity functioned better than it does today. The social bargain stuck. If you worked hard and followed the rules, you could expect the benefits. Growth helped immensely to lubricate this system, but growth was not all there was to it. The success of the *de facto* social contract of the first decades after World War II reflected our splendid isolation from the global economy. Auto- and steelworkers could expect to be laid off and called back to work periodically with the swings of the business cycle, but they were well insulated from economic ruin because they were isolated from global pressures. Some industries, such as textiles, did go through wrenching dislocations, but new and usually better-paying industries came along to replace them. Agricultural policy stabilized commodity prices, and though the exodus from America's farms continued, it continued at a socially manageable pace. Moreover, most of the people who left farms did so not because farming was unattractive or financially disabling but simply to improve their living standards. Industrial change, more often than not, led to improvements not only in statistical productivity but in job opportunities and higher living standards.

Blacks and women were not full-fledged members of this social contract. Blacks—denied voting rights and equal education, employment, or housing rights—were effectively an inferior class of citizen; women were not granted full rights as economic individuals and, in effect, were proxy members of the social contract only via marriage. Despite these large exclusions, at a mythic and practical level the social contract seemed to function for those who were party to it, in just the way that eighteenth-century America functioned as a "democracy" which happened to exclude blacks, Indians, women, and children.

Today the problem is reversed: while blacks, women, and working-class whites are full-fledged *de jure* members of the American political system, the *de facto* social contract has broken down. Trade unions are no longer effective guarantors of the social contract for labor. Wage-earners can give a full day's work for a day's pay, but then they can be dumped unceremoniously when a distant entrepreneur discerns a more profitable opportunity to invest the company's resources elsewhere, or when a corporate raider suddenly acquires the company and radically reduces costs, or when it becomes more economical for the company to make the product in Korea. Neither the union, nor the paternalism of the employer, nor public policy serves to enforce the implicit social bargain. Public schools are stuck in time as if the family still operated on the 1953 model. Most parents, fathers and mothers, have jobs outside the home, yet the school system assumes that kindergarteners can go home to their mothers in the afternoon, and that primary-school pupils have someone to come home to at three o'clock and during school vacations. And aid to Families with Dependent Children (AFDC) functions as if it were addressing the 1930s problem of widows and orphans, when the 1980s problem is teenage mothers and divorced women with poverty-level incomes.

The *de facto* system of social comity that flourished during the decades after World War II came at a fortuitous historical moment, but it was also built on explicit public programs. Political progressives had sponsored many programs fostering economic opportunity and security for the middle class, and they suited the social structures and aspirations of the period.

Consider the famous GI Bill. In June 1944, President Roosevelt signed the Servicemen's Readjustment Act, popularly known as the GI Bill of Rights, which provided tuition payments of up to five hundred dollars a year, and subsistence payments of up to fifty dollars a month (increased to seventy five dollars in 1948). During the twelve years of the original program, 7.8 million World War II veterans received these subsidies for education and training: 3.5 million in vocational and technical schools, 1.4 million on the job, almost 700,000 in agricultural courses, and 2.2 million in colleges and universities. Although some prominent educators of the time opposed the virtual open enrollment of veterans, the veterans mostly outperformed the average college students. The total cost of this education and training under the GI Bill was $14.5 billion, or something like $55 billion in current dollars. Another 2.4 million Korean War vets received the same benefits under successor legislation, at a cost of $4.5 billion.

The GI Bill had almost universal support, though it represented a sizable government intervention into a largely private sector— higher education—and a sizable outlay of public funds. But nearly everyone agreed that veterans had earned the benefits, by serving their country in wartime, and the outlay was not considered a giveaway, since it was serving the eventual self-sufficiency of the recipients. Thus the beneficiaries were considered "deserving" in both senses. Significantly, they were not income-tested. This was what we would now call an entitlement; to qualify, one only had to have served in wartime for at least ninety days. The GI Bill came at a time when economic horizons were expanding. It served industry's need for a better-trained workforce and individual economic opportunity.

In the same manner, the two notable housing programs of the era, VA-guaranteed home loans and FHA-insured loans, were almost universally supported. Unlike the education grants under the GI Bill, these programs were mainly loan guarantees, not subsidies, and they were also in the service of individual economic opportunity and advancement. VA mortgages, initially at an interest rate of 4 percent, eventually served more than 11 million vets and their families; FHA loans served another 15 million families.

The higher education subsidies that began in the Johnson administration—the Great Society era—can be considered part of the same tradition of making government outlays to promote individual advancement. Under the present program of so-called Pell grants (named for Senator Claiborne Pell), students from low- or moderate-income families can get up to $2,100 per academic year and half of their total educational costs. In 1986, some 2.6 million students benefitted from this program. This program also enjoys wide support: it is not a safety net, but a ladder of opportunity.

However, as federal social spending has come under increased budgetary and ideological pressures, Congress has de-emphasized student grants and put greater reliance on loans. A decade ago, in the academic year 1975–76, funding for grants and loans was about equal. By 1984–85, loans outstripped grants by three to one. As tuition expenses have risen much faster than family incomes have, and as the minimum wage paid in most part-time student jobs has lagged behind inflation, millions of college graduates enter the work world saddled by huge debts.

Life chances, and the view of government as an ally of opportunity, can be strikingly different for different generations. Compare the perspectives of a man born in 1921 and one born in 1961. A person born in 1921, who is at retirement age today, was a teenager during the Great Depression. He probably had the unsettling experience of family expectations being lowered when he was a boy in the early 1930s. An early memory might be of Father bringing home a paycheck from a public-works job. He probably fought in World War II and quite possibly got educated on the GI Bill and bought a house with a GI loan at 4 percent. As he matured and raised a family, he almost surely participated in the remarkable rise in real incomes between 1945 and 1973. During that period, he watched the government provide tangible, useful things—new public schools, an interstate highway system. And on reaching retirement age, he will enjoy the benefits of medicare and an inflation-indexed social security pension far in excess of his lifetime social security tax contributions.

It is all radically different for the man born in 1961. He was born into a far more affluent world than the older man; his family, in all likelihood, never experienced the steep reverses in economic status of the older man's family during the Depression. But as he enters the world of work, government as a provider is not very noticeable, and government as taxer is omnipresent. His real disposable income cannot keep pace with inflation. (As Frank Levy and Richard C. Michel have documented, before 1973 the average man passing from age forty to fifty saw his real earnings increase by 30 percent; after 1973 his disposable income dropped by 14 percent. Although overall taxation as a fraction of the GNP increased only slightly between 1953 and 1980, the burden of those taxes changed dramatically—from corporate to personal, and from upper-income to middle-income. In 1953, the average-income family paid just 8.7 percent of its income in federal income and payroll taxes; by 1980, that had grown to 16.2 percent.)

As the younger man looks at what he gets for the taxes he pays, he doesn't see very much that benefits him directly. There are very high taxes to finance social security and medicare—14.1 percent of payroll compared to 3 percent in 1944—but retirement is forty-some years off and medicare doesn't cover the working population. All told, more than 70 percent of the entire federal budget is now in just four categories—defense, social security, medicare, and interest on the public debt.

If our 1961 man is a college graduate, government may have helped with his tuition payments, but more likely with a loan than a grant, and the loan payments are now due. If he wants to buy a house, there are no more cheap government loans and virtually no more subsidies on moderately priced homes. Even after the recent drop in mortgage interest rates, an FHA or VA loan is in the 10 percent range. (Levy and Michel calculate that an average-income thirty-year-old could buy a medium-priced house for monthly payments equal to just 14 percent of his income in 1949; by 1985 it took an astonishing 44 percent.)

There are still the "safety-net" programs—AFDC if the young man fathers an illegitimate child; food stamps and medicaid if he finds himself in sudden poverty; short-term unemployment compensation if he has a work history though no entitlement to a job or to job training. But most of the working-age population does not receive these benefits. So it is not surprising that young people today seem so self-directed, so skeptical about government. This is likely to remain the case until public policy is realigned to fit popular economic and social needs of today and tomorrow. It is hardly the case that everyone disdains government intervention on behalf of economic opportunity because they are too affluent. Living standards have been dropping steadily since 1973. They have been maintained largely via the two-income family—and with other social costs. The problem is that policies and programs have failed to address people's needs. There are too few counterparts of the GI bill, FHA loans, college grants, and the whole *de facto* social contract that worked to serve popular wants. The not very surprising consequence is voters like Milwaukee's Bill Gapolinsky. The Democratic challenge today is to put government back on the side of solidarity and opportunity.

IV.

The first need for Democrats is to re-create the conditions that allow them to *have* an economic policy. This involves the interrelated issues of trade, industrial strategy, currency values, and global economic interdependence. As I have suggested in Chapter Five, even Democratic economists are educated to be skeptical of government interventions, and nowhere can we find this disjunction between the party and its economic advisors more dramatically than on issues concerning the integrated world economy. As intuitive politicians, most Democrats have been dismayed at the recent erosion of the United States's position in the world economy. The "hollowing" of the American industrial economy cries out for remedy. But most economists advising the party have argued that the invisible hand will solve most of these problems if politicians will only manage to balance the federal budget. They tend to view an activist trade policy as nothing more than political pandering to injured industries and special-interest union constituents. If left means interventionist and right means *laissez-faire*, this general stance puts the Democrats' own economic advisors well to the right of the party's politicians, in some respects even to the right of the Reagan administration.

Most economists have held that the effort begun in September 1985 by Treasury Secretary James A. Baker III to stabilize the dollar and create a system of managed exchange rates is in the long run futile. "Economists don't have much faith that these exchange agreements can do more than perhaps quiet short-term speculative markets," says Robert Litan, a Brookings Institution economist who advises Delaware Senator Joseph Biden. "Over the long run fundamental market forces determine exchange rates." In this prevailing view, the trade imbalance is mainly the result of the overvalued dollar, which dollar reflects the big U.S. budget deficit, which forces the Federal Reserve to keep real interest rates high. The only solution is to get the budget in balance.

Politically, however, this syllogism deprives Democrats of policy levers. In the immediate postwar period, Democrats were economic activists both at home and abroad. As leaders of the Western alliance, American statesmen built institutions of a global mixed economic system that worked well until the 1970s, the era of oil-price shocks, and the 1980s, the era of giddy financial deregulation. Like their domestic economic strategies, these institutions were created in the spirit of moderately Keynesian economics. The Marshall Plan, the GATT* system of liberal trade, the World Bank, the International Monetary Fund, and the Bretton Woods system of fixed, managed exchange rates served both stability and growth. Today, this system has been overwhelmed by the new realities of the private global economy. It offers neither the stability nor the growth, and it desperately needs overhauling.

But if one follows the standard economic counsel, it is impermissible to reinvent a Bretton Woods kind of system, though it worked well for twenty-five years; it is even more improper to devise "managed trade" or industrial policies; and the emphasis on deficit reduction renders moot any major government spending initiatives to retrain the work force or to restructure uncompetitive industries. Taken together, the usual advice discards the machinery of a mixed economy and creates a policy paralysis where the only available remedies are balanced budgets and lower wages—policies that make neither economic sense nor political sense for Democratic voters. As the value of the dollar sinks to compensate for

---

*General Agreement on Tariffs and Trade, referring both to the treaty governing trade rules, and to its enforcement bureaucracy in Geneva.

America's growing uncompetitiveness, it also means that we as a nation grow poorer and poorer. Eventually, a cheaper dollar may balance our trade accounts, but it will balance them at a level where it takes far more American bushels of wheat to buy far fewer Japanese cars, and our economy regains "competitiveness" the same way Bangladesh does—by having a cheap currency and paying low wages.

The American diplomatic stance in international trade negotiations has been quite at odds with our national interests. The United States fancies itself the guardian of the free-trade system. In practice, this has meant that our prime objective in trade talks has been to get other nations to rid their markets of barriers to our goods. The problem with this is that most other nations are much more eclectic in their view of economic development than we claim to be (though the United States actually engages in a lot of back-door industrial planning, if one counts the Pentagon). But the American posture does not allow us to accord any legitimacy to economic planning and this reality. Instead of looking for a global arrangement that treats free trade as the first-best and allows for some legitimate exceptions, the United States uses up its scarce diplomatic capital in pressuring other nations to make themselves over in an image that fails even to describe the American reality. In the process, we deny ourselves needed tools of economic redevelopment, and we squander our international influence.

Our recent negotiations with the Japanese illustrate this pattern all too graphically. The Reagan administration's diplomatic strategy vis-à-vis the Japanese has been to prod them to open their markets. It has proceeded as if Japan were a liberal, U.S.-style economic system rather than the state-managed form of capitalism that it is. The assumption has been that if Japan would just dismantle "barriers" and raise the value of its currency, our trade imbalance with Japan would subside. This policy has failed, in three distinct respects. First, it has been a conceptual failure: in good American legalistic fashion, it has been process-oriented, whereas Japanese economic strategy is goal-oriented. American negotiators keep looking for needles in the Japanese protectionist haystack, when in fact, since the entire Japanese system is designed to set economic goals and meet them. It would be better to negotiate an overall scheme of trade reciprocity and let the Japanese figure out how to manage it within their own domestic economy.

Second, in practice the United States has put military goals ahead of economic ones. The administration behaves as if our geopolitical relationship with Japan were more important than our economic one. As a result, we have been quick to give away trade objectives in exchange for military ones—such as Japanese concessions on the basing and billeting of U.S. troops and an increase in Japan's defense budget. Whereas Japan defines its economic well-being as *the* national security issue, we accord it a second strategic priority. "America wants a harmonious relationship with Japan, as a key member of the Western alliance," according to Clyde Prestowitz, formerly the administration's chief negotiator with the Japanese. "We think of trade policy not as an integral part of our grand strategy, but as a handmaiden. For Japan, trade is the strategic objective." Only rarely have American negotiators linked Japanese objectives like fishing rights or quota liberalizations or technology transfer to real trade reciprocity. Repeal of the automobile quota, which should have been used as a bargaining counter, was given up unilaterally because it bothered the American free-trade conscience, as was access to our telephone market. If American negotiators employed the same bargaining strategy in, say, East-West arms talks, they would be dismissed as craven unilateralists.

Third, the diplomatic practice vis-à-vis Japan has been wildly inconsistent, oscillating between a demand for "market-opening" measures and crude, furtive violations of free trade by means of bilateral agreements for trade restraints that plainly violate the GATT rules. The Reagan administration has negotiated agreements to limit Japanese shipments into the United States of machine tools, semiconductors, computers, and autos—all of which transgress the stated principles of liberal trade. Often these have proven self-defeating. For example, the United States encouraged Japan "unilaterally" to limit the number of cars exported to the United States—an overt bilateral quota would have been a flagrant violation of the GATT—but neglected to limit the dollar value of such shipments. As a result the Japanese simply shifted from exporting cheap autos to exporting expensive ones, and the dollar value of the trade deficit widened. In the critically important field of semiconductors, the illegitimacy of our national strategy left us helpless as Japan gradually overtook our lead. A belated 1986 agreement limited Japanese exports and put a floor under prices, but this quasi-protection only encouraged Japanese dumping of cheap semiconductors in third-country markets, and injured U.S. producers. Eventually, in early 1987, when the damage was done, the administration fell back on a "national security" justification for the semiconductor policy that it should have had all along on plain economic grounds.

Globally, our goals vis-à-vis the GATT have suffered from the same ideological paralysis. Because U.S. negotiators have been obsessed with the first-best—i.e., absolute free trade—we have continued to press nations to abandon industrial policies which they need to develop. Our trade policy and our debt policy with respect to the Third World have been totally at odds with each other. The International Monetary Fund, as the collection agent for creditor American banks, has pressed debtor nations to run big export surpluses in order to earn foreign exchange to service their debts. This has the unfortunate side effect of depressing their domestic markets for U.S. products. But meanwhile, our trade negotiators are pressing these countries to open their economies to more U.S. goods and, especially, to exports of financial "services," meaning American banking and insurance. But Third World countries take the position that before they will open their markets further, they want debt relief, and they want the United States to get rid of its own forms of limited protection, such as restraints on imports of farm products and textiles. Diplomatically, the grand American *laissez-faire* dream is to negotiate a once-and-for-all trade deal in which all countries would simultaneously abandon all forms of protection, and totally free flow of capital, technologies, and products would follow. This, in theory, would produce the long-sought textbook world of perfect efficiency. But just as individual *laissez-faire* economies can suffer from bouts of overproduction, deflation, and depression, the world economy can slip into a self-deepening whirlpool of overcapacity, price cutting, product glut, and competition to cut wages. Most of our competitors are too worldly to seek an Adam Smith economy. They are content to search for second-bests and for an international system that at least offers some comity. In a world of sovereign nation states, where labor (which is to say people) is not so mobile as capital is, the *laissez-faire* dream is dangerous because it keeps us from negotiating the achievable second-bests.

Trade, debt, and world economic growth are intimately linked in both logic and economics, but they are seldom linked diplomatically. The diplomats who bargain over trade are not the same as the ones who bargain over debt. Growth is not part of the official GATT agenda, nor is macroeconomic harmony the concern of the world's bankers. The real trade-offs that should occur in the trade negotiations are not so much a matter of you-liberalize-bank-branches/I'll-liberalize-textiles as they are more imaginative trades: the Third World could pay off its debt if world growth were restored; Japan and the United States could stop fencing if each accorded the other the right to a dose of economic planning and negotiated some serious reciprocity.

The Republican Treasury Secretary, James Baker, in 1985, took a big step into the real world. He ignored the advice of the Republican supply-side economists and embarked on some serious economic diplomacy—the only farsighted statecraft to distinguish the Reagan administration's benighted foreign policy. At the now-famous Plaza Accord of September 1985, Baker abandoned the experiment in floating exchange rates and began working with the West Germans and the Japanese to coordinate a series of reductions in interest rates, and to work jointly to gradually depress the value of the then inflated dollar. In an integrated global market, economic stabilization depends on international coordination of macroeconomic policies. But Baker had less success in devising a common program of economic stimulus. His power to proceed beyond a series of *ad hoc* ententes was hobbled by his own administration's commitment to *laissez-faire* economics.

Democrats ought to pick up where Baker left off. There is a pressing need for a coordinated program of restored economic growth, debt relief for Third World nations, and a revision of the trade regime to acknowledge the reality of national economic planning. Often, Democrats have been browbeaten into pledging allegiance to pure free trade. As a result, when some Democrats guiltily decide to embrace protectionist measures, they are denounced as opportunists; others, proclaiming their fidelity to free trade, find themselves unable to show the voters any advantage in it. That usual political question—who is a free trader, who is a protectionist?—is a fatal trap for Democrats. The real question ought to be: What is the most efficient version of a mixed economy, both globally and domestically? Democrats, let us recall, do not believe in pure *laissez-faire*. The party gave it up in 1933. And the voters, with their social security and their medicare and their public schools and their membership in a political community, gave it up a long time ago, too. The voters are not Adam Smith purists, and they grow appropriately confused whenever good Democrats begin bowing to the invisible hand.

For Democrats to put forward a practical version of a mixed global economy, they must propose the sort of economic diplomacy that they championed in the late 1940s: to reinvent a stable world economic system, with shared goals, public as well as private institutions, and real reciprocity among nations. That means, surely, that multilateral development agencies, as well as money center banks, must be in the business of Third World development. It means acknowledging that the American national interest is not identical to the interest of the shareholders in Citibank. As far as trade is concerned, it means reinventing the rules of trade to allow a place for economic planning instead of pretending that no such planning exists or ought to. Perhaps free trade should be the residual norm, but in any case every trading nation should be permitted a certain number, or proportion, of exceptions, for purposes of development. If an advanced nation such as Japan wishes to target semiconductors as a key industry, perhaps the trade rules should prohibit it from targeting ten other advanced industries as well. Perhaps industries that are truly creatures of the invisible hand should enjoy free market access with no tariffs or quotas, but other industries that are creatures of domestic economic management should be subject to trade management and market-sharing rules when they are traded internationally. It is legitimate to suggest overall limits on import shares in certain key industries, for each nation, and to demand some symmetry and reciprocity in the system as a whole. At a minimum, we need to begin seriously debating the specifics of such an alternative trade regime. This would have the twin benefit of adjusting the rules to fit the reality, and would also give the United States the ideological license to engage in some necessary planning at home.

Even economists are beginning to come around, reluctantly, to this approach. For example, though they don't like import quotas at all, several prominent neo-classical economists recently proposed that import quotas be accepted as a necessary part of the trading system, and auctioned. At present, when the U.S. government negotiates a *de facto* import quota, say on Korean steel, the price of the import rises to meet the higher U.S. price. The foreign producer reaps a windfall, the American purchaser pays, and the U.S. government gets nothing. But if, instead, quotas were auctioned, the most efficient foreign producers would bid for them; there would be no windfall profit for the foreign manufacturer, and the U.S. Treasury could collect revenues of as much as $10 billion a year.

In the same manner, several good neo-classical defenders of free trade, including Brookings's Robert Lawrence, and Jeffery Schott and Gary Hufbauer of the Institute for International Economics, have proposed "retariffication"—a system of temporary tariffs for purposes of industrial adjustment. With a tariff, the government receives revenue, and the domestic manufacturer receives temporary shelter with which to restructure. There is less distortion of prices than with quotas. Robert Litan, also of Brookings, who advocates auctioned import quotas as a temporary expedient, would prefer temporary tariffs.

Proposals such as these have far more potential than merely as useful "new ideas." They represent a long-sought middle ground on trade policy that acknowledges the need for a mixed economy globally as well as domestically, and they show professional economists rejoining the real world. As long as economists lectured politicians that all forms of protectionism were equally evil, they guaranteed that the politicians would ignore their advice altogether and guiltily reach for the most expedient form of protection available. By abandoning the "first-best" world of the textbook, and recognizing that second-bests can be preferable to fourth-bests, these economists are performing a real service that can allow the Democratic Party some effective practical politics.

Many progressive Democrats have endorsed the slippery proposition that economic growth is necessary before a social agenda can proceed. Growth is surely a *sine qua non,* but the mistake many Democrats make is to accept the Republican belief that the only possible or desirable form of growth is *laissez-faire* growth. That reflects a political preference, not a technical imperative. In reality, our recovery from the Great Depression, our extraordinary leap in technological knowledge and living standards during World War II, and our stable Keynesian advances after the war were not the fruits of *laissez-faire* growth. Yet they were the years of the most dynamic, sustained growth in our economic history.

Finally, taking an activist stand on world trade, debt, and growth issues is a way for Democrats to redefine the national-security and foreign-policy debates. The Reagan administration defined national security almost exclusively in military and geopolitical terms. As long as that is the accepted standard, and as long as Democrats have a neo-conservative flank to protect, Democrats will be tempted to adopt as hard-line a foreign policy and as costly a military program as the Republicans. But the more serious threat to our national security, for the remainder of the century, is likely to be economic, as American industry loses standing to foreign producers. By redefining foreign-policy firmness as economic leadership, Democrats can play to their natural strength and show up the Republicans' failure to defend America's true national interests.

This does not mean that Democrats ought to be as belligerent about trade as Republicans have been toward the Soviets, say. On the contrary, a realistic trade policy, which acknowledges the reality of mixed economies, can diffuse a lot of unnecessary tensions. It would be self-defeating for Democrats to view trade simply as chauvinistic raw meat to throw a hungry electorate. The more pressing need is for real statecraft, and institution building, of the sort that rebuilt the global economy after World War II. I have chosen not to dwell on foreign policy in this book. Here, Democrats spend an inordinate amount of political energy attempting to shore up what is perceived as a weak flank. During and after World War II, Democrats were both the party of economic recovery and the party of patriotism. Roosevelt had been both Dr. New Deal and Dr. Win-the-War. Since the beginning of the Cold War, and especially since the Vietnam War, Democrats have been divided into foreign-policy soft-liners and hard-liners, and party leaders have often worried that voters perceived them as the soft-on-communism party. This has led some analysts to advise that Democrats must win the hearts of voters by demonstrating foreign and military toughness. Candidates like Georgia Senator Sam Nunn and former Virginia governor Charles Robb are trotted out as exemplary patriots.

I suspect that foreign and military policy does present Democrats with opportunities—to demonstrate that a strong defense need not be spendthrift, that assertiveness includes economic issues as well as geopolitical ones, and above all that true national security ought to include arms control as well as arms. The voters are hungry for real American leadership on arms control; they perceive that the Reagan administration has passed up historic opportunities to lessen world tensions and to demonstrate leadership. In the spring of 1987, polls all over Western Europe showed Mikhail Gorbachev with higher approval ratings than Ronald Reagan. American voters miss the United States that played the role of friendly giant on the world stage, with initiatives like the Marshall Plan, the Peace Corps, and more recently Jimmy Carter's human rights initiatives and the Camp David accord. A careful foreign-policy approach—imaginative, assertive but not belligerent, emphasizing steady and cooperative leadership—can probably gain Democrats votes. But even if the schisms within the party on foreign policy can be overcome, and a latter-day version of John Kennedy can be found who advocates a policy that is both toughminded and idealistic, I would still counsel Democrats that the next election ought not be fought primarily over foreign-policy issues, and that candidates ought not be chosen mainly on that basis. Like every other left-of-center party in the parliamentary West, the Democrats' strong suit is economics.

V.

One weakness of the Democrats as a coalition party is a tendency to try to be all things to all people. The logical conclusion of that approach is to do nothing very well and to leave every constituency vaguely dissatisfied. At some point, a beleaguered President like Jimmy Carter begins to blame the party's own voters and to talk like a Republican. This part of the neo-liberal critique of Democrats as interest-group politicians is accurate. Moreover, except in the exemplary cases of social security and medicare, Democrats have too often sponsored approaches that fragmented rather than unified their base. In the 1960s, when Democratic progressives had a working majority in the Congress, they made the fatal mistake of concentrating on "poverty programs" that isolated the poor as a distinct category, which invited a backlash against broad, universal programs in key areas such as health, housing, and employment, rather than working to expand them.

The next Democratic President needs to do a few big things well, in areas that serve the broad wage-earning and salaried class of voters. The single most important area for real leadership in domestic policy is that closely interconnected set of issues involving education, labor-market policies, employment opportunities, and related family supports. The conservative solution is radical individualism: the free market produces the jobs, individual incentive provides the motivation, the traditional family offers the social support. But in the real world, the market often doesn't provide enough good jobs and distributes opportunities unjustly; personal initiative doesn't help when unemployment rises; and many families can't provide the necessary supports because the old-style family model can no longer exist. The conservative formulation of personal initiative versus dependency is another false dichotomy. Effective public policies can promote economic opportunity and family autonomy, not undermine them. Nothing is more pro-family than a good public school or a good training program or a career opportunity that offers a living wage. A related problem is that as the private market economy shifts from manufacturing and industry to services, it is producing too many jobs that pay too little to sustain a middle-class standard of living. The political consequence is diminished opportunity for the next generation and pessimism about the economic future.

Everybody agrees, in the abstract, that the ultimate source of American wealth and economic competitiveness is the quality of our work force. Yet the policies we have for creating a world-class work force are patchwork, expressing the contradictory goals of different administrations and constituencies during the past fifty years. We spend a great deal of money on education, and we have a set of labor-market programs, but these do not function well as a coherent system. If public education is the most fundamental citizen entitlement, Democrats ought to be champions of public education. In the current economic climate, they also need to champion a relatively new educational concept for the United States—lifetime learning and continuous job upgrading. As the labor market shifts from manufacturing into services, it means that fewer human workers are needed to produce life's material products. In principle, this is a net gain for society because it allows workers to be liberated to do other work. But in a pure market economy, it is not necessarily a gain for the displaced workers or for wage-earners generally. A service economy can mean new jobs for people who help to provide society with better education, medical care, and cultural endeavor, or it can mean millions of low-wage jobs serving meals to investment bankers, typing briefs for lawyers, and entering data for insurance companies.

The United States spends \$30–\$40 billion a year on labor market subsidies. Most of this goes for unemployment compensation, which pays people with a work history for being involuntarily idle during downturns of the business cycle. We also have a patchwork of training, retraining, and vocational education programs, some of which are under the umbrella of the Job Training Partnership Act, the Republican successor to the much maligned CETA (Comprehensive Education and Training Act). What we do not have is any systematic approach to continuous upgrading of the work force, as many other nations do. In Sweden, which has the most advanced such system, a national labor market board has a budget equal to approximately 3 percent of the entire Swedish gross national product. The comparable figure in the United States would be \$120 billion a year. The Swedish board operates a national employment service that has listings of every job opening in the country. It subsidizes job training and retraining. It can offer funds for training sabbaticals during phases of the business cycle when private employers would otherwise lay workers off, and thus serves to soak up excess labor while that labor is retrained. Conversely, when labor

markets are tight, it can target resources to train people for speciali-
ties where skilled workers are scarce, so as to keep labor shortages
from excessively bidding up costs. The national board also gives
grants to local boards to facilitate a community's adjustment out of
a declining industry into a growth one. For example, a town in the
far north of Sweden may be losing a major shipbuilding firm and
with it hundreds of jobs. The local labor market board, made up
of representatives of business, labor, and the town government,
formulates a plan to attract new industry. The national board ap-
proves the plan and provides a grant to subsidize temporarily a new
employer's wage or job-training costs. In effect, this uses a labor
subsidy to subsidize capital. Employers are encouraged to locate
new facilities in communities that need jobs, through the device of
a carefully targeted wage or training subsidy. In the United States,
all too often, local governments compete with each other to attract
industry by promising a "good labor climate," which means few
unions and plenty of workers who are willing to work for less, and
by bartering away needed tax base.

Sweden's approach should not be seen as merely an ingenious
technical fix. It is the logical outcome of a set of frankly ideological
and political goals, carefully developed by trade unionists and their
close allies in the governing Social Democratic Party. Sweden's
labor market board is the centerpiece of what's known as an "active
labor market policy," designed to serve several broad solidarity
goals as well as narrow economic ones. First, it keeps the country
at or near full employment, which is the alpha and omega of the
Swedish system. Without full employment, labor solidarity col-
lapses, employed workers are played off against unemployed ones,
and social subsidies are consumed paying the costs of the idle
instead of being saved for genuinely needy cases. Second, the active
labor market policy serves to adjust and upgrade the workforce,
which makes the entire economy more competitive and productive.
Third, it gives workers *employment* security independent of their
current job, and that allows the workers to welcome rather than
fear innovation. In the United States, workers understandably resist change because their own security and status are often linked
to a specific job. With an active labor market policy, employment
security is underwritten by the system as a whole. Moreover, Swe-

den's national commitment to a fairly narrow spread between the
wages paid for different kinds of jobs means that a worker suddenly
shifting from auto assembly to electronics assembly or clerical work
doesn't suddenly suffer a 50 percent drop in pay. Finally, this approach reinforces organized labor's constructive position as an
institutional guarantor of a functioning social contract, which is a
crucial political and electoral underpinning for the entire system.

Though in the popular caricature, Sweden is "socialistic" and
socialism connotes bureaucracy, in fact the Swedish labor market
system is highly decentralized and reliant on flexible tripartite part-
nerships among local business, labor, and government. Of course,
the United States has neither the Social Democratic Party nor the
pervasive trade-union movement of Sweden. But we have the same
political and economic need to socialize the costs of industrial
transitions, so that the costs don't fall solely on displaced workers
and communities. An American version of this approach would
produce similar political benefits for our "social-democratic" party,
the Democrats, in the sense that it would deliver real economic
benefits to wage earners who ought to be Democratic voters and
would nurture public planning at the local level as a counterweight
to purely private economic decisions.

An American labor market board would have to combine our
several disparate programs, each with its own bureaucracy, into a
functioning, coherent system, with a clear set of goals. What we
have now is, on the whole, marginal to the actual labor market. Few
private employers or workers get much benefit, and yet we are
spending a lot of money on it. The public Employment Service
functions mainly as an agency of last resort for employers who
cannot find workers anywhere else, or for workers with few skills.
Its steadiest source of clients are people drawing unemployment
checks, who are required to sign up with the local Employment
Service in order to collect benefits. Fewer than 5 percent ultimately
get their jobs through the Service.

It is time to merge the system of unemployment insurance into
a general re-employment, job-creation and job-retraining system.
A few states have allowed people to convert AFDC checks into
retraining and wage subsidies. The same could be done with unemployment compensation. And the separate system of vocational

education needs to be merged with the existing employment and training apparatus. It is also time to recognize that training is what economists call an "externality." The employer does not acknowledge the benefits of investments in worker training because a better-trained worker is more likely to quit and take a job with a competitor. As a result, firms systematically underinvest in the upgrading of their work forces. A few states have understood this and have created training programs financed by a separate payroll tax. For example, California's Employment Training Panel invites employers to submit plans for job upgrading, and then underwrites most of the cost of the training, usually at local junior colleges. This not only improves the work force and pumps employer-specific resources into the community college system, but it encourages employers to focus on the structure of their own internal labor markets. And, in line with our political goal, it provides concrete services to the public.

If the United States government had a strategic commitment to lifetime learning, workers would be able to take periodic training sabbaticals, subsidized by public funds. Displaced workers could also be given vouchers that would pay part of the cost of their wages for, say, two to five years. This job-creation technique would allow such workers to go to the head of the job queue. The government might also require large employers to set up affirmative-action plans whose goal would be to create more explicit career ladders within firms, and the gradual conversion of bad jobs into good ones. In highly unionized countries, there is less of a problem of low-wage service-sector jobs, because service jobs pay nearly the same wages as industrial jobs. As a result, employers cannot afford to squander costly human labor on dead-end scut work and are motivated to invent mechanical substitutes. Workers are then free to perform jobs in human services, or in other more advanced activities, where they are truly needed, and the whole society operates at higher levels of productivity.

There are other mechanisms that could unite the related goals of job creation, job upgrading, employment security, and national productivity. My intent is not to offer an encyclopedia of technically elegant "new ideas" but to shed some light on the necessary politics. The trouble with many of the ideas that enjoy currency today is their political innocence. For example, the popular proposal for an Individual Training Account—in which workers would get a tax deduction for setting up a bank account like an IRA which they could tap to pay the costs of retraining if the worker was laid off—has the drawback of being privatized; it exists in isolation from any coherent, social commitment to upgrading, and as a self-financed, tax-subsidized mechanism it would tend to favor relatively well-paid workers and do little for social solidarity. Moreover, there is little evidence that good jobs are going begging for absence of a $4,000 retraining subsidy. The greater social need is to create an ongoing system of training and job upgrading that also serves to take up slack in the labor market, so that workers don't find themselves involuntarily on the street.

In the absence of a coherent world view about market and society, thinking up new ideas like Individual Training Accounts places the cart before the horse; the cart ends up looking like something more appropriate to a Republican elephant than a Democratic donkey. Full employment, lifetime learning, and worker flexibility are logically interrelated. The logic has to be political as well as economic. Democrats stand for the proposition that civic man is a social animal as well as an individual one. In that respect, policy always has a politics, and it must be consistent with the deeper social logic. It must serve the broader goals of solidarity while it serves the immediate programmatic ones.

Lately, there has been an almost uncanny convergence of themes articulated by Democratic candidates. In place of the chronic fragmentation and ideological infighting, virtually the entire spectrum of Democratic candidates for the presidency, as well as other party leaders, are singing the same songs. The songs have to do with making the United States economy more "competitive," better education, productivity, a commitment to "families," and an emphasis on workfare rather than welfare. One could read a position paper articulating these themes, and not know whether it was the handiwork of Hart, Biden, Babbitt, Gephardt, Robb, Nunn, Bradley, Dukakis, Cuomo, or whomever.

This surprising thematic unity is cause for celebration, yet tempered by concern. It is encouraging because for once there is no overt split between party right and party left, no bitter combat over divisive, morally irreconcilable issues, like Vietnam. Even the recent habit of bashing "interest groups" has mercifully muted. Broadly speaking, all Democrats seem to share the same goals. But at the same time there is the danger that this superficial conformity will lead the party to beg hard questions. Does "competitiveness," for example, require a serious social contract between industry and labor with a constructive role for unions, or only a cheaper dollar and lower wages? Does support for education translate into a serious commitment to lifetime learning, and the enlargement of public education to encompass daycare, or only the passage of teacher-certification rules as an on-the-cheap substitute? Does productivity entail tax breaks for industry and further deregulation, or a different conception of reciprocity? These questions require Democrats to be serious, and explicit about their public philosophy.

VI.

A different social contract for employment policy necessarily requires not only a new scheme of full employment and labor-market upgrading, but, concomitantly, a changed view of the corporation and the role of employees as parties to the social contract. The recent uproar about hostile takeovers has highlighted the ideological premise that a corporation has only one obligation to society—to maximize the yield to its shareholders.

When corporations were first invented as legal forms, they were chartered by the state for specific, narrow purposes; in return for serving these purposes, they received certain privileges and immunities, such as the protection of their owners from personal liability. But in this century, corporations have been allowed to behave as if their sole function were to maximize shareholder wealth. Even the most radical constraints on corporate behavior, under the antitrust laws, accepted the *laissez-faire* premise that a corporation was breaking the rules of the game only when it colluded with competitors and cheated on the invisible hand. Other predatory activities were perfectly legal, and even laudable, if they served to increase dividends or the values of shares. Economic planning and a more social conception of the corporation enjoyed a short-lived vogue early in the Roosevelt administration and re-emerged covertly only in the context of planning for national defense. But our stated philosophy has never really conceded that corporations are social institutions, with reciprocal obligations to workers as well as to owners. The implicit assumption, once again, has been Adam Smith's—that a corporation maximizing the yield to shareholders must also be serving society, by definition. If the shareholders are different individuals today and tomorrow, if one set of managers devours another, if the company manufactures steel this week and imports video games next week, if it maximizes its yield by decamping for Taiwan, no matter.

Merger mania usefully forces the issue. Until a decade or so ago, the contractual obligations between corporation and society may not have been specified in law, but they were implicit in social custom. What made them explicit were norms of corporate behavior. One corporation did not use borrowed money to devour another corporation over the objection of the target firm's own management. The financial establishment did not permit it. Corporations normally gave their salaried employees something close to lifetime employment, subject to good behavior. Their industrial employees were hired and fired subject to a strict set of rules, based on the social contract as negotiated during the Great Depression. Unions could win legal recognition, by majority vote, under the Wagner Act. Hourly employees were normally allowed to bid for better-paying jobs, as these became available, by seniority. If layoffs occurred, they occurred by reverse seniority. Nonunionized firms were not compelled to follow these rules, but most of them did, if only as union-avoidance medicine. This system had its drawbacks, but it provided a measure of predictability, reciprocity, and loyalty. Some scholars have concluded that what it lacked in flexibility, it made up for in stability and teamwork.

Whatever its pluses and minuses, the old corporate social contract is defunct. In the frenetic industrial restructuring of the 1980s, firms feel no obligation to repay the loyalty of their workers. Investment bankers feel no loyalty to managers. The holders of shares, as always, are happy to sell the firm out for an eighth of a point gain—this was always the case—but lately the pace of speculative trading has dramatically increased. Nobody is responsible for the health of the enterprise in the long term. In the mythology of *laissez-faire* capitalism, all of this social dislocation "must be" good for the real economy, because it "proves" that financial assets are being redeployed to more productive uses; the new managers must have some skills that the old managers lacked; otherwise the market would not entrust them with the assets. The laid-off workers must have been overpaid relative to what they accomplished; otherwise the market wouldn't find them expendable.

The trouble with this *ex post* deductive reasoning is that it ignores the serious disruptive costs to the corporation as a social organization. It discounts the destructive effects on loyalty and on teamwork. In their myopia, financial economists have argued that "golden parachutes" (multimillion-dollar consolation payments to displaced executives) are actually good for the system because they minimize the management's resistance to enforced restructuring. But it does not occur to these economists that perhaps the loyalty of lowlier employees might be enhanced by economic security as well.

In the orgy of hostile corporate takeovers, the "raiders" have been able to pose as the invisible hand incarnate because the group they are challenging is entrenched corporate management. If corporate management is self-perpetuating and no social forms of corporate accountability exist, then raiders like T. Boone Pickens provide the only mechanism available to discipline managers on behalf of shareholders and shake the system up. Editorialists have accepted this defense of raiding far too credulously. The problem is that we have failed to provide alternative mechanisms of accountability that are less disruptive of the system as a social organism.

As takeover abuses have mounted, the usual public debate has been framed too narrowly. Congress has begun taking measures to restrain the worst abuses on both sides of the takeover game, which supposedly will make it more difficult for purely speculative raiders to mount hostile takeovers, as well as preventing managers from insulating themselves from legitimate shareholder pressures. In a characteristic exposition of the issues, Felix Rohatyn, an investment banker with a statesmanlike persona, began an essay entitled "The Blight On Wall Street" with the astonishingly uncapitalist assertion that "A cancer has been spreading in our industry. . . . the cancer is called greed." When Rohatyn got around to his list of remedies, it included the usual proposals for tempering the worst abuses on both sides—limit "junk bond financing" of takeovers, restrict the tax advantages that fuel hostile takeovers, prohibit "greenmail," restore "one-share/one-vote," and so on.

But once you concede that "greed," otherwise known in the economics textbooks as "profit maximization," is not an unmitigated economic good, you must begin to consider what else is necessary to reclaim the corporation as an economically defensible social organization. It is not enough to restore comity between the two existing parties to the contract—managers and shareholders. The existing corporation is a creation of law, not of the invisible hand. Once we concede that it has some social function beyond mere greed, we ought to be more venturesome in thinking through its broad economic purpose and designing the machinery of its governance.

It remains an anomaly of our political democracy that democratic governance does not extend to the workplace. Somebody who buys shares today and sells them tomorrow has legal control over a corporation—total control if she acquires 51 percent—but a worker who has served the corporation loyally for twenty years has no legal standing whatsoever. Obviously, it is the employee, with no "golden parachute" and no prospect of a quick financial killing, who has the most stake in the corporation's long-term viability.

The Wall Street scandals offer a rare political opening to achieve fundamental changes in the conception of a corporation. Congress is poised to revise the securities laws in order to make it more difficult for speculative raiders to take control of corporations. This, on balance, will give more security to managers. But instead of giving this protection away, Congress should devise other forms of accountability, and give employees standing as members of the corporate community.

There are many ways of doing this, ranging from placing workers on boards to creating European-style works councils, to mandating profit sharing. The neo-liberal version embraces profit sharing, without altering the corporation as a legal and social organization. In Martin Weitzman's conception of a "share economy," for example, workers take on some of the risks of entrepreneurship by agreeing to adjust their compensation to the firm's profitability. But Weitzman does not confer upon workers the more basic perquisite of the entrepreneurship—the power to control management. If workers are exposed to the downside risk of bad management in the form of wage cuts, it is only fair that they also have some influence to keep management as efficient as possible. The conservative assumption is that innovation requires constant institutional turmoil—what the economist Joseph Schumpeter called "creative destruction." But creative innovation within the context of institutional stability and accountability is probably sounder economics and certainly better social policy.

One strategy for giving workers this enlarged standing in corporate governance would be through a drastic revision of the social role of pension funds and employee stock-ownership plans (ESOPs). At present, nearly all pension funds and ESOPs operate as totally passive forms of deferred compensation. They give workers shares but no effective influence over corporate governance. Pension funds are managed by professional experts instructed to look for the highest yield. They are viewed purely as market instruments, not as social instruments. Similarly, management carefully structures the vast majority of ESOPs—to make sure that the workers do not get voting rights in the stock. But if workers got some of their compensation in the form of stock that collectively conferred voting rights and other management prerogatives on a worker council, and managers came under closer worker scrutiny, it would also be far more difficult for a raider to capture a corporation over the objections of its workforce.

As a beginning, Congress might pass a chartering law creating a new, experimental corporate form, which would enjoy certain tax advantages and regulatory protections against hostile takeovers, but in return would be structured institutionally to give workers coequal power with shareholders.

In the absence of any standing for employees, many worthwhile and innovative experiments in employee involvement, work-quality circles, flexible job classifications, and so on have been stillborn, because the workers had no assurance that their sacrifices would pay off. At an LTV Steel facility in Cleveland, the steelworkers union and a farsighted company labor-relations team negotiated a pioneering agreement getting rid of job classifications and tying pay to generic skill levels. The agreement even shifted workers from hourly wages to weekly salaries, and it provided for labor cost cutting in exchange for enhanced employee involvement. What the bargain could not guarantee was job security. The ink was barely dry when LTV, in a new round of cost cutting, went into Chapter 11 bankruptcy, rendering the agreement moot. Autoworkers have encountered the same dilemma. Since the late 1970s, the UAW has pioneered employee involvement teams and wage-restraint-for-profit-sharing-deals, but plants keep closing and pressures for further restraints persist.

Perhaps the saddest recent case of a narrowly missed opportunity to invent a new social contract for labor is the case of Eastern Airlines. At Eastern, with a bitter history of labor strife and high labor costs, the machinists union and the company hammered out a radically different bargain: the union agreed to steep wage cuts in exchange for 25 percent of the company stock; more importantly, the company granted the union something approaching genuine codetermination, in which workers got access to confidential management financial projections and participated intimately in all aspects of corporate planning. In 1985, this bargain led to concrete productivity improvements that saved the company at least $30 million and dramatically improved morale.

But in a newly deregulated industry subject to relentless cost-cutting pressures, Eastern workers were pressured to take even steeper cuts whenever another industry downturn came. Management was able to stash profits in capital investments, to avoid paying out profit shares to workers. Ultimately, the company was sold at a bargain-basement price and merged with Continental Airlines. Although workers owned 25 percent of Eastern stock, their offer to buy controlling interest was not seriously entertained, nor were the worker representatives on the Eastern board party to the negotiations. At this writing, Eastern's morale and quality are deteriorating in tandem.

These anecdotes make a common point: an *ad hoc* new deal between management and labor that would trade labor flexibility for labor influence or wage restraint for job security cannot work in the current industrial climate if it is just a one-company, bilateral deal between workers and executives. It needs a third-party guarantor. The next Democratic administration should encourage new forms of labor-management bargains by offering subsidies, models, management training, and—most importantly—by insisting that the bargain be honored. A company in the throes of a historic restructuring agreement with its unions should not be permitted abruptly to seek further cost reductions via a technical bankruptcy or a fire sale, or to raid pension funds, or to wriggle out of profit-sharing commitments. There also has to be a place to put loyal workers when productivity improvements render them redundant. The job-security promise must be social, because the individual firm can't guarantee it. To stick, such deals have to guarantee authentic worker influence, as well as worker employment security, and this cannot be done in isolation; government needs to be a party to the bargain.

The federal government's rescue of the Chrysler Corporation in the late 1970s was an *ad hoc* attempt to fashion just such a social bargain. For a deal concocted in great haste, it did not work all so badly, but the profit-sharing aspect was weak, as was the guarantee of worker influence and job security. The bargain was a triumph at the corporate level because the company survived and returned to profitability. But it was only a limited success as social policy because there was no framework or set of criteria for its enactment. On the contrary, it violated the principle that only the marketplace should determine which firms survive.

The idea that workers need many kinds of skills training and that management needs to be able to redeploy them as necessary enjoys great popularity as a remedy for America's poor productivity record. Conservatives and many neo-liberals contend that the only thing we need is more such "flexibility" on the part of workers, and that flexibility is best attained when unions are weakened or nonexistent. This is all wrong. What is needed is a successor social contract to replace the informal one that expired in the late 1970s. By all means, the United States does need a flexible work force, trained in generic skills rather than artificially narrowed job categories. But worker flexibility in the absence of management reciprocity makes for insecurity, vulnerability, and exploitation. Eventually that hardens into worker cynicism, and society pays the price. Windfall corporate profit from the breaking of established social contracts can be understood as a one-time cashing-in of accumulated institutional good will. Just as cheating a customer does not produce renewed business from that customer, cheating the work force does not lead to long-term productivity for the economy.

By brokering reciprocal labor-management bargains, the next Democratic administration can also serve the institutional goal of helping the labor movement adjust to the realities of the changing economy. Democrats did this, albeit under markedly different circumstances, during the New Deal. In 1933, progressives in Congress wrote into the National Industrial Recovery Act a provision giving trade unions legal recognition and the right to bargain collectively for their members. Under the NIRA scheme, industrial restructuring was supposed to be a three-way partnership involving business, labor, and government. When the NIRA was declared unconstitutional in 1935, the union recognition was retained, under the successor Wagner Act. That legislation did not create the industrial labor movement, but it provided legal and political space for the movement to organize itself. When CIO president John L. Lewis went around the country telling meetings of workers, "President Roosevelt wants you to join the union," he was exaggerating only slightly.

The Wagner Act framed a social entente between management and labor that came to be known as business unionism. Management conceded labor's right to exist and permitted unions to recruit members and to bargain for a share of profits via industry-wide "master contracts" and for job security via seniority and work rules. Labor agreed to stay away from "management prerogatives," including decisions involving capital investment, pricing, product lines, deployment of personnel, location of facilities, and so on. When the UAW president, Walter Reuther, demanded "a look at the books," he was told this was none of the union's business.

Today, in a fiercely competitive, deregulated global economy, the Wagner Act framework provides neither the job security nor the stable wages, and management feels entitled to attack unions as institutions. In these circumstances, unions today are both more docile and more venturesome. They are willing to give up the once-sacrosanct work rules and master contracts; they are also prepared to involve themselves deeply in issues involving capital investment, technology, work organization, and other management prerogatives, and to make a series of mutually beneficial trade-offs. Thus the preconditions exist either for a more cooperative, less adversarial form of labor relations, or for a predatory labor market with no social contract at all. Conservatives would prefer the latter. Democrats must create a new legal framework to institutionalize a set of labor-management relations that fits the needs of the 1980s and 1990s. Just as in the 1930s, government cannot create a labor movement, but it can help labor to reinvent itself.

The Labor Department currently has a small division that oversees cooperative labor-management programs, and a few million dollars annually are used to encourage collaborative labor-management experiments. Under a conservative Republican administration, this program obviously has no ideological goal of helping revive the movement. The office's resources are meager, thanks to the Reagan budget priorities, and its work must be cloaked in a Republican-sounding version of collaboration. But under a more imaginative and pro-labor administration, one could devise a program of grants to support pilot labor-management arrangements whose avowed purpose would be to increase the managerial and financial sophistication of unions and to devise homegrown models of codetermination.

There is a fine precedent for this, which was pioneered by the Carter administration in another area of labor law. In previous years, the Occupational Safety and Health Administration (OSHA) suffered from a terrible reputation of being bureaucratically onerous to industry, and so myopic and driven by rulebooks as to be ineffective for labor. Under its new Carter appointee, Basil Whiting, a former Ford Foundation executive, and Labor Secretary Ray Marshall, a program of New Direction grants was started to increase labor's competence and sophistication in health and safety matters, as an alternative to more policing. "At the time, the expertise was all one-sided," Whiting recalls. "There were a grand total of six industrial hygienists in the entire labor movement. If a union saw a problem, its only recourse was to call the cops. But you can't have good health and safety just by relying on the cops, and you'll never have enough cops." So the Labor Department grants helped to train and subsidize industrial hygienists on union staffs, to sponsor joint labor-management reviews to improve health and safety, and to pay the cost of union "COSH" (Committee on Safety and Health) initiatives. According to Whiting, the initial reaction of some union officials to the New Direction budget of $10–$15 million a year was, "If the government has a spare ten million dollars to spend on health and safety, why don't they hire another hundred inspectors?" But other unionists grasped the strategic value of the approach. In health and safety, as in other arenas, knowledge is power. By becoming more empowered about health and safety, trade unionists inevitably found themselves tackling more fundamental issues of plant design, work organization, and capital investment—which is to say, management prerogatives.

The New Direction program died with the Carter administration before it had a chance to take the next step. In other industrial nations, trade unionists are the front line of health and safety enforcement. Government inspectors are a backup; they are called in when labor and management reach an impasse, and they occasionally do spot checks. But unionists often find that their own highly trained health and safety teams are far more reliable than an army of bureaucrats. And, of course, union responsibility for health and safety adds to the union's authority and stature generally. Thus, allowing the union to play an expanded role in health and safety enforcement is what has been called a "nonreformist reform"—a seemingly incremental step whose logic fundamentally changes power relationships.

Government funds might also be used to train unionists to cope with a variety of management issues, going far beyond health and safety. A few unions, such as the Bricklayers, the Amalgamated Clothing and Textile Workers, and the International Ladies Garment Workers, have perceived the potential of working with their industry counterparts to develop new technologies. The Bricklayers, working with their industry trade association, cosponsor a masonry institute. ACTWU and the ILGWU have a joint program with industry to develop automated apparel technologies, operated at the Draper Laboratories at MIT. Unions conventionally are seen as enemies of automation, but in this case the needle-trades unions have realized that if advanced technologies and higher productivity can keep some jobs in the United States, that is preferable to losing the entire industry to cheap labor. The apparel project, which also dates to the Carter administration, has a small Commerce Department grant, and this is another practical case of tripartism, which allows labor to increase its sophistication about production technologies, capital investment, and industrial strategies at the same time.

A creative Democratic administration could help reinvent a labor movement that would function as a genuine social partner, committed to a productive, safe, remunerative workplace in which sacrifices would be repaid. As politics, this set of goals is vastly superior to mere profit sharing. The next Democratic administration ought to sponsor a wide variety of experiments to encourage the labor movement to play a constructive, collaborative industrial role, and in the process rejuvenate labor's own capacity as a key part of the Democratic base.

VII.

Democrats must also put a number of key programmatic objectives back on the national agenda. These include national health insurance and comprehensive child care. The health system we have now blends elements of national health insurance (medicare), pauper medicine (medicaid), private insurance, and gold-plated, profit-motivated medicine for those with the means to pay the bill. The government backs into a regulatory role, but without consistent criteria, and is always one step behind the private providers. Politically, the average working-age voter identifies his health insurance with his private employer, not with his membership in a civic community. Health care is a superb instance where a universal public program is plainly more efficient, as well as more equitable, than a private one.

The modern family, with two wage-earners, or often with just a single parent, has to juggle career and child rearing. For childcare during working hours, society provides only a vestige from an earlier era, the public school. But the myth is still that a school is in the business of formal education, and of custody and socialization only incidentally; nobody has thought to align the school's calendar with the parent's work calendar. If you can afford private help, of course, this is not a problem. If you are on welfare, the state will sometimes pay to stash your children somewhere if you agree to take a job. But for most Americans the absence of a childcare policy is a gaping policy default. Democrats should put this issue on the agenda—even if they begin modestly, with experimental all-day school grants, or more encouragement and subsidy of parent cooperatives, or longer parental leaves, or employer-provided childcare.

Housing, likewise, has become a national policy default. We lavishly subsidize housing for the haves, through the mortgage interest tax deduction, which underwrites tax-favored equity buildup for those who already own houses and bids up the cost of those houses for new buyers. But with the near demise of the FHA and the VA, we do almost nothing to promote first-time home buying for those without family wealth. In the rental market, the dismantling of subsidized construction, the condo conversion boom, and the absence of a cooperative housing sector have created ever wider gaps between family incomes and available rents. Rent control in some localities serves as a stopgap; conservatives attack it, but in the absence a great deal of affordable new housing offer no strategy to replace it. A Democratic administration should devise a national housing policy, emphasizing first-time home purchase, and the creation of a nonprofit, co-op sector for apartment dwellers.

True reform of the welfare system is also overdue. Here, a bipartisan consensus about welfare reform has been in the making for several years, but progress has been blocked by the ultraconservatism of the Reagan administration. In this emerging consensus, liberals recognize that the Aid to Families with Dependent Children (AFDC) system often creates dependency and that many if not most welfare recipients ought to work. At the same time, many conservative critics have acknowledged that benefit levels are indecently low and that shifting the emphasis from welfare to workfare cannot easily be done on the cheap, unless the intent is purely punitive. A woman who goes off AFDC to take a minimum-wage job finds herself with new childcare expenses and without medicaid (fewer than half of former AFDC recipients get health insurance from their new employers). By itself, a minimum-wage job produces a family income far below the poverty level. Without transitional subsidies—for childcare, health insurance, and job training—shifting from welfare to work often produces an absolute reduction in family living standards. Congressional Democrats and moderate Republicans have proposed fairly stringent workfare and child-support requirements, in exchange for increased transitional benefits to families where the mother works. However, the Reagan budget priorities and the administration's opposition to new federal mandates has blocked any such grand compromise. Democrats should champion a national policy of reducing the welfare rolls by providing work opportunity—not just to dismantle the separate welfare culture, but to improve living standards. This will also take money.

There are other policy areas, without going into great detail, where public programs can promote both immediate benefits as well as social cohesion. A program of work opportunities for welfare recipients should be part of an overall employment and training framework, and not an isolated, punitive scheme for the dependent poor. A public works program should repair long-neglected public infrastructure and at the same time provide good jobs.

The obvious advantage of these goals is that working toward them will unite many diverse constituencies, and achieving them will give the American people tangible services. But all of this, of course, will cost money. For Democrats, one of the most paralyzing aspects of the Reagan era has been the contrived budgetary strait-jacket. Until early 1987, most Democrats accepted Reagan's premise that there could be no tax increase and, as a consequence, were constrained to join the Reagan administration in hacking away at what remained of programs that served the Democratic electorate. In part, this situation reflected the continuing trauma of the Mondale defeat and its association in the minds of many Democratic legislators with Mondale's ill-fated call for a tax increase (and little else). Then-House Speaker Thomas P. "Tip" O'Neill vowed that Democrats would never support a tax increase unless the White House moved first.

Reagan's political collapse in the fall of 1986, the recapture of the Senate, and the election of a new House Speaker converged to liberate Democrats from these immobilizing assumptions. House Speaker Jim Wright of Texas, viewed in liberal-conservative terms, looks like a moderate conservative. But Wright, like his fellow Texan Jim Hightower, has a shrewd populist streak. On assuming office in January 1987, Wright began calling for a tax increase. Unlike Mondale, who viewed tax issues solely in technical and fiscal terms, Wright understands that taxes have a populist aspect: he proposed taxing the rich. Specifically, he proposed that the top tax rate, scheduled to drop to 28 percent in 1988, be held at 38.5 percent for taxpayers with incomes of over $75,000. He also shrewdly took advantage of Wall Street's bad odor to propose a transfer tax on stock sales. Politically, the beauty of the transfer tax is that it reaches few wage-earning voters. In economic terms, it has the further virtue of taxing speculators each time they trade, while long-term investors need pay the tax only when they sell. Most importantly, the new revenues would help liberate Democrats from their fiscal paralysis.

At this writing, the projected federal budget deficit is in the range of $150 billion. The Gramm-Rudman Act of 1985, a bipartisan desperation measure, required that the deficit be gradually reduced to zero. But by early 1987, many Democrats felt emboldened to call for the repeal of Gramm-Rudman as unrealistic and unnecessary. A reasonable, and economically sustainable deficit for the long term is about 2 percent of gross national product, or some $80 billion. In order to achieve that, Democrats need to find about $70 billion worth of tax increases and program cuts.

A sensible Democratic program would raise about $80 billion in new taxes through a combination of income tax increases on the wealthy, stock transfer taxes, and specific new levies such as a tax on energy. Democrats could also reduce military spending by about $30 billion without damaging national security. Taken together, this would generate a total of $110 billion—$70 billion for deficit reduction and the remaining $40 billion for necessary new public spending.

Once in office, the next Democratic administration will have to go well beyond even these measures. The United States during the Reagan years kept its economy afloat by irresponsibly borrowing money. We borrowed from each other to finance consumer spending, and in the process we depleted savings and capital for investment. We kept the public sector solvent only by borrowing from abroad. We financed the illusion of prosperity by importing almost twice what we export, which entailed further borrowing. Economists of every persuasion agree that this pyramid of borrowing must soon end and that when it does there is a serious risk of a decline in living standards. The great danger for the next Democratic administration is that by articulating responsible policies, it will herald austerity. "The Democrats are back, tighten our belts" is not the sort of image—or reality—the party needs.

It is desperately important that Democrats create the fiscal and political space to pursue effective policies of high growth and social cohesion. The United States finally blasted out of the Great Depression on the economic surge created by the massive public spending of World War II, and in the process we created a generation of new technologies and highly skilled workers, as well as the economic growth to buy a generation of social peace. The next administration will have the twin task of putting the nation's fiscal house in order *and* enhancing economic growth at the same time. The Reagan administration accomplished modest growth, mediocre productivity, excessive unemployment, and left a fiscal shambles.

The next president will almost surely have to turn to some form of broad-based Value Added Tax (VAT), which is a form of national sales tax, to finance much of the basic social overhead, such as health care and retirement, and still leave public funds available for other needs, such as an active labor market policy and industrial restructuring. A Value Added Tax, as a sales tax, has a bad reputation among liberals because it can be regressive in its incidence, but it can also be designed to be progressive by encorporating exemptions. Value added taxes help nations like West Germany and Sweden to have high rates of economic performance and generous social spending simultaneously. Because a VAT taxes only consumption, it has the further virtue of stimulating savings, and a higher savings rate is needed to avoid continued borrowing from abroad. I do not think Democrats should make a VAT a centerpiece of their campaign—that would indeed be an overdose of "tax and spend"—but I suspect that in the early 1990s both parties will have to share the responsibility for enacting one, just as they shared credit for the politically difficult tax reform law of 1986.

VIII.

Democrats have come through two wrenching decades in which their most fundamental precepts were called into question, their electoral base fragmented, their instrumental means immobilized. As the party heads into the 1990s, it stands better positioned to reclaim both its historic soul and its electoral majority than most observers would have thought possible at the height of Ronald Reagan's popularity. But the chronic pressures to abandon a mixed economy in favor of simple *laissez-faire,* and thereby to abandon the party's natural base, will persist.

In writing at a moment when the country is headed into an election, one normally dwells on candidacies and elements of a party program. But platform writing can be a sterile exercise. It is easy enough to call forth policies from the vasty deep. The trick is to get them to come when you call. As the reader who has gotten this far will have gathered, my effort here has not been mainly about individual politicians or about election-year platform-building. Rather, I have tried to understand the political logic that has allowed Democrats to be the majority party and has created the political space for egalitarian policies. I am rooting for the Democrats, and I have suggested some policies which seem to fit that logic. But I am not commending these policies mainly as a campaign blueprint. They are far more important as agendas to pursue in office than as slogans along the campaign trail; it is by governing well that Democrats rebuild their alliances with voters. From my own observation of recent Democratic office-holders, I have detected little strategic planning intended to cement links among party, program, individual voter, and political community. According to the historians, Roosevelt is said to have intended precisely that in his design of social security; Lyndon Johnson may have understood something of the same thing in programs like higher education aid and medicare (though the structure of his poverty program and medicaid had largely the opposite effect). Yet for the past two decades, there has been precious little such strategic use of governance to create the political conditions for cohesive and egalitarian policies. The several caprices that determine elections—personality, business cycle, timing, luck, as well as strategy—will sooner or later give Democrats another turn at governing, and they had better not squander it.

Leadership, obviously, will be a key determinant of the party's resurgence. The American people have a latent idealism that astute politicians can tap. A leader can inspire the best in people, as well as inspiring them to go to the polls. Progressive politics is not only about delivering tangible benefits to constituencies; it is also about membership in a civic community. Neo-liberals are right when they put forth that aspect of Democratic politics, best symbolized by John Kennedy. But they are wrong to present idealism as a substitute for political self-interest. Under the best Democratic presidents, the two have been complements. The Democratic field is unusually large this year. I do not have a candidate to recommend; I suspect that any of several contenders could do the job, if they can free themselves from the immobilizing assumptions of the Reagan era and move the party to its high ground of articulate economic populism.

There will be microscopic examinations of personalities in future elections. This book has endeavored to anchor those examinations in an understanding of party fundamentals: the philosophy, the program, the politics, and the necessary function of a progressive party as the guardian of a mixed economy and a social conception of citizenship. The life of the party, of course, includes its candidates, its professionals, its office holders, fund raisers, policy intellectuals, and pollsters. But ultimately the life of a Democratic party is the democratic electorate. How the party serves that electorate will determine its future.

NOTES

Epigraph, p. vii: William L. Riordan, *Plunkitt of Tammany Hall* (New York: E. P. Dutton, 1963), p. 88.

CHAPTER ONE
DEMOCRATIC DILEMMA

Page 13. Lloyd Free and Hadley Cantril, *The Political Beliefs of Americans* (New Brunswick, N.J.: Rutgers University Press, 1967).

Page 16. Gergen: in *Public Opinion,* June–July 1985, p. 56.

Page 17. Hartz: Louis Hartz, *The Liberal Tradition in America* (New York: Harcourt, Brace, 1955), p. 263.

Hirschman: Albert O. Hirschman, *Rival Views of Market Society* (New York: Elisabeth Sifton Books · Viking, 1986), p. 134.

Page 25. Mondale: on "Meet the Press," October 24, 1982.

Page 27. Galston: William Galston, *Brookings Review,* Winter 1985, p. 19.

CHAPTER TWO
MONEY

Page 34. Many of these insights on how campaign finance whip-saws Democrats should be credited to Thomas Byrne Edsall, in his path-breaking *The New Politics of Inequality* (New York: W. W. Norton, 1984).

Page 35. Sabato: Larry J. Sabato, *PAC Power* (New York: W. W. Norton, 1984), pp. 169, 186.

Page 38. History of money and politics: see Matthew Josephson, *The Politicos* (New York: Harcourt, Brace, 1938); George Thayer, *Who Shakes the Money Tree?* (New York: Simon and Schuster, 1974); William Domhoff, *Fat Cats and Democrats: The Role of the Big Rich in the Party of the Common Man* (Englewood Cliffs, N.J.: Prentice-Hall, 1973); Herbert Alexander, *Financing Politics,* third edition (Washington, D.C.: CQ Press, 1984).

Page 40. Campaign finance statistics from Federal Elections Commission, except where otherwise noted. Statistics on expenditure by independent committees from Sabato, *op. cit.,* p. 99.

Page 42. Coelho: interview with the author.

Dependence by challengers on party committees. Sabato, *op. cit.,* p. 154.

Page 43. Ann Lewis: interview with the author.

Page 44. Perkins estimate: interview with the author.

Value of labor volunteers: *Sabato, op. cit.,* p. 69.

Page 45. See Thomas Ferguson and Joel Rogers, *Right Turn* (New York: Hill and Wang, 1986), pp. 46–49.

Page 48. Hoenlein: interview with the author.

Page 49. Palevsky: interview with the author.

Page 50. Jacobsen and Kernell: in Michael Malbin, ed., *Money and Politics in the United States* (Washington, D.C.: American Enterprise Institute · Chatham House, 1984), p. 62. See also Gary C. Jacobson, *Money in Congressional Elections* (New Haven: Yale University Press, 1980), and Jacobson, *The Politics of Congressional Elections* (Boston: Little, Brown, 1983).

Alexander: interview with the author.

Page 51. Landow: interview with the author.

Page 52. Kipnes: interview with the author.

Page 55. Kipnes: interview with the author.

Page 58. Sheinbaum: interview with the author.

Page 59. McGovern campaign finances: in Gary W. Hart, *Right from the Start: A Chronicle of the McGovern Campaign* (New York: Quadrangle Books, 1973), pp. 118–19.

Page 62. Marta David: interview with the author.

Coelho: interview with the author.

Page 63. Pat Williams: interview with the author.

Gregg Easterbrook, "The Business of Politics," *The Atlantic,* October 1986, p. 28.

Page 65. Ralph Whitehead: interview with the author.

Page 66. John Sasso: interview with the author.

Page 67. Frank O'Brien: interview with the author.

CHAPTER THREE
PARTY

Page 73. Key: V. O. Key, Jr., *Politics, Parties, and Pressure Groups,* fourth edition (New York: Thomas Y. Crowell, 1968), pp. 182–85. For the seminal discussion of parties as aggregating and integrating agents, see Key's *Southern Politics in State and Nation* (New York: Alfred A. Knopf, 1949), especially pp. 298–310.

Page 75. Wattenberg: Martin Wattenberg, *The Decline of Political Parties, 1952–1984* (Cambridge, Mass.: Harvard University Press, 1984), p. 57.

Page 76. Wattenberg, *ibid.,* pp. 84, 66.

Note. See Thomas B. Edsall, *The New Politics of Inequality* (New York: W. W. Norton, 1984), and David Ademany's essay in Malbin, *op. cit.,* and David Price, *Bringing Back the Parties* (Washington, D.C.: CQ Press, 1986).

Page 77. David Broder, *The Party's Over* (New York: Harper and Row, 1971).

Xandra Kayden and Eddie Mahe, Jr., *The Party Goes On* (New York: Basic Books, 1985), p. 183.

William Crotty, *American Parties in Decline* (Boston: Little, Brown, 1984).

Page 79. E. E. Schattschneider, *The Semisovereign People* (New York: Holt, Rinehart and Winston, 1960), p. 35. See also Schattschneider, *Party Government* (New York: Farrar and Rinehart, 1942).

Walter Dean Burnham, "Elections as Democratic Institutions," paper presented to Third Annual Thomas P. O'Neill Symposium, Boston College, October 1985, p. 11.

Verba: interview with the author.

Maurice Duverger, *Political Parties* (New York: John Wiley, 1960), p. 270.

Page 80. Price, *op. cit.,* p. 111.

Walter Dean Burnham, *Critical Elections and the Mainsprings of American Politics* (New York: W. W. Norton, 1970), p. 133.

Page 81. James Q. Wilson, *The Amateur Democrat* (Chicago: University of Chicago Press, 1962).

Huey Long: Quoted in Thayer, *op. cit.,* pp. 68–69.

Page 83. Brookover: interview with the author.

Page 86. Brookover and Caddell: interviews with the author.

Page 87. Pounian and Mahe: interviews with the author.

Page 88. Wirthlin: interview with the author.

Page 89. Allsop: interview with the author.

Page 90. Wirthlin: to the author.

Page 96. Gohmann: interview with the author.

Page 100. Nelson Polsby, *Consequences of Party Reform* (New York: Oxford University Press, 1983).

Austin Ranney, *Curing the Mischief of Faction* (Berkeley: University of California Press, 1975).

Page 103. Whitehead: interview with the author.

Page 104. Hart; in R. W. Apple, "Voters' Rebuff to Reagan's Vision," *The New York Times,* November 7, 1986, p. 1.

CHAPTER FOUR
VOTERS

Page 110. Whitehead: interview with the author.

Page 112. Analysis of electoral college: interview with Pat Caddell.

Page 114. Warren Miller, "The Election of 1984 and the Future of American National Politics," paper presented to the Third Annual Thomas P. O'Neill Symposium, Boston College, October 1985, p. 11.

Page 115. Polls: from various Roper Reports and Gallup Polls. See also Miller, *op. cit.,* table 4. See also Yankelovitch Poll for *Time,* February 17–18, 1987.

Page 116. January Poll indicating 54 percent wanted a change of direction: NBC–Wall Street Journal national poll of January 12, 1987. February 1987 government spending: Washington Post–ABC Poll of February 9, 1987.

Page 118. Whitehead: to the author.

Page 120. David Gopoian, "Q Analysis of Parma, Ohio Swing Voters," paper prepared for Ohio Public Interest Campaign, September 1986.

Stanley B. Greenberg, "Plain Speaking: Democrats State Their Minds," *Public Opinion,* Summer 1986.

Page 121. Jonathan Schell, "History in Sherman Park," *The New Yorker,* January 5 and 12, 1987.

Page 123. Voting statistics from U.S. Bureau of the Census, P-20 series. Raymond E. Wolfinger and Steven J. Rosenstone, *Who Votes?* (New Haven: Yale University Press, 1980), pp. 17ff.

Page 124. Michael W. Traugott and John P. Katosh, "Response Validity in Surveys of Voting Behavior," *Public Opinion Quarterly* 43 (1979), pp. 359–77, statistic at p. 367.

Page 125. Walter Dean Burnham, "The Democratic Party Goes Upscale," *Boston Globe,* November 2, 1986, p. A-1.

Page 127. Income and voting statistics: CBS–New York Times election day exit polls, November 1986.

Page 129. Ann Beaudry and Robert Schaeffer, *Winning State and Local Elections* (New York: The Free Press, 1986), p. 18.

Page 130. Black voting turnout: Darryl D. Woods, "The Chicago Crusade," in Thomas E. Cavanagh, ed., *Strategies for Mobilizing Black Voting Participation* (Washington, D.C.: Joint Center for Political Studies, 1987), pp. 29, 30.

Page 131. Linda Davidoff: interview with the author.

Pages 131–32. Edward Schwartz, testimony before the Democratic Party's Leland Commission, Philadelphia, August 15, 1981.

Page 134. Davidoff: to the author.

Page 135. Burnham, *Critical Elections,* turnout statistics at p. 21.

Page 136. Joseph Harris, *Registration of Voters in the United States* (Washington, D.C.: The Brookings Institution, 1929), pp. 67–68. Quoted in Ron Hayduk, "The History and Politics of Voter Registration in the United States," unpublished paper, Columbia University School of Social Work, 1986.

Participation decline: Burnham, *Critical Elections,* p. 21.

Page 137. Davidoff: to the author.

Page 138. Richard A. Cloward and Frances Fox Piven, "How to Get Out the Vote in 1988," *The Nation,* November 23, 1985, p. 547.

Page 142. Strict nonpartisanship: "Pathways to Power," by Hamilton, Rabinovitz & Alschuler, Inc. (New York, 1986), p. 50.

Page 143. Committee for the Study of the American Electorate report, "Voter Registration 1984," Washington, D.C., 1985, p. 23.

Page 147. James Q. Wilson, *The Amateur Democrat* (Chicago: University of Chicago Press, 1962), pp. 274, 288.

CHAPTER FIVE
IDEOLOGY

Page 153. Peter Steinfels, *The Neoconservatives* (New York: Simon and Schuster, 1979), p. 6.

Page 156. Midge Decter, *Liberal Parents, Radical Children* (New York: Basic Books, 1975).

Page 158. Nathan Glazer, "Why Are the Poor Still with Us?" *The Public Interest,* Fall 1985, p. 81.

Page 159. John C. Pittenger and Peter Kuriloff, "Educating the Handicapped: Reforming a Radical Law," *The Public Interest,* Winter 1982, pp. 72–96.

Page 160. Aaron Wildavsky, "Richer Is Safer," *The Public Interest,* Summer 1980, pp. 23–39.

Martin Feldstein, "The High Cost of Hospitals and What to Do about It," *The Public Interest,* Summer 1977, pp. 40–54.

Page 161. Sidney Blumenthal, *The Rise of the Counter-Establishment* (New York: Times Books, 1986), p. 123.

Page 162. Kelman, quoted in the *Washington Post* (national edition), February 2, 1987.

Richard M. Scammon and Ben J. Wattenberg, *The Real Majority* (New York: Coward, McCann and Geohegan, 1970), p. 21.

Page 164. Kevin Phillips, *The Emerging Republican Majority* (New Rochelle, N.Y.: Arlington Press, 1969).

Scammon and Wattenberg, *op. cit.,* pp. 80, 198.

Page 165. Schneider: to the author.

Page 167. Steinfels, *op. cit.,* p. 294.

Civil Service: *Manifesto,* reprinted in Charles Peters and Phillip Kiesling, *A New Road for America: The Neoliberal Movement* (Lanham, Md.: Madison Books, 1985), pp. 3–4.

James Fallows, "Entitlements," *The Atlantic,* November 1982, p. 58.

Peters's social security quote: Aunt Alice line, quoted in David Osborne, "Now Bob . . . But Charlie," *Mother Jones,* May 1985, pp. 26–27. A variation in the same line is in his *Manifesto, op. cit.*

Page 170. The Villers Foundation, "The Other Side of Easy Street: Myths and Facts about the Economics of Old Age" (Washington, D.C., 1987), p. 54.

Page 172. Babbitt: interview with the author.

Philip Longman, "Taking America to the Cleaners," *Washington Monthly,* November 1982, p. 30.

Page 173. Gregg Easterbrook, "Voting for Unemployment," *The Atlantic,* May 1983, p. 43.

Page 174. Robert M. Kaus, "The Trouble with Unions," *Harper's,* June 1983, p. 32.

Page 175. Martin Weitzman, *The Share Economy* (Cambridge, Mass.: Harvard University Press, 1985).

Page 176. Peters: in "A Neoliberal Manifesto," *Washington Monthly,* May 1983, p. 12.

Theodore Lowi, *The End of Liberalism* (New York: W. W. Norton, 1969).

Page 177. Irving Howe, "Intellectuals, Dissent, and Bureaucrats," *Dissent,* Summer 1984, p. 272.

Page 178. James Fallows, "America's Changing Economic Landscape," *The Atlantic,* March 1985, pp. 47–68.

Fallows book: *National Defense* (New York: Random House, 1981).

Page 180. Lomasny: Lincoln Steffens, *The Autobiography of Lincoln Steffens* (New York: Harcourt, Brace, 1931), p. 618.

Page 181. Mickey Kaus, "The Work Ethic State," *New Republic,* July 7, 1986, quote at p. 33.

Page 185. Eizenstat and Cutter: see Robert Kuttner, "Revenge of the Democratic Nerds," *New Republic,* October 22, 1984, pp. 14–17.

Page 188. Rayburn, quoted in David Halberstam, *The Best and the Brightest* (New York: Penguin Books, 1983), p. 53.

Page 190. Isaiah Berlin, *The Hedgehog and the Fox* (New York: New American Library, 1957), pp. 7–8.

Page 191. Van Dyk: to the author.

Page 192. Van Dyk: to the author.

Page 193. Molander: to the author. See also Robert Kuttner, "What's the Big Idea," *New Republic,* November 28, 1985, pp. 23–28.

Page 196. Economic Policy Institute. Disclosure: I currently serve on EPI's Board.

Page 197. Schneider: in "Revolt of the American Public: Left, Right, or Both?" *New Perspectives Quarterly,* Fall 1986, p. 4. (Transcribed from a conference organized by the New Populist Forum, May 1986.)

Page 198. Phillips: *ibid.,* p. 5.

Frank Reissman: in Harry C. Boyte and Frank Reissman, eds., *The New Populism* (Philadelphia: Temple University Press, 1986), pp. 54–55.

Page 199. Boyte: in Boyte and Reissman, *ibid.,* p. 10.

Robert Kuttner, *The Economic Illusion* (Boston: Houghton Mifflin, 1984).

Pages 201–3. Hightower: in Boyte and Reissman, *op. cit.,* pp. 242–44.

Page 203. Leuchtenberg speech to DLC: Text provided by Leuchtenberg.

CHAPTER SIX
DEMOCRATIC OPPORTUNITY

Page 206. Howard Phillips, "Let's De-Fund the Left," *Conservative Digest,* April 1982, pp. 50–51. (The entire issue was devoted to this theme.)

Page 212. GI Bill: U.S. Veterans Administration. Various annual reports. FHA: Memorandum "Federal Housing Administration Mortgage Insurance Programs," Washington, D.C.: Congressional Research Service, November 25, 1985.

Page 213. Pell Grants: "Guaranteed Student Loans," Washington, D.C.: Congressional Research Service, November 11, 1985.

Page 214. Frank S. Levy and Richard C. Michel, "An Economic Bust for the Baby Boom," *Challenge,* March–April 1986, pp. 33–39.

Page 216. Litan: to the author.

Page 218. Prestowitz: to the author.

Page 222. Gary Clyde Hufbauer and Jeffrey J. Schott, "Trading for Growth: The Next Round of Trade Negotiations" (Washington, D.C.: Institute for International Economics, 1985), pp. 15–17; and Robert Z. Lawrence and Robert E. Litan, "Saving Free Trade" (Washington, D.C.: The Brookings Institution, 1986), pp. 4–5.

Page 228. "Re-employment system": see Robert Kuttner, "Getting off the Dole," *The Atlantic,* November 1985.

Page 234. Felix Rohatyn, "The Blight on Wall Street," *New York Review of Books,* March 12, 1987.

Page 240. Basil Whiting: to the author. See Robert Kuttner, "Unions, Economic Power, and the State," *Dissent,* Winter 1986, pp. 33–44.

"Nonreformist reform": the phrase and concept are Andre Gorz's.

INDEX